Pictorial encyclopedia of the animal kingdom

Pictorial encyclopedia of theanimal kingdom

by V. J. Stanek

Consultants for the American Edition:

FISH   C. Lavett Smith, The American Museum of Natural History, New York
REPTILES   Herndon Dowling, New York Zoological Society
INSECTS   Jerome J. Rozen, Jr., The American Museum of Natural History, New York
BIRDS   Peter L. Ames, New York Zoological Society
MAMMALS   George G. Goodwin, The American Museum of Natural History, New York

Crown Publishers, Inc., New York, New York

Graphic design by Julius Hauf
Translated by George Theiner
© 1962 Artia, Prague
Published by
CROWN PUBLISHERS, INC.,
NEW YORK
Printed in Czechoslovakia
S 1488

CONTENTS

PROTOZOA

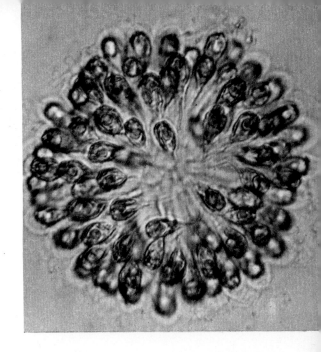

The first and fundamental group in the ex
tensive animal kingdom is that of the Protozoa, microscopic animals consisting of a single
cell which performs all the vital functions.
Over ten thousand different kinds of Protozoa
have been described. The picture at the
top shows flagellates of the order Chryso-
monadina. These are among the most primitive creatures, not far removed from the
vegetable kingdom. The chromatophores in
their bodies enable them to use the sun's
energy to make their own foodstuffs in much
the same way as do green plants. All other
animals feed on other living organisms.

The flagellates shown here are *Synura uvella*. They live in
colonies about $1/_{500}$ in. in size. Between spring and
autumn they float like a mass of globules in streams and
ponds and usually in such numbers that they colour the
water brown.

The bottom picture shows a colony of *Volvox aureus*
belonging to the order Phytomonadina. Like *Synura*, they
inhabit fresh water. Their colonies, however, are coloured green and reach a size of about $1/_{25}$ in.

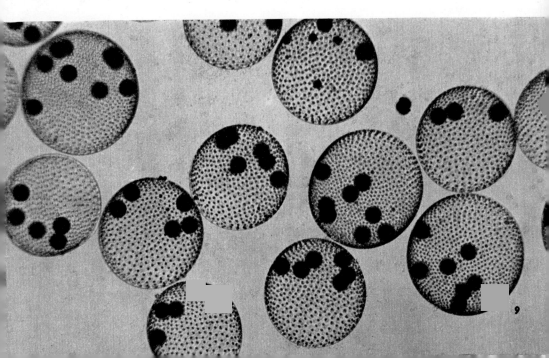

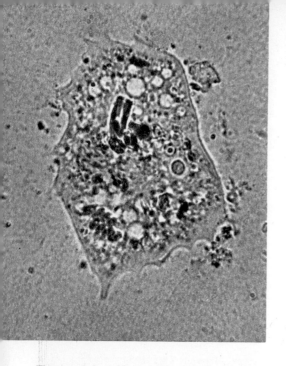

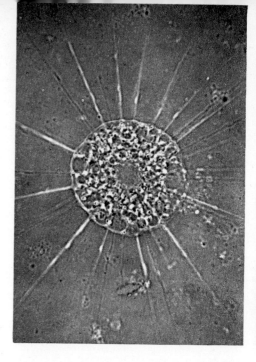

The second class of Protozoa consists of rhizopods — Rhizopoda. Above is one of the largest species of Gymnamoebaea, or naked Lobosa, *Pelomyxa palustris*, reaching a maximum size of $^{1}/_{25}$ in. The *Pelomyxa* live on the muddy bottom of freshwater pools and puddles, feeding on minute organisms, particularly bacteria and algae, by ingesting them in their cells.

Actinosphaerium eichhorni (top right) is a sun animalcule belonging to the order Heliozoa ($\times$ 500).

Shown below are the microscopic calcareous shells of the Foraminifera, of the genus Globigerina.

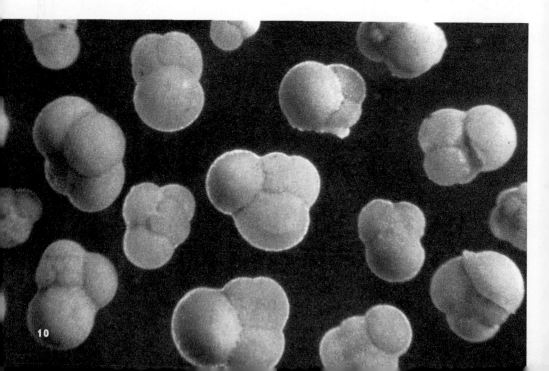

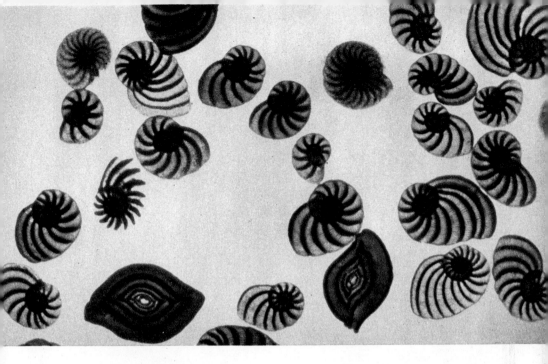

Above are calcareous shells of Mediterranean For-aminifera. The two which are roughly pointed at each end are called *Spiroculina planulata*, the large spiral ones are *Peneroplis pertusus*, and the smaller coiled ones *Peneroplis planatus* (× 30).

Below are siliceous shells of Radiolaria from deposits in the deep seas near Barbados (× 100).

When alive, the Foraminifera and Radiolaria have threads of protoplasm, often branched, protruding from their shells. They float in the ocean, preying on minute algae and bacteria. Their empty shells fall to the bottom, forming Globig-erine ooze, which covers about one-third of the ocean floor at great depths.

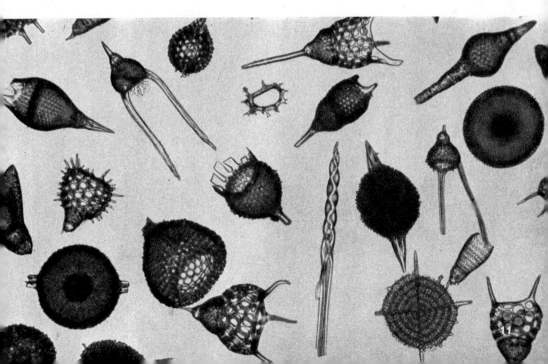

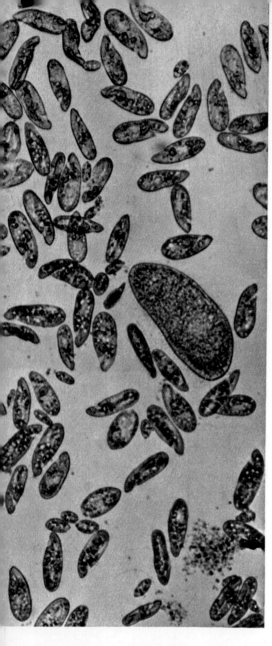

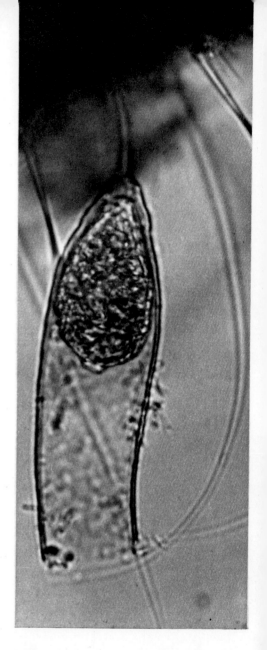

The subphylum Ciliophora includes Ciliata (Infusoria). These live in fresh water and are too small to be distinguished by the naked eye, the largest species alone forming minute dots. *Paramecium aurelia* (the smaller on the left) and *Stylonychia* *mytilus* (the larger on the left) are the species most frequently found in stagnant waters. Some ciliates like *Cothurnia (right)*, live attached to various objects in the water, forming a protective cup on a stalk. They measure about $3/10000$ in.

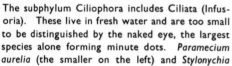

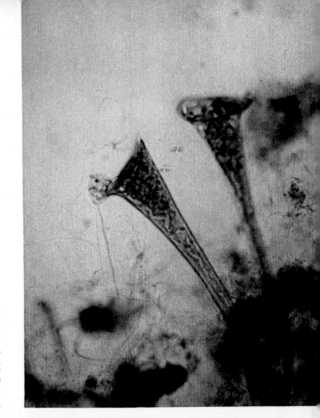

Stentor coeruleus (right), which may sometimes be almost $1/10$ in. long, floats about for much of the time. Undulating membranes at the wider end of its body create water currents, sweeping the food into its mouth opening. Other species of Ciliata, such as *Opercularia (below)*, form branching colonies on various water organisms.

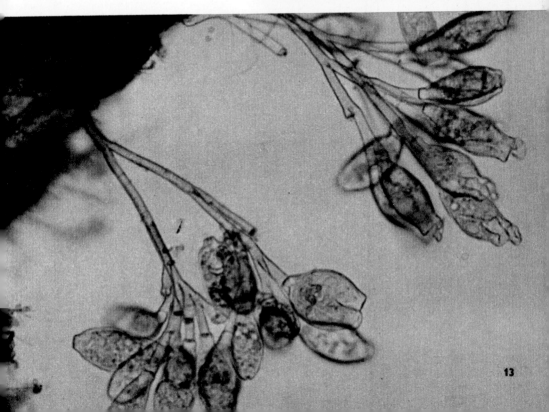

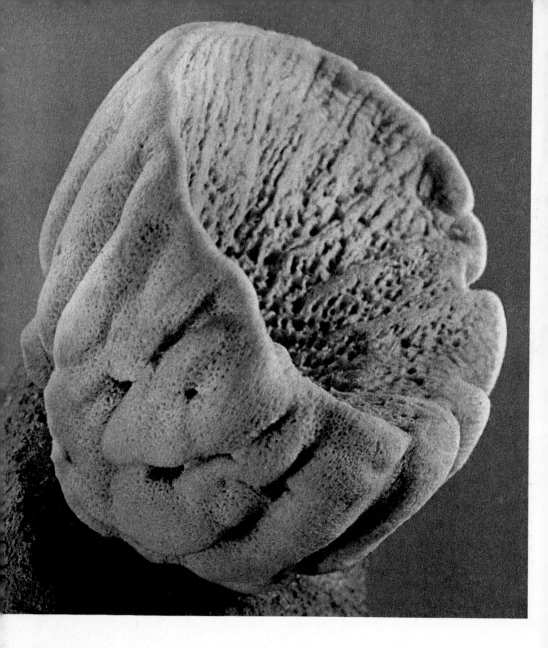

PARAZOA

The second group – Parazoa – includes the most primitive cellular animals: the sponges – Porifera. The bath sponge is the best known of the marine forms. Here is the finest species, *Euspongia mollissima*, which is found along the shores of the Mediterranean.

The same order of Keratosa or horny sponges, i.e. sponges with a horny or siliceous skeleton, also includes the South African species, *Dactylochalina cylindrica*, with a widely branched body *(top left)*. At top right is *Spinosella sorroria* from the shores of the Antilles. Below is the beautiful Australian *Janthella basta*, a horny sponge with no mineral skeleton.

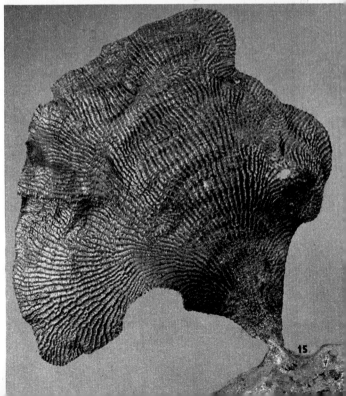

15

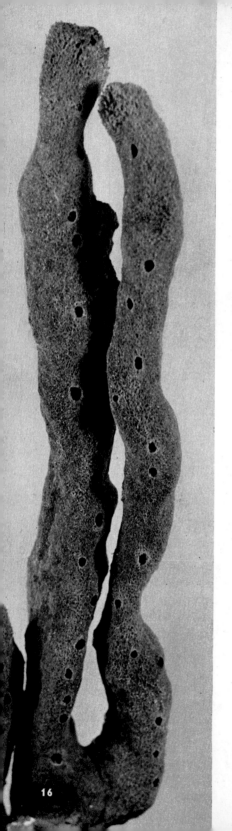

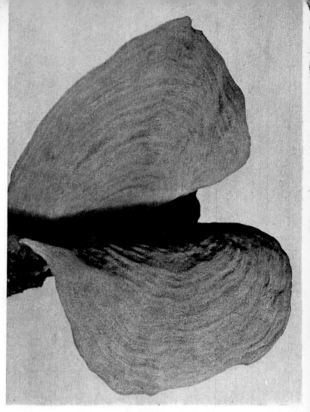

The horny *Pachychalina rubens* forms tall, stalk-like formations, which are rarely branched. The specimen shown on the left comes from Florida. *Cavochalina bilamellata (above)*, from the Antilles. This species is thin and two-leafed.

On page 17 are skeletons of glassy sponges living in the cool depths of warm seas. Left, *Euplectella oweni*, centre, *Semperella schulzei*, and right, *Hyalonema sieboldi*. These species are found mostly in the seas around Japan, living in the mud at great depths.

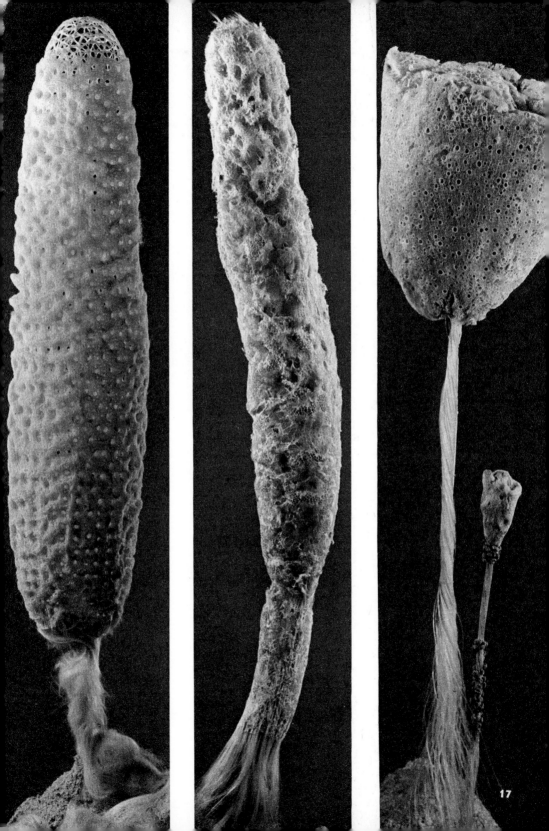

17

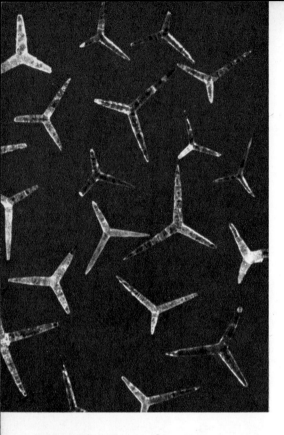

The sack-like bodies of marine sponges are generally reinforced by firm inorganic spicules, as well as the organic spongin fibres. The larger skeletal spicules called megascleres may be an inch or so in length, whereas the smaller microscleres are not usually visible to the naked eye. At top left are the three-branched calcareous spicules.

Top right are silica needles of oxyaster type belonging to the *Tethya* sponge; below, a simple curved spicule from the coast of California. The circular shapes in the corners are Diatoms.

The picture opposite is of the *Hexactinella ventilabrum* glass sponge from the seas around Japan.

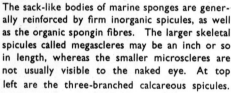
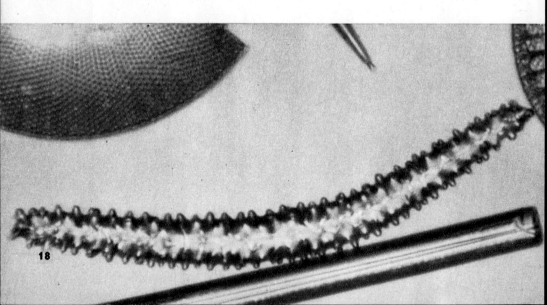

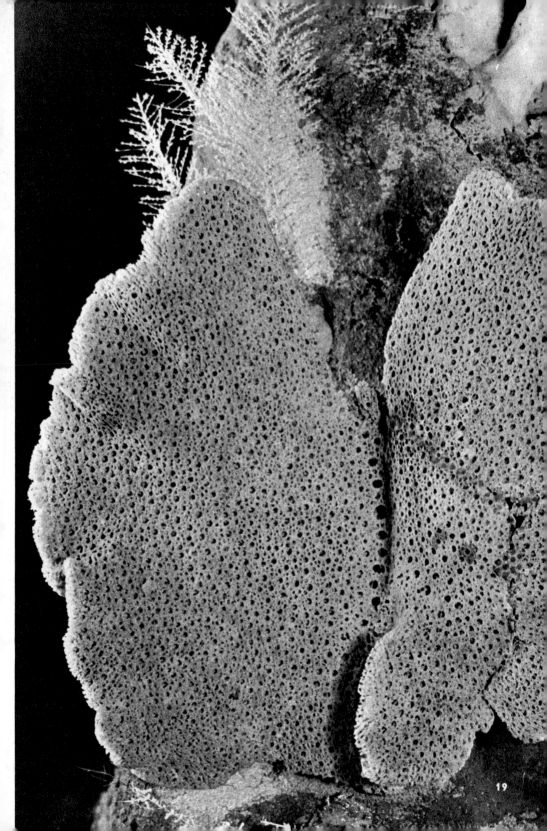

19

The siliceous skeletons of many kinds of marine sponges, after removal of the organic parts, are extremely beautiful and ornamental. *Aphrocalistes beatrix*, a Japanese deep-sea sponge, for example, resembles a fragile cockade of Meissen porcelain (*magnified*).

The photograph opposite shows the naked skeletons of a group of the beautiful *Euplectella aspergillum*, or Venus's Flower Basket, from the ocean depths near the Philippines and the coasts of equatorial Africa.

21

METAZOA

The third large group (sub-kingdom) of animals is that of the Metazoa, higher animals with multi-cellular, differentiated bodies with tissue, a muscular system and various organs. The simplest of these are the Coelenterata. The Brown Hydra *(Pelmatohydra oligactis)*, shown on the left (× 10), belongs to the Cnidaria. It lives in ponds and lakes overgrown with vegetation, feeding on small swimming organisms, which it captures with its tentacles and then conveys to a distensible mouth situated between the shoulders.

Below is the Mediterranean Red Coral *(Corallium rubrum)* whose polyps project from a calcareous skeleton, and live in the sea similarly to the freshwater hydras.

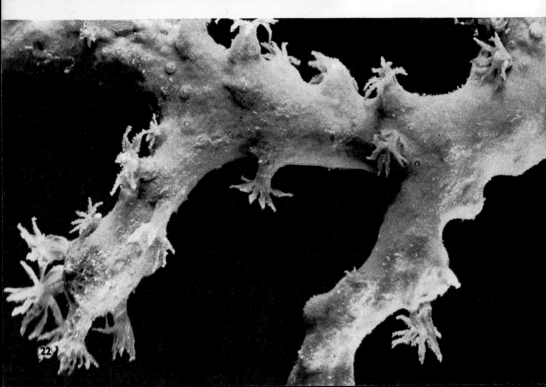

Like the red coral, which is extensively used as an ornament, the Organ-
Pipe Coral *(Tubipora hemprichi)* also
belongs to the subclass Octocorallia.
It grows in colonies in warm waters,
either on reefs or on isolated objects
on the ocean bed, such as the empty
shell in this picture.   Green polyps
project out of the red, organ-like
tubes. As the older layers of tubes
die off, new ones grow on top of
them.

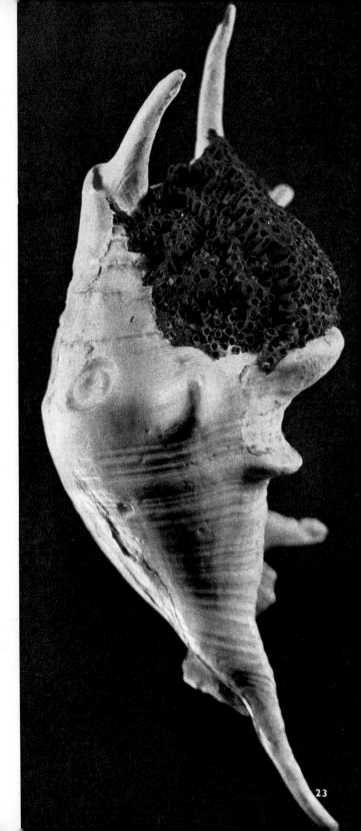

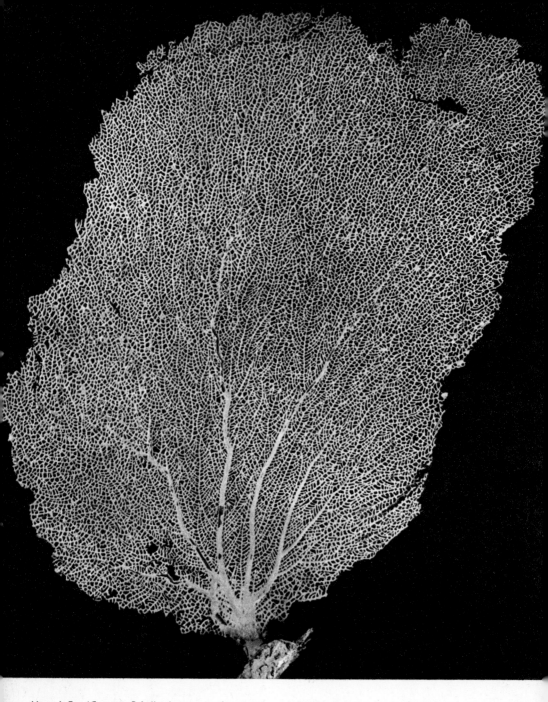

Venus's Fan (*Gorgonia flabellum*) grows on the ocean bed, especially in the West Indies. It is one of the Octocorallia in the order Gorgonacea, the Horny Corals, forming large, fan-shaped colonies with a horny skeleton, covered on both sides with a soft layer of retractable polyps.

Related genera from the warm waters of the West Indies appear in a wide variety of shapes. *Eunicea anceps (top left)* forms bushes whose branches seem to be made of cork. *Hymenogorgia querci-* *folia (top right)* resembles a leaf. Below is *Isis hippuris*, a striking colony of branches with alternating horny and calcareous sections.

Coral-like growths, though not corals proper, can sometimes be found among the colonies on coral reefs. They are in fact Hydrozoa which have acquired a calcareous skeleton. Various forms of living growths project from these skeletons, some of them small medusas. At the top is a picture of *Distichopora violacea*, a species found in the Pacific, coloured a beautiful violet. At the bottom is the red *Distichopora coccinea*, also from the Pacific.

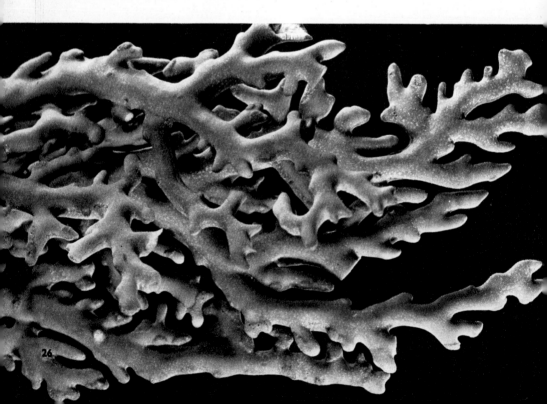

Sea anemones – Actiniaria – are large marine polyps of the subclass Hexacorallia. They live singly and have no skeletons; there are thousands of different kinds. *Anemonia sulcata*, the Opelet Anemone, grows to 16 in. and is common in the Mediterranean. It can distend its mouth widely enough to devour small fish.

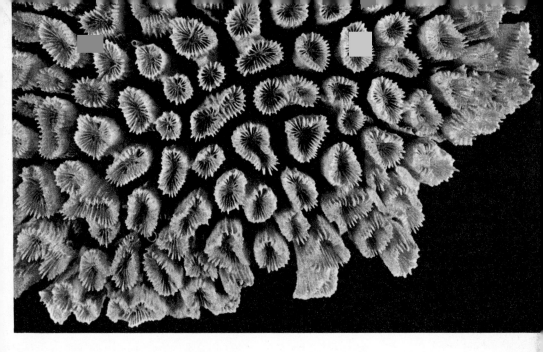

Acropora (Madrepora) cervicornis is a West Indian reef coral. The picture on the left shows its calcareous skeleton. Above is another member of the Hexacorallia, *Dasyphyllia echinulata*, which is found in the Indian Ocean. Below is a skeleton of the *Galaxea lamarcki* coral from the Red Sea (actual size).

30

A cluster of the *Dendrogyra cylindrus* coral from the Bahamas *(top left)*. Part of the skeleton of a cluster of *Diploria crassior* from the China Sea *(top right)*, and, *(bottom left)*, the same cluster removed from the reef. The radiate structure can be seen clearly in this picture, showing how the coral attaches itself to the reef. Neptune's Brain *(Diploria cerebriformis)* from the Bahamas, shown at bottom right, resembles a human brain in both size and shape.

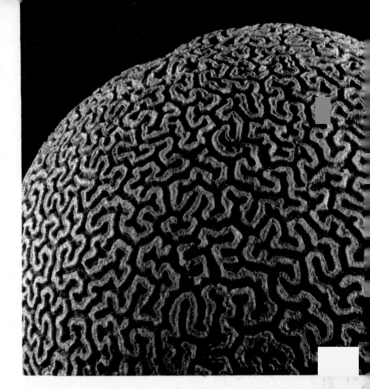

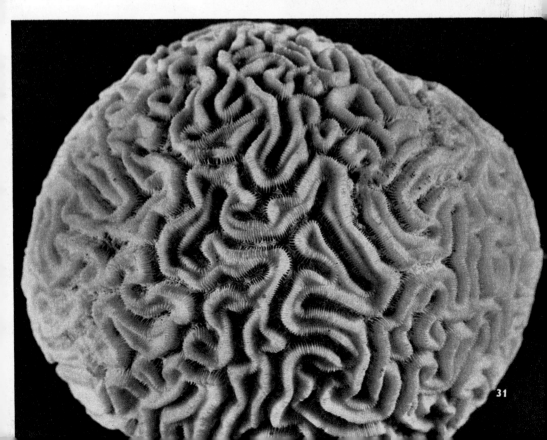

31

Pocillopora eydouxi, a Pacific coral (approximately actual size). Minute polyps, together making a constantly growing, living entity, protrude from openings in the hard, calcareous skeleton. The dead coral on the bottom of the formation becomes part of the shore or barrier reef.

Another species of typical reef coral, *Plesiastrea curta*, from the Pacific island of Samoa (approximately × 2).

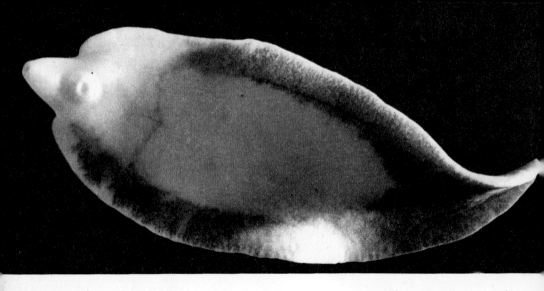

WORMS

The Liver-fluke of the sheep *(Fasciola hepatica)*, is classified among the Platyhelminthes, or Flat Worms, in the class Trematoda. It is a parasite which infests the bile-duct of sheep and other ruminants. It has also been known to cause disease in other mammals, and on rare occasions even affects humans *(above, × 7)*.

Diplozoon paradoxum is unique in that two individuals join together to mate and remain permanently united in an X-shape. It is parasitic on the gills of Cyprinoid (carplike) fish *(below, × 12)*.

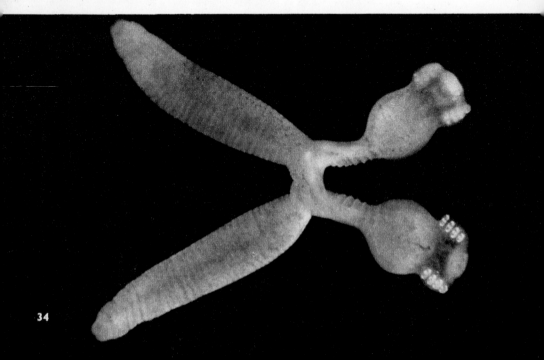

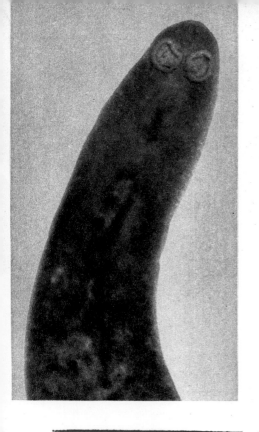

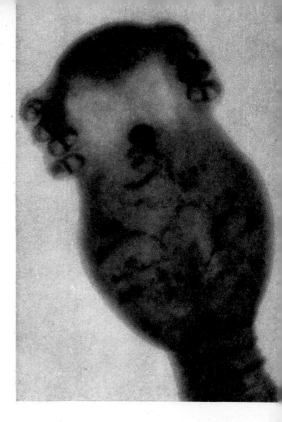

At top left is the front part of *Diplozoon paradoxum* showing two suckers; at top right the hind part with eight suckers. Below are egg capsules of the Dog Tapeworm *(Dipylidium caninum)* (× 40).

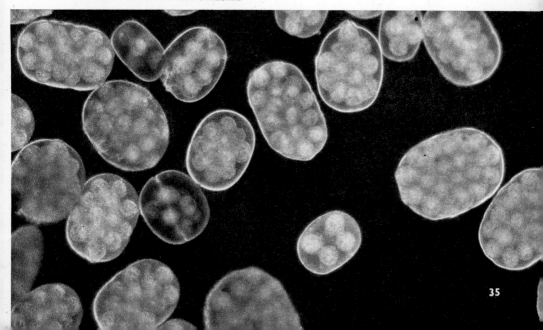

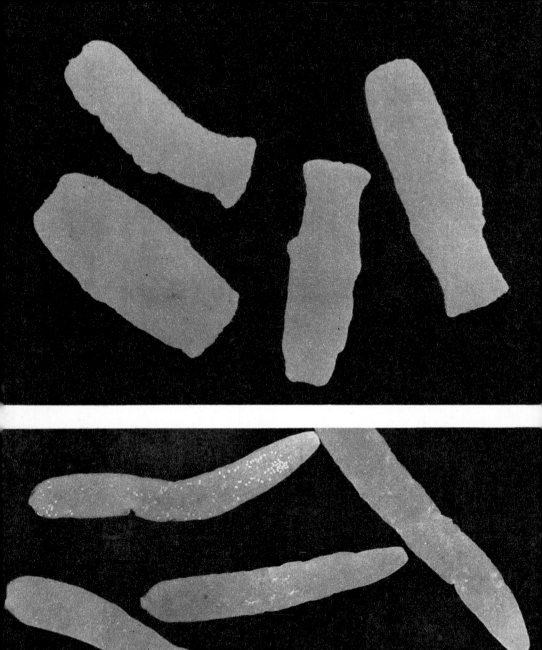

Segments of the Rabbit Tapeworm *(top left)*, and of *Dipylidium caninum (bottom left)*, with transparent, light-coloured egg capsules, like those on the previous page. Both of these were found in dog excrement ($\times$ 5). On the right can be seen the ring of hooks of the Rabbit Tapeworm with which it attaches itself to the dog's intestines. At bottom right is a bunch of cysts of the Rabbit Tapeworm, from a rabbit's abdominal cavity ($\times$ 5); at bottom left a single cyst – a young Tapeworm ($\times$ 10).

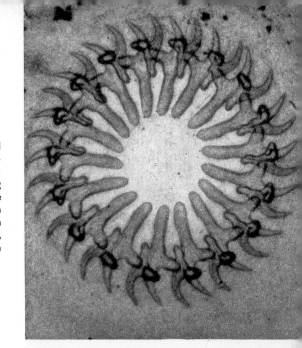

37

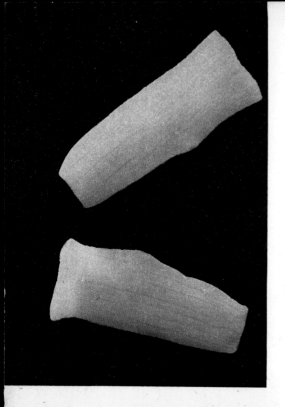

On the left are two segments of the Beef Tapeworm *(Taenia saginata)* from a human intestine ($\times$ 2½). The cysts of this Tapeworm live in the flesh of cattle and are transferred to the human intestine when the infected meat is eaten raw or half-cooked.

Below is *Ascaris suum* of the class Nematoda (Roundworms). It lives as a parasite in the small intestines of pigs. The Roundworm which inhabits the human alimentary canal looks exactly the same, but is slightly smaller ($\times$ $^1/_3$).

The opposite picture is of a Rabbit Tapeworm *(Taenia serrata)* ($\times$ 2). In the middle is the head, or scolex, which is usually attached to the inside of the victim's intestinal wall. New segments are continually growing from this head.

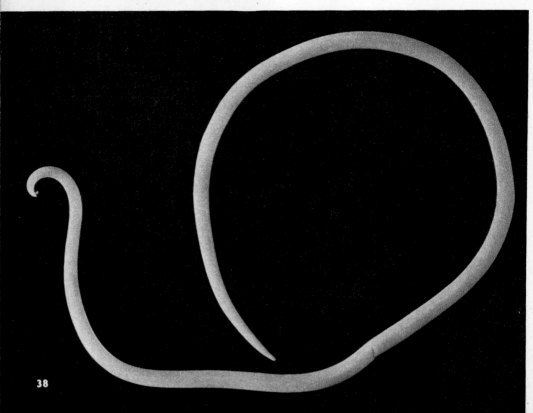

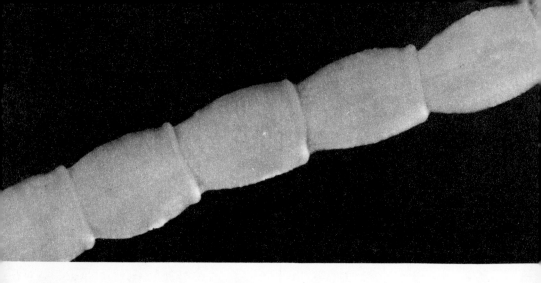

Segments of a Tapeworm (*top*, × 7). Shown below
are the eggs of the Pork Tapeworm *(Taenia solium)*.
The adult is a parasite in man, and may measure
up to 14 feet.

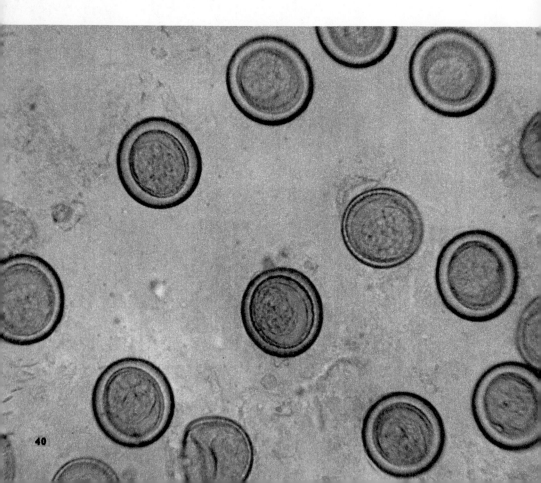

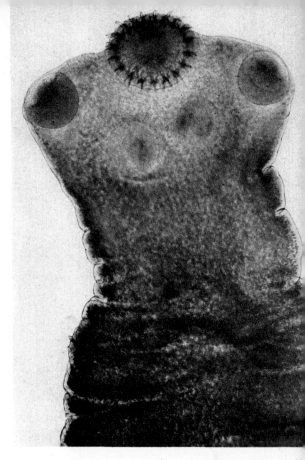

The head of a Rabbit Tapeworm (approximately × 70). In front is the ring of sharp hooks and on the sides four suckers, all of which enable the Tapeworm to attach itself to the intestine.

Tapeworms also have a different phase, usually found in a different species of host. Known as cysts (Cysticercus) they are membranous sacs with scolex inside. The adult tapeworm can develop only in the intestine of a suitable animal that has swallowed a cyst. The cyst of the Liver Tapeworm *(Echinococcus granulosus)* may grow to the size of a child's head, and contains thousands of microscopic scolices *(below)*. These grow in the dog's intestine into small Tapeworms, about $\frac{1}{8}$ to $\frac{1}{5}$ in. in length. It is possible for humans to be infected by eggs from a dog's muzzle, even with fatal consequences.

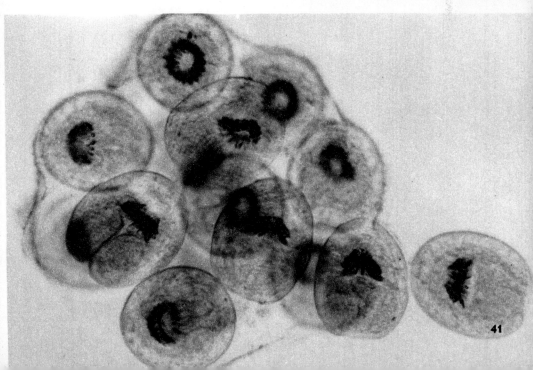

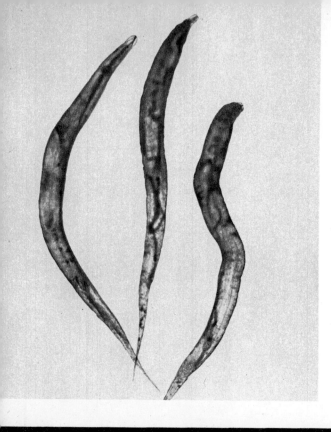

Oxyuris vermicularis (left) belongs to the Nematoda, and is known as a Threadworm. It is white, about $1/6$ to $1/2$ in. long, mobile, and inhabits the human intestine, causing severe irritation. A mature female will produce as many as 12,000 microscopic eggs, one of which can be seen in the lower picture, above the female's head. These eggs contaminate food, either through unclean hands or occasionally by means of dust, and infection may recur frequently.

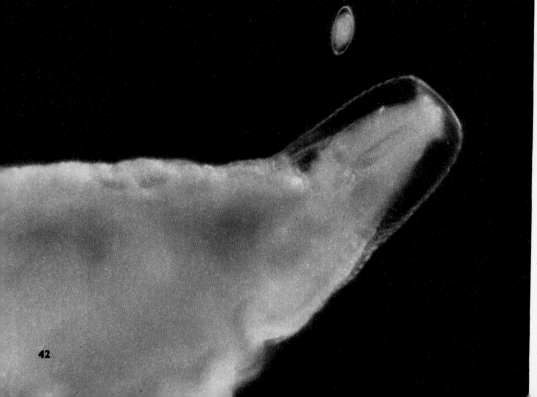

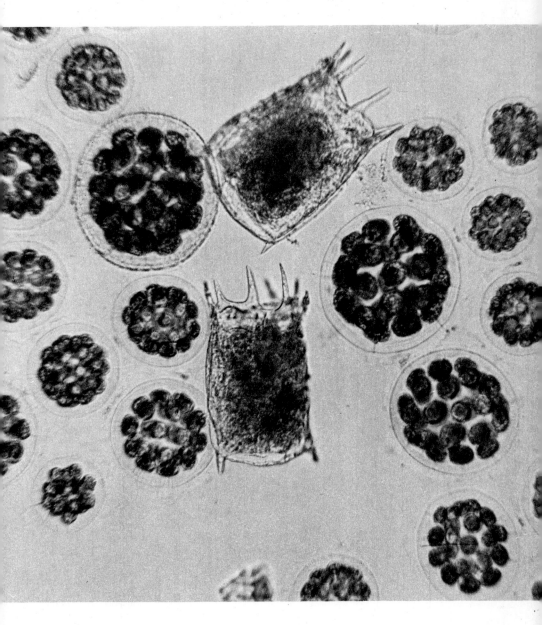

The Rotifera or Wheel Animalcules are microscopic, freshwater creatures, about $^{1}/_{25}$ in. long. The whirling movements of two rings of cilia at the front of the body propel them through the water, and are also used to convey food to the mouth.

Some species, such as *Keratella quadrata* have ornamental cases. The two illustrated here are surrounded by green colonies of *Eudorina elegans* (Flagellata).

MOLLUSCS

The class Amphineura includes what are considered to be the most primitive of the Molluscs. Best known among these is the genus *Chiton*. Their soft bodies are covered by a number of plates, and they are able to coil and uncoil freely. *Chiton* have neither eyes nor feelers. They live on the ocean bed, feeding on organic matter with a mouth situated on the underside of the body (actual size).

Bithynia tentaculata, about $\frac{1}{2}$ in. long *(above)*, lives in stagnant and gently flowing waters in Europe, Asia and Africa. It belongs to the Prosobranchiata Molluscs, most of which are marine animals. The beautiful *Mitra papalis* from the Indian Ocean *(below)* has a white shell decorated with reddish-brown specks. Very many Gastropods (with single shells) live in the sea, varying greatly in size and shape; some are elegant and beautifully coloured.

The Triton's Horn *(Tritonium tritonis)*, from the coastal shallows of the Pacific.   The shell of a young specimen, actual size.   Below is the shell of *Murex tenuispina* from the Indian Ocean.

The shell of *Cypraea argus* from the equatorial zone of the Pacific. The picture shows the underside of the shell.

Below are two *Cypraea tigris* shells from the shores of Polynesia (actual size).

Above, the shell of *Pterocera rugosa* from the shores of Tahiti (actual size).

Below, *Conus textile* from Polynesia. Care must be taken in collecting these, for their bite is poisonous. *Conus princeps* is found on the west coast of Central America.

Shells of Sea Snails. From left to right and top to bottom: *Murex radix, Murex microphyllus, Murex approximatus* – taken from the Atlantic: *Cypraea tigris, Cypraea aurantium, Cypraea testudinaria* – from the Pacific. Below, centre: *Turbo sarmaticus* (shell worn away to the mother-of-pearl layer). Below: *Murex regius* – from the Panama Canal, *Ranella elegans* – from the Atlantic, *Cassis rufa* – from the Indian Ocean (approx. half natural size).

With very few exceptions, all the land molluscs belong to the order Pulmonata. *Zebrina detrita (right)*, which is about an inch long, lives in dry regions of the European Mediterranean, extending its habitat to parts of south-west and central Germany, and as far as north-western Iran.

Below, a picture of *Cochlodina laminata* which lives in forest gorges throughout central and northern Europe (approximately × 13).

Many land molluscs have either no shell or an underdeveloped one. The Slug *Arion hortensis (left)* is a familiar pest in vegetable gardens. It is yellowish-brown or dark grey in colour and measures between 1–1$\frac{1}{2}$ in.

Below, the large *Limax maximus*, light grey with black markings. These Slugs spend the day sheltering in the shade, emerging at night or on a rainy day to search for food.

A well populated site of the Striped Snail *(Helicella candicans)*, which inhabits dry fallow land, grassy slopes, chalky or sandy hillsides, embankments and fields. They are widespread in south and central Europe.

Although the Pulmonata are hermaphrodites, sexual union takes place among them, the eggs being laid by the individual acting as the female, usually in the earth or under stones. Below, the Snail *Monacha incarnata*, a European forest species. It has just laid a batch of eggs, from which the young will emerge in twenty days ($\times$ 9$^1/_4$).

In rare instances mollusc shells are decorated with spikes or hairs. *Isognomo-
stoma personatum* from the mountain forests of Europe is covered with regularly
spaced hairs, all of the same length.
Three 'teeth' protrude from its lip.

Below, Roman or Edible Snail *(Helix pomatia)*, attached to the bark of a tree. Alongside is a picture of the same species, partially burrowed into the ground while laying eggs. Above, a photomicrograph of a snail's tongue (radula) with which it rasps its food.

The sexual union of two *Helix pomatia*. Though hermaphrodites, they exchange the products of their gonads. Below, a cluster of eggs of *Helix pomatia*, after being uncovered. On the right, *Cepaea vindobonensis* (× 4). This Snail lives on dry rocky hillsides and in woods in parts of central and eastern Europe.

Helicigona faustina (left), one of the most beautiful European Snails, lives chiefly on the chalk formations of the Carpathians, hiding in damp, rocky crevices ($\times\ 4^1/_2$).

The somewhat larger *Helicigona banatica (below)* favours drier rocks, especially under forest cover, in the mountains of eastern and southern Europe. The shell of this attractive species is an inch across and coloured light brown.

The Bivalves (Lamellibranchiata) are another large class of Molluscs. They live in water and breathe through gills. The most typical of these are the Cockles. The Prickly Cockle *(Cardium echinatum) (opposite page,* $\times$ 8) is found in European waters, particularly along the south coast of England. It has a long, red, hooked foot, which enables it to move about on the sea bed. Its flesh is very appetising.

The vivid, pastel-coloured shells of the genus *Spondylus*, widespread in warm seas, are very attractive. In the live shell the two valves are pressed together, held by a strong muscle. There is a raised part on the inside of the shell where the muscle was originally attached. *Spondylus pictorum (opposite)* is found on rocks round the southern coasts of North America.

The Cephalopoda are an extremely specialised and highly organised group of Molluscs. Those with a shell nowadays represent only a small remnant of the numerous and very varied fossil Cephalopods which have existed since the Cambrian period.

Cephalopods are predators which attack other marine animals, overpowering them with strong tentacles, and crushing them with hard, beak-shaped jaws. Some genera (including *Architeuthis*, the Giant Squid) are veritable monsters, with tentacles as long as 14 ft. and bodies up to 6 ft. Not surprisingly, divers have found these huge creatures to be formidable adversaries.

In all Cephalopods the sexes are separate and they reproduce by means of eggs. Some 600 living and 10,000 extinct species are known, the great majority of which belong to the Octopoda (8-armed) or Decapoda (10-armed).

Below is the Common Octopus *(Octopus vulgaris)*, which occurs in all the warmer seas. It reaches a maximum length of 3 ft. On the right is a smaller Mediterranean species of Octopus, *Philonexis catenulata*.

The mouths of Cephalopods are encircled by eight or more tentacles, equipped with formidable suckers, which enable them to move and to capture their prey. Some species, as, for instance, *Eledone (Ozaena) moschata* from the Mediterranean, seen on the left, have these tentacles joined by a web of thin skin which enables them to grasp their victims more firmly.

The Decapoda are here represented by the Common Cuttlefish *(Sepia officinalis)*, seen at lower left. Cuttlefish or Sepias live in all the warmer European waters. They swim by means of undulating movements of their fins, unlike the Octopuses which swim by expelling water through a muscular funnel. When it senses approaching danger or is disturbed in any way, the Sepia excretes an inky brown substance. The calcareous cuttlebone or sepion inside its body is used for feeding cagebirds. Most living Cephalopods have no outer shell – only a few develop one in the same way as other Molluscs.

The female of the Mediterranean Paper Nautilus *(Argonauta argo)* builds a thin shell which looks as if it were made of opaque glass *(right)*; the eggs are incubated there. The males are small, with no shell, and resemble Octopuses.

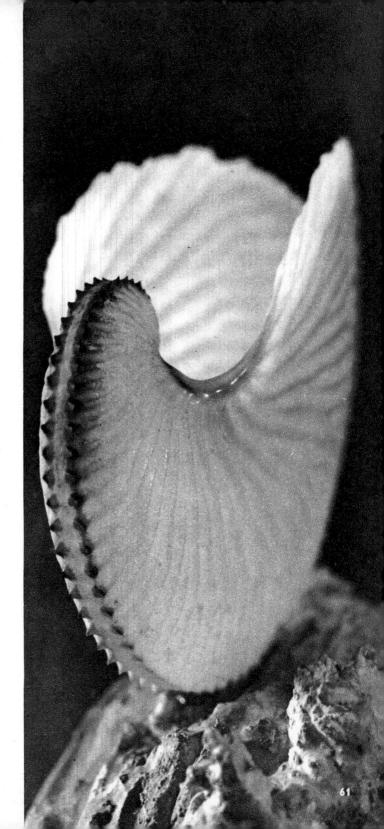

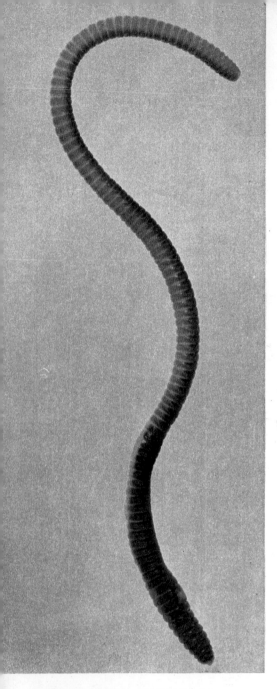
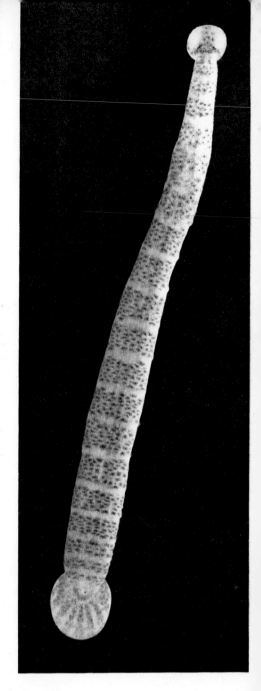

SEGMENTED ANIMALS

A large group known as the Annelida (Segmented Worms) includes the class Oligochaeta in which are the many species of Earthworms as, for instance, *Lumbricus rubellus*, frequently found in garden or forest soil. In the picture on the left, the head is at the bottom (× 2).

Piscicola geometra, or Freshwater Leech, belongs to the class Hirudinea, order Rhynchobdellida. It has a protrusible proboscis with which it sucks blood, chiefly of fishes *(right-hand picture, × 6. The head is at the top)*.

Glossiphonia complanata, an ordinary small Leech inhabiting European ponds (the left-hand picture shows it from above, the right-hand picture from below – both × 8). It can elongate the front part of its body.

Below, the membranous, transparent cocoons of *Herpobdella octoculata*. Eggs and embryos are at various stages of development The newly-hatched Leeches leave the cocoon through a small opening (× 6).

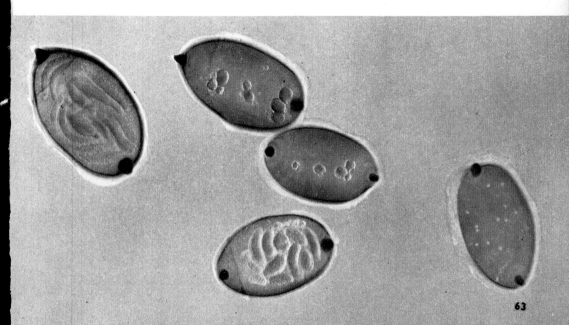

ARTHROPODS

The largest phylum of all is the Arthropoda. The earliest of them were creatures belonging to the class of Trilobites – Trilobita – which lived and became extinct some two hundred million years ago. Some descendants of the Chelicerata, however, have survived to this day. The strange-looking King Crab *(Limulus (or Xiphosura) polyphemus)*, about 20 in. long, lives in the mud along the Atlantic coast of North America, feeding on small creatures. It swims on its back with its legs in the air, turning 'right way up' when crawling along the bottom of shallow waters. The sharp pointed spine at one end of its body helps the Crab to turn over, a particularly difficult operation on dry land. Several related species live in the coastal waters of South-east Asia.

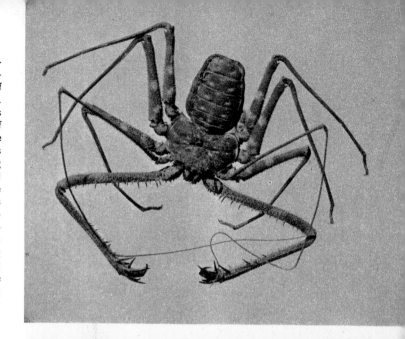

Among the Spiders – Arachnida – one of the most ancient forms is the order of Scorpions – Scorpionida. These nocturnal predators inhabit the warmer parts of the globe. They spend the day concealed under stones or in the ground, preying at night on insects and spiders which they seize with their pincer-like claws and paralyse with their tail-sting. They crush their victim with their scissor-like feelers but feed by injecting digestive juices and sucking the prey dry. Scorpions are viviparous, i.e. they bring forth living young. The top picture is of a Whip Scorpion of the genus *Phrynichus* from tropical Africa, belonging to the order Pedipalpi. The front legs have been transformed into exceptionally long, whip-like feelers; the strong, clawed appendages in front are the pedipalps which seize the prey. This Whip Scorpion is not poisonous ($\times$ 1^1/$_2$).

Below, the Scorpion *Buthus eupeus*, found in the Caucasian area and farther east in central Asia ($\times$ 2).

There are a number of interesting kinds of 'False Scorpions' – Pseudoscorpionida – and 'Harvestmen' – Phalangida. The Book Scorpion, (Chelifer cancroides) illustrated on the right, is found in books and in old warehouses. It is only about ¼ in. long and feeds chiefly on mites.

Best known among European Harvest Spiders or Harvestmen are: the Common Harvester (Phallangium opilio), shown on the left (× 2¹/₂), and Opilio parietinus (lower right, × 2). The feelers of the male Common Harvester are so long that they look like a fifth pair of limbs. Opilio parietinus is somewhat smaller. Harvesters feed on both vegetable and animal refuse, some of them also preying on various insects. None of them spin webs. Both these species, especially the latter, find their way into houses towards the end of summer. Some 2,500 species of Harvest Spiders are known.

Of more than 20,000 different species of true Spiders – Araneae – four are illustrated here. One of the most decorative is *Argiope bruenichi (top left)*, an inhabitant of southern Europe and the warmest parts of central Europe, and which has been found in southern England. It builds its webs in the grass above streams, spinning globular cocoons for its eggs.

Below is a picture of *Teutana grossa* (× 6), one of the commonest of all Spiders, which makes its home in dilapidated houses.

Opposite is a female Garden or Diadem Spider *(Araneus diadematus)*, lying in wait in her web.

The largest Spider in the eastern part of central Europe and the neighbouring warm Mediterranean regions is *Hogna (Trochosa) singoriensis*. Owing to the present swing towards a warmer climate it is now spreading to central Europe itself, where it inhabits dry hillsides and open scrub forests.

The large order of Ticks and Mites – Acarina – also belongs to the Arachnids. This order includes the best known Ticks, the Sheep or Castor-bean Tick *(Ixodes ricinus)*, shown below (× 7). It lives mainly in deciduous woods with dense undergrowth. Ticks in various stages of development live as parasites, usually on warm-blooded vertebrates. They may carry a variety of diseases.

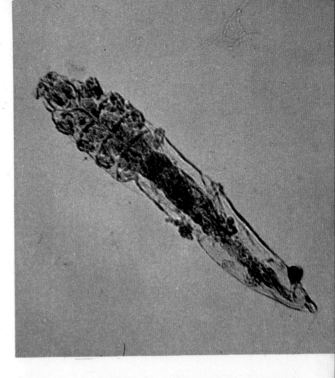

Of the very numerous Mites the most objectionable to humans and to various domestic animals is *Acarus siro (Sarcoptes scabiei)*. It is transferred mainly by actual contact and causes the skin disease known as scabies or sarcoptic mange. The female is larger than the male, but both are under $1/_{50}$ in. long. This variety is typical in man, while many others infest domestic animals exclusively.

The top picture shows another Mite, *Demodex folliculorum*, which infests humans – and causes follicular mange. It is roughly the size of *Sarcoptes*, but oblong in shape. It may be found in the pus of facial skin eruptions, and many similar species infest mammals in all parts of the world.

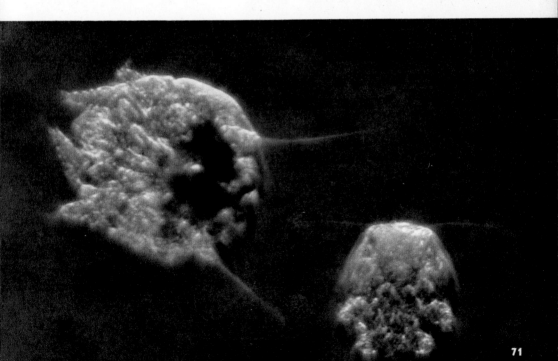

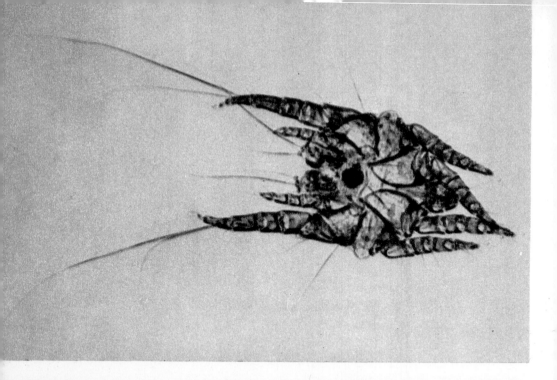

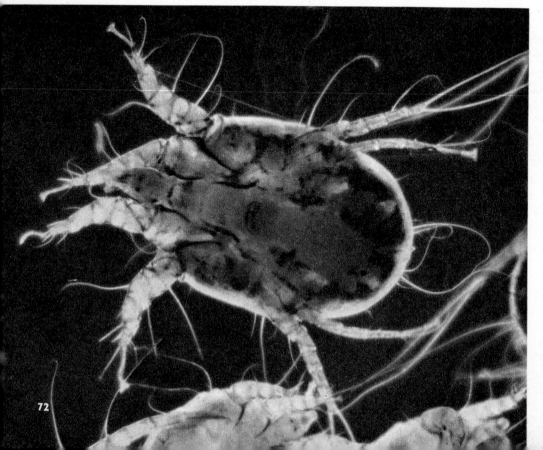

On the left is a parasitic Mite, *Otodectes cynotis*, which infests the ears of dogs and cats. It is $1/8$ in. in length.

Below it is a picture of another parasitic Mite, *Psoroptes cuniculi*, which infests the inner ears of animals, especially domestic rabbits, causing severe pain ($\times$ 120).

On the right are the legs of a hen suffering from scaly leg. *Cnemidocoptes mutans* Mites, of which the females are shown below, live under the thick scabs covering the fowl's feet.

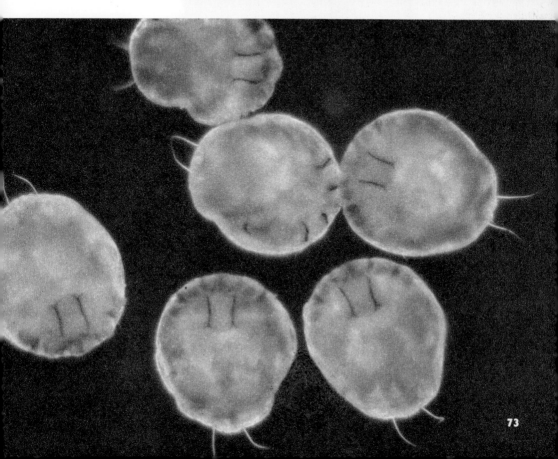

CRUSTACEANS

The Lower Crustacea — Entomostraca — include the order Phyllopoda, the oldest and most primitive of all crustaceans. *Chirocephalus grubei* is almost an inch long and lives in freshwater pools in central Europe. The picture on the left shows a male (*at top*) and a female, while below is a female with a sac full of eggs. Right, *Lepidurus productus*, also from freshwater pools in central Europe (actual size).

Above are two specimens of *Triops cancriformis* (× 2). This species is found in summer, whereas those on pp. 74–5 are found mainly in early spring. They occur very irregularly, being absent for a number of years and then, when particularly favourable conditions occur, quickly build up to large numbers. Their eggs can survive for several years in the bottom mud. These Branchiopods feed on minute aquatic animals.

The order Cladocera (Water Fleas) also belong to the Lower Crustacea, as do the Copepoda. Most of them are tiny transparent creatures inhabiting both marine and fresh waters. They form the chief part of plankton, important for the nutrition of fish and other aquatic animals. On p. 77, top left, is a *Daphnia magna*. Inside its body it has a brood chamber containing two winter eggs (× 20). The picture at top right shows a brood chamber with a fertilised winter egg of the *Alonopsis ambigua*.

The Cyclops (*bottom of p. 77*) lives in fresh water in central Europe.

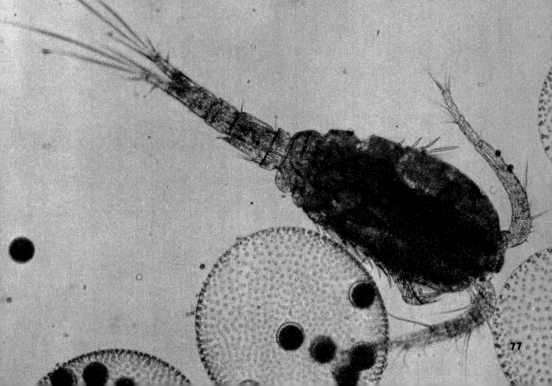

The order Ostracoda contains small, mostly microscopic, marine and freshwater Crustacea whose bodies and heads are completely enclosed in bivalve shells. They have seven pairs of appendages and feed on plants or on the organic matter on the bottom. Some are parasitic. Over 2,000 different species have been described. Fossil shells with their characteristic shapes are important indicators for identifying sedimentary rocks.

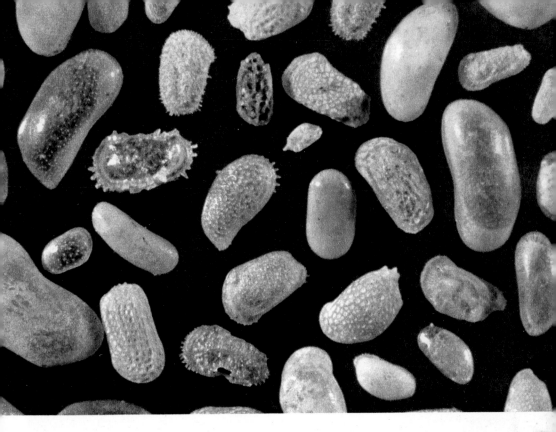

Left, the whole animals, enclosed in their double shells. Above, the individual single shells of various species. Below, a degenerate unarmoured Crustacean: the Carp Louse (*Argulus foliaceus*) (× 8).

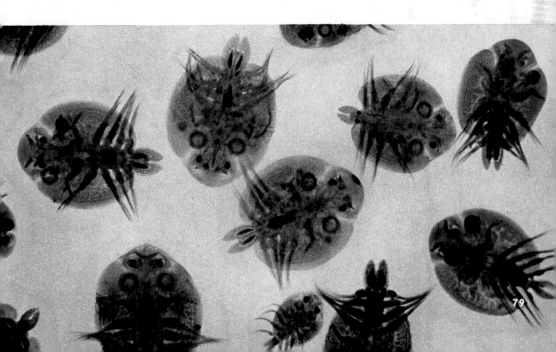

shells often cast up on the shore in large numbers. Below, Acorn Barnacles (*Balanus balanoides*), on the shore of Iceland; a slightly enlarged detail appears in the picture at the bottom of p. 81. Both *Lepas* and *Balanus* belong to the Cirripedia. They can be found on rocks and floating objects, concealed in segmented, calcified carapaces. Their spiral-shaped appendages agitate the water and drive food into their mouths (× 4).

At top right is a picture of a Carp Louse (× 26), a white, transparent Crustacean belonging to the order Branchiura. It is a parasite on freshwater fish.

At top left are some Goose Barnacles (*Lepas anatifera*),

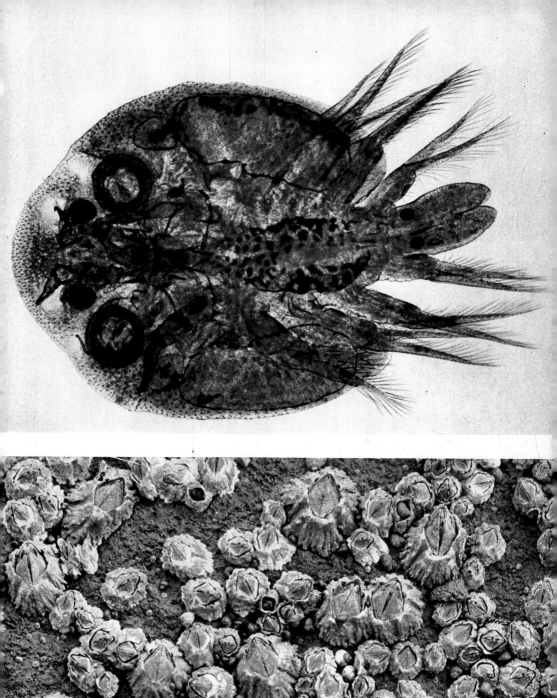

81

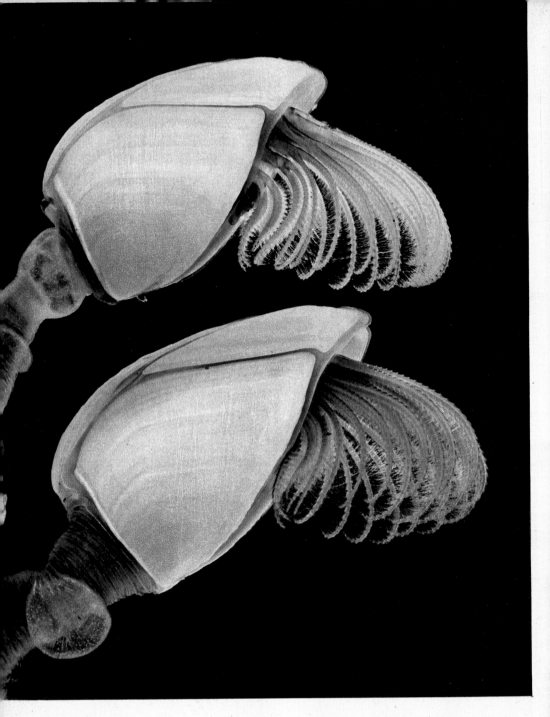

Above, Goose Barnacles *(Lepas anatifera)* (× 3).
The order Isopoda includes most Crustaceans adapted for life on dry land, though they tend to seek damp places to live in. The pictures on the opposite page show two different species of Wood-louse, *Porcellio scaber (above)* and *Oniscus asellus* (× 7). They are commonly found in cellars and old buildings.

Tertiary seas, which took refuge below ground and became adapted to this new mode of life when the sea disappeared. The species shown on the left is *Niphargus tatrensis agtelekiensis* from the subterranean caves of Slovakia.

Below, the Common Freshwater Shrimp *(Gammarus (Rivulogammarus) pulex fossarum)* (× 9), an inhabitant of ponds and brooks. The pictures on p. 85 show two species of Crayfish belonging to the order Decapoda. At the top is the River Crayfish *(Astacus fluviatilis)*, below, the Mud Crayfish *(Astacus leptodactylus)* (actual size).

The most interesting member of the order Amphipoda is the Blind Well-Shrimp *(Niphargus)*, a blind, white freshwater animal, about $\frac{1}{2}$ in. long. It is thought to be a living relic of the

A third species, shown on this page from the side and above, is the Stone Crayfish *(Astacus torrentium)*, which lives in mountain streams.

At the top of p. 87 is the best known of the marine Crustaceans, the Lobster *(Homarus vulgaris)*. The American variety is known as *H. americanus*. It is up to 18 in. long, bluish in colour and lives in the deeper waters, especially in the North Sea.

Below, opposite, is the Langouste or European Rock Lobster *(Palinurus vulgaris)*, also found in Bermuda, where it is known as *P. argus*. It is reddish purple in colour, and lives in the Atlantic Ocean and the Mediterranean. The flesh of both Lobster and Langouste is considered a great delicacy.

87

The Hermit-crabs – Anomura – form a transition group between Crayfish and Crabs. The rear part of their bodies is well developed but usually soft and without any protecting carapace. The Crab inserts it into the shell of a marine snail, which it carries about with it. When it grows bigger, it finds itself a new, larger 'house'. The Common Hermit-crab *(Eupagurus bernhardus)*, shown above, is a frequent inhabitant of both the coast and deeper water of the North Sea and the Atlantic. Sea-anemones are often found growing on the shells of these Crustaceans, living in symbiosis with them. The picture opposite shows a pair of Velvet Crabs *(Portunus holsatus)*, from the coasts of the Atlantic, the male lying on its back.

This typical freshwater Crab, *Potamon potamii*, lives in Armenia where it can be seen running about in the vicinity of rivers, breeding in the lakes from which they flow.'

Below, the Mitten Crab (*Eriocheir sinensis*), which originated in China but at the beginning of this century was transported in ships to the estuaries of the Weser and the Elbe. It has since gradually extended its range to various river systems, returning to brackish waters to breed.

On p. 91 is an interesting small Spider-crab, *Inachus scorpio*, from the Mediterranean. Like all Crabs, it is omnivorous.

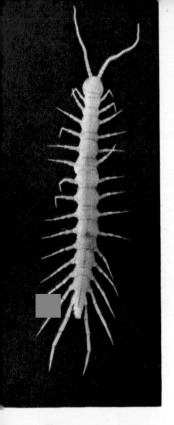

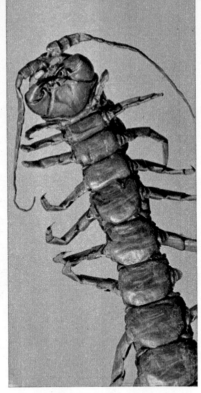

left shows *Lithobius mutabilis*, a very common European Centipede, which lives under stones and in the ground, feeding mainly on small insects. Next to it is the front part of the body of a large tropical Centipede, *Scolopendra gigantea*, which measures 10 in. and feeds on large insects. If forced to defend itself, its poison claws can be dangerous to man.

Below left is *Glomeris guttata* (approx. × 4). Its food consists of vegetable waste lying under stones or fallen leaves. *Schizophyllum sabulosum* (centre), 1½ in. long, has similar habits. Right, the Giant Millipede, *Spirobolus*, from tropical America (actual size). Millipedes are not harmful to man.

The superclass Antennata includes the Centipedes – Chilopoda – and the Millipedes – Diplopoda. The Myriapods belonging to these two classes (over 8,000 species) have a long, segmented body which is not made up of three distinct parts as is the case with adult insects.

Myriapods have separate sexes and lay eggs. The picture on the far

INSECTS

Insects – Insecta – are the most numerous of all forms of animal life. Of these, the Springtails, belonging to the order Collembola are among the most primitive. *Tetrodonthophora bialiensis* is one of the largest *(above, left)*, measuring about $^1/_5$ in.

Lepisma saccharina, the Silverfish *(above, right)* is a well-known nocturnal visitor to the larder in the United States and Europe.

Lepismachilis notata (below, × 6), an inhabitant of sun-warmed rocks of central Europe, has similar-appearing relatives in the United States. Both these and the Silverfish belong to the order Thysanura.

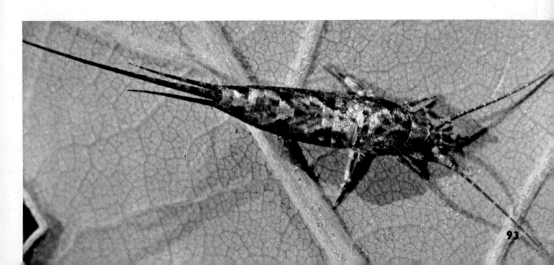

The orders Ephemerida, Mayflies, and Plecoptera, Stoneflies, are the most primitive members of the Pterygota, the large section containing winged insects. Today we know over 1,500 species of Mayflies and about 1,500 species of Stoneflies in various parts of the world. In both the immature stages develop in fresh water, mostly under stones. The development takes up to three years, according to the species. In the May-flies, the immature stages and the adult are separated by a distinct stage, called a subimago, that is unable to feed or breed. The subimago soon sheds its delicate skin and turns into a mature individual or imago, which usually lives only a few hours or days.

The picture on the left (× 4) shows a subimago of the Mayfly *(Ephemera danica)*, while at top right is a mature insect of the same species (× 2). The two stages are at once distinguished by the length of the tail appendages. Members of Ephemera occur in the United States as well as Europe.

The lower picture on p. 95 is of a typical Stonefly, *Perla abdominalis* (× 3).

The immature stages of the order Odonata – Dragonflies – also live in fresh water. Some species take as long as five years to mature.

At top left is *Sympetrum sanguineum*, which in late summer leaves the water and takes to the fields, sometimes migrating in large swarms.

Most of the American species of this genus are reddish in colour.

Right, the Blue Damselfly (*Calopteryx virgo*), usually found near water. Similar-appearing *Calopteryx* are found in many parts of the United States. Below, a nymph, or immature stage, of *Lestes sponsa* (× 4).

Top left, the nymphal skin out of which a Damselfly *(Cordulegaster)* has just emerged *(top right).* This large, vividly coloured species lives near mountain streams.

Below, the larva of *Aeshna*, the Brown Dragonfly, photographed under water (× 3). This genus is quite common in the United States.

The common Green Grasshopper (Katydid) of central Europe *(Tettigonia viridissima)*, shown in its male form in the upper picture, and the Glasshouse Grasshopper *(Tachycines asynamorus)*, of which a female is illustrated below, both belong to the order Orthoptera. Orthoptera live on a wide range of vegetable food and forms similar to these are abundant in the United States. The Glasshouse species, which came to Europe from China, eats only live plants, in particular germinating ones, and is therefore a serious pest. On the right is the Migratory Locust *(Locusta migratoria)*, a widespread

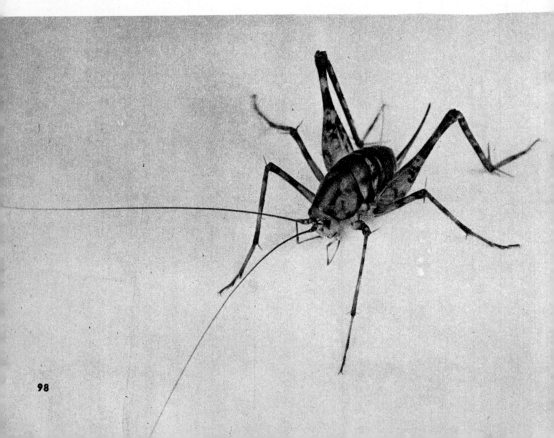

pest which has several sub-species and two ecological phases in the warmer parts of Asia, in Africa, and in South-east Europe. The hoppers of the solitary phase hatch in sandy reed-beds, while from time to time individuals of the migratory phase come into being. Plagues in which huge swarms of these insects invade and devastate large areas have been a well-known phenomenon since ancient times. The Migratory Locusts in the United States belong to the genus *Melanoplus*.

Below is a well-known European garden and field pest, the Mole-cricket *(Gryllotalpa gryllotalpa)*, said to have been introduced into North America. It is a member of the family Gryllidae – Crickets. Towards evening and at night its strong, uninterrupted chirping can be heard, produced by rubbing together its fore wings. Curiously, this relatively heavy insect is capable of flight. (All pictures on pp. 98 and 99, × 2.)

Above is a picture of House Crickets (*Gryllus domesticus*) which live in the warmer parts of the Old World. They usually live near human habitations, while in colder climates are only to be found in constantly heated houses. They are nocturnal animals and feed on both animal and vegetable waste. Most of the Crickets shown here are in larval stages, only those with wings being adults.

On the left, a male Old World Field-cricket (*Gryllus campestris*) (× 4), which lives in southern and central Europe, North Africa, and western Asia. In cultivated regions this attractive, harmless creature gives 'concerts' in the fields and dry hillsides on which it lives. It is omnivorous.

The Indian Stick Insect (*Carausius morosus*), shown on near right, resembles a dry twig. It is a close relative of American Walkingsticks. On the far right are its eggs (× 8).

Below, a Leaf Insect (*Phyllium*), also from India. Its shape, colour and trembling movement give it a remarkable likeness to a green leaf. Both these species belong to the family Phasmidae and are typical examples of plant mimicry by insects.

The Common Earwig *(Forficula auricularia)*, shown above, feeds on vegetable food and upon small insects such as green fly. It is nocturnal and spends the day hiding under the bark of trees or in cracks in timber (× 7). It is widely distributed around the world and is considered a pest in parts of the United States.

The Praying Mantis *(Mantis religiosa)* is the only central European species of a large family found mainly in the hotter parts of the world. A powerful flier, it frequents dry, grassy regions, and is carnivorous. Shown below is a male *Mantis* (× 2). Several American species resemble closely this European form.

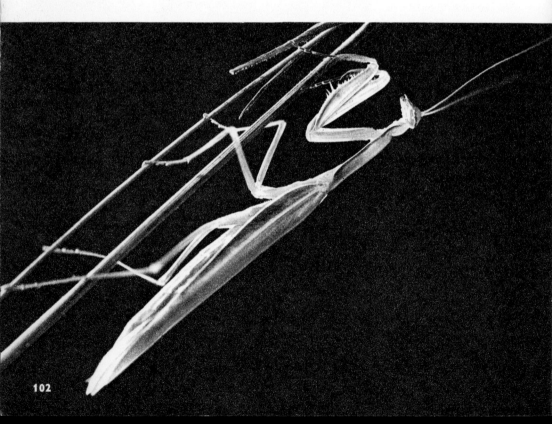

Above, a colony of the American Cockroach *(Peri-planeta americana)*. Most of the insects in this picture are wingless nymphs. This species of Cock- roach occurs in all the warmer regions of the world; in temperate parts it is found only in well-heated places or in deep mines.

Cockroaches lay their eggs in special capsules. On p. 104 is one such capsule of the European Cockroach (Blatella germanica), with several adult insects. This species has a similar range to the American Cockroach (× 4).

Above, a pair of Oriental Cockroaches (Blatta orientalis) (× 2), with the female on the right. This species, too, needs a warm environment. Both of these species are common pests in the United States.

Termites form the order Isoptera and very few species live outside the tropics. Calotermes flavicollis is found around the Mediterranean. Two soldiers are shown below, right (× 4). On the left are a wingless specimen and a winged male at swarm time. This species lives chiefly inside rotting trees, but will also attack planks and beams in buildings. Termites found in the United States are similar to these in appearance.

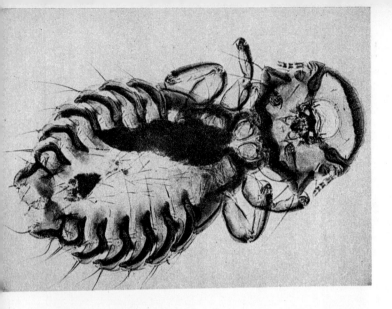

Biting Lice (Mallophaga) and Sucking Lice (Anoplura) are all parasitic on animals. The upper picture shows *Goniodes colchicus*, a species of Mallophaga infesting pheasants. The female measures only $1/10$ in. This louse lives among the feathers of its host, feeding on horny particles of the skin and on the feathers themselves. Below are two specimens of the widely distributed Biting Louse, *Trichodectes canis*, which lives on the dog. This is an even smaller species (about $1/20$ in.) which penetrates the dog's fur, and feeds on the blood and lymph. At top right, two Crab Lice *(Phthirus pubis)* attached to a human hair. These insects, about $1/16$ in. long, infest hairy parts of the human body other than the head, piercing the skin and sucking blood and lymph. The adjoining picture shows their eggs, deposited on a hair.

Lower right (p. 107) shows *Pediculus humanus capitis*, a Sucking Louse infesting the

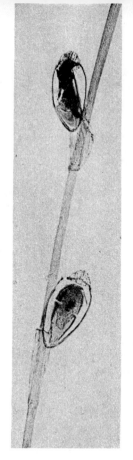

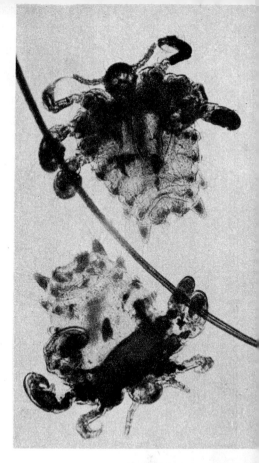

hair of the head, measuring about $1/10$ in. The third form of human Louse is *Pediculus humanus corporis*, about $1/8$ in. long, living on the body and in clothing, and responsible for the spreading of typhus and other epidemics. The use of insecticides has greatly reduced the numbers of these parasites in most parts of the world. The Sucking Lice that infest man are found around the world.

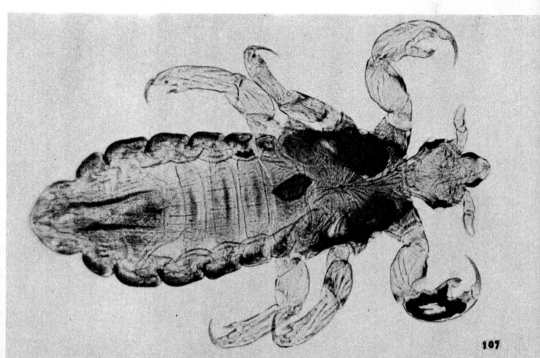

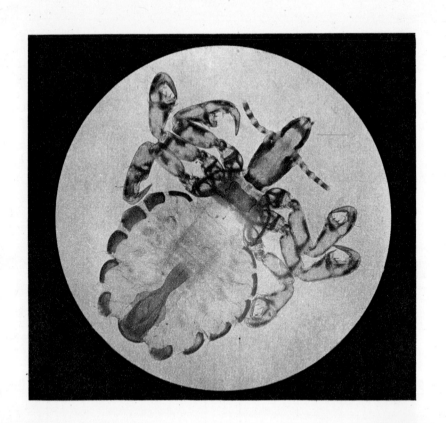

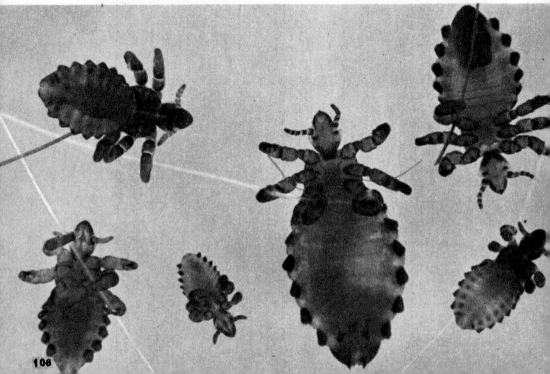

Most animals have specific parasites. For instance the large Swine Louse *(Haematopinus suis)*, which measures $1/_5$ in. and has rudimentary eyes, lives on the domestic pig. It is shown at the top of p. 108.

The lower picture is of *Haematopinus eurysternus* which parasitises various species of cattle. Both Sucking Lice, they are cosmopolitan in distribution.

From our own point of view, the most unpleasant of the Bugs (order Hemiptera) is the Bed-bug *(Cimex lectularius)*. It remains hidden during the day, emerging at night to suck human blood. Above is a picture of several of these pests, young as well as adult, shed skins, and *(top left)* an egg ($\times$ 11).

The picture on the right shows the small predatory *Empicoris vagabunda* ($\times$ 5), which also lives in human dwellings but is useful because it attacks and kills flies and other harmful insects.

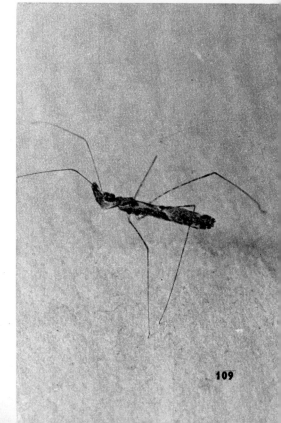

Many insects belonging to the order Hemiptera (True Bugs) are known in nature. The largest of the European aquatic species is the Water Stick-insect *(Ranatra linearis)*, which is illustrated in the picture on the left. With its legs it measures 3 in. This curious insect seizes its prey with its long, prehensile front legs, impales it on its pointed proboscis and then sucks it dry.

Below is the common Water Scorpion *(Nepa cinerea)* ($\times$ 3^1/$_2$). It is the colour of mud and is reddish on the underside of the wings. This stinging insect inhabits freshwater pools, ponds and canals, like the related Water Stick-insect. Both species have close relatives in the United States. At top right on page 111 are three specimens of the Fire Bug *(Pyrrhocoris apterus)*. These insects are a little over ^{2}/$_5$ in. long. They are beautifully coloured red and black, and live in colonies, sunning themselves and seeking their food together. They are to be found on the lower parts of the trunks of old lime or elm trees, usually on the side facing the sun. They suck the body fluids of dead worms, snails and insects, and also suck various juicy berries which they find on the ground. Some related North American species are considered pests by farmers.

At top left are two individuals of the Swallow Bug *(Oeciacus hirundinis)* ($\times$ 12), found hibernating in a martin's nest. They are paler, more yellow, and more hairy than Bed-bugs and do not infest man. *Oeciacus vicarius* has similar habits in North America. At the bottom of p. 111 are two Striped Bugs *(Graphosoma italicum)* ($\times$ 6). These brightly coloured, harmless insects are usually found on the blossoms of umbelliferous plants. Although members of this family occur in North America, none of them is striped.

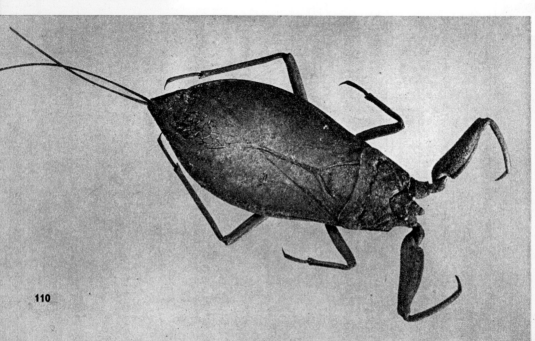

The order Homoptera includes among others the Cicadas (Cicadidae), Green-flies (Aphididae), and Mealybugs (Coccidae). Most Cicadas live in warm regions and are extremely varied in colour and shape. There are only a few species in Central Europe. Of the larger species the most northerly is the Blackhorn Cicada *(Cicadetta tibialis)*, which is illustrated top left. It is about 1 in. long and can be found on vegetation in sunny places. The Periodical Cicada is the best known North Ameri-

Leaf Insect from Ceylon ($\times$ 2½).

can species. The front part of the head of
the Central American Lantern Fly *(Later-
naria phosphorea)*, shown top right, p. 112, is
swollen. People once believed that this
gave off light. At the bottom of p. 112 is
a small European Spittlebug (Cercopidae),
the brown *Aphrophora alni* (× 9). Its larva
feeds on various bushes and herbs. On the
right is a group of Green-fly, or Plant-lice,
of the Aphididae family, seen on a willow
leaf. Members of this family, which are
found around the world, suck the sap of
plants.

On the branches of untended fruit trees
we often find Scale Insects, one of which
(Lecanium corni), is illustrated below. These
are the dead bodies of females which protect
the eggs and later the young of the next
generation (× 4).

Some species of Scale Insect are active throughout their lives. One of these is *Orthezia urticae*, a strange insect about $^2/_5$ in. in length, which is to be found in spring and summer on tall nettles. The females have bodies covered with strips of a chalk-white, waxy substance. The winged males live for a very brief period in early spring. Relatives of this species can be found in the United States.

The order Hymenoptera includes the Pine Sawfly (*Lophyrus pini*), a well-known forest pest in Europe. Close relatives cause heavy damage to coniferous forests in North America. The male, which is only some $^3/_{10}$ in. long, is black in colour and has comb-like feelers (p. 115, *top left*). The female is a little over $^2/_5$ in. in size, and is brown in colour. A female which had just laid her eggs on a pine-needle is illustrated top right on p. 115.

The larvae of Sawflies resemble those of butter-flies, but they can be recognised by their curied tails. Their body is often in the shape of an S, the tail being elevated (picture below).

Small insects which cause the growth of so-called galls on various plants are known as Gall Wasps (Cynipidae). The female makes an incision in the plant tissue and then lays one or more eggs in it. The plant reacts by producing a special growth in which the larvae hatched out of the eggs live and feed. The picture on the left shows a rose gall of *Andricus fecundator* (× 3), on an oak twig.

At the bottom on p. 116 can be seen the hard, ligneous marble galls made by *Cynips kollari* ($\times \frac{1}{3}$). Although neither species occurs in the United States, many other Gall Wasps do. The true Wasps belong to the Aculeata, a group of the Hymenoptera. Above is a picture of German Wasps *(Vespa germanica)*.

A nest of the Saxon Wasp *(Dolichovespula saxonia)* is shown below (both pictures in actual size). These two species look very much like American Hornets (or Yellow Jackets) to which they are closely related.

The open nest hanging on a stalk in the picture on the left is that of *Polistes bimaculatus* (× ¹/₄), a central European Wasp, usually found in rocks, quarries and sandpits among fields. Other species of *Polistes* are a common sight in the vicinity of houses and garages in the United States.

Below is a Hornet *(Vespa crabro)* (× 3¹/₂). It has exceptionally long feelers and can safely be taken in the hand, for only the females have stings. This species has been introduced into the eastern United States. There are also innumerable parasitic Wasps, both large and small, which lay their eggs inside other insects or spiders. The larvae then literally 'eat up' their unwilling host. The top picture on p. 119 is of a caterpillar of the moth *Diloba caeruleocephala*, almost destroyed by the larvae of Braconid Wasps of the genus *Microgaster* (× 5). The larvae had eaten their way up to the surface of the caterpillar's body and formed pupae there in cocoons. Shortly afterwards, the adult Wasps cut off the tops of the cocoons and crawled out. Sights such as these are not uncommon in the United States.

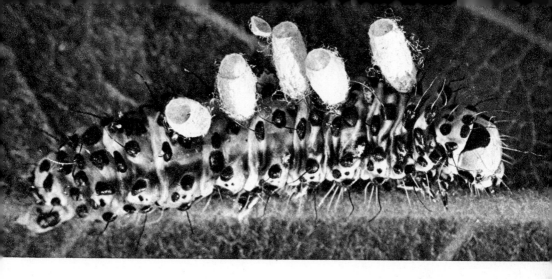

Below, Red Ants or Wood Ants *(Formica rufa)* (× 2), crawling over a slice of apple placed on the ant-hill. All the Ants in the picture are workers, the males and females only coming out at swarming time.

Above are live workers of the Red Ant (greatly magnified).   On the left is a Queen Bumblebee *(Bombus terrestris)* – a hibernating fertilised female (× 3).   In spring she can be seen as one of the first pollen-seekers, flying from plant to plant.   She investigates every crevice, seeking a suitable place for a nest.   Nearly 50 species of Bumblebees are found in North America.

The picture on p. 121 shows a worker Honey-bee *(Apis mellifera)* with its proboscis inserted into the newly opened floret.   On its hind leg the Bee has a full pollen basket.

The Great Water Beetle *(Dytiscus marginalis)* (× 2¹/₄), which is illustrated above, belongs to the Coleoptera, suborder Adephaga. It is carnivorous and lives in freshwater pools and ponds. Its larva is likewise predacious and burrows into the bank to form pupae. Both adult beetle and larva must surface at intervals to breathe. This species is thought to occur both in Europe and North America.

Below is *Chalcophora mariana* (× 3), of the suborder Polyphaga, which includes the majority of Beetles. It is a beautiful bronze colour, but is usually covered with a fine layer of white 'sawdust' which renders it practically invisible against the trunk of the pine-tree. The larvae tunnel in the live wood of these trees. Species of this genus are widely distributed in the United States.

The family Lampyridae includes the Glow-worms *(Lampyris noctiluca)*. A male is illustrated above (× 10). These luminescent little Beetles can be seen on summer nights flying on the fringes of woods and in damp forest clearings, as they look for the wingless females on the bushes. The females too give off a light. These insects feed on small snails. This family is common in North America, where the adults are called Fireflies.

Below is the larva (× 3½) and the pupa (× 8) of the cosmopolitan Meal-worm *(Tenebrio molitor)*. Its yellowish-brown larva has a hard integument and lives in old flour and among refuse.

Above is a Meal-worm (× 5). It lives on the refuse it finds in the dark corners of flourmills, larders and warehouses, and will sometimes breed in such large numbers as to become a serious pest. Its larvae are used to feed a wide range of small insectivorous animals in captivity, and are 'mass-produced' for this purpose.

Below is another Tenebrionid Beetle, *Blaps lethifera* (approx. × $\frac{1}{3}$). These Beetles inhabit cellars, stables and various dark places, living on vegetable refuse and scraps of food. They used to be much persecuted in Europe owing to a superstition that their appearance heralded a death in the house. This species has been accidentally introduced into the United States.

On p. 125 is the Bacon and Skin Beetle (*Dermestes lardarius*) (× $6\frac{1}{2}$). Two adult beetles are shown at the top, and below is a larva. Surrounding them are the shed skins of larvae, excrement and remains of food. These insects eat dry animal matter and destroy badly prepared skins and zoological collections.

Of the Lady-birds (Coccinellidae) the best known European species is one of the largest, *Coccinella septempunctata*, the Seven-spot Lady-bird (× 6). This is a very useful destroyer of aphids, its larva accounting for as many as fifty of these pests a day. Above right are two pupae of the somewhat smaller *Coccinella bipunctata*, the Two-spot Lady-bird (× 6). This species is widely distributed over Europe and North America.

The largest European Beetle – not counting the length of the antennae of some other species – is the male Common Stag Beetle *(Lucanus cervus)* (× ¹/₃). Its large larvae and pupae develop in the rotting wood of old oak trees. Smaller, but still impressive Stag Beetles occur in the United States.

An exotic Stag Beetle from Chile *(Chiasognathus granti)*, is illustrated on p. 127 (× 3). The male's mandibles are longer than its body.

The best known European Dor Beetle (family Scarabaeidae) is the forest species *Geotrupes silvaticus*, illustrated above. It has a shiny, blackish-blue body. The female lays her eggs in a ball of dung which she then buries in the ground. The young Beetles emerge the following year. Closely rela-

ted species with similar habits are found in North America.

Below is a pair of Dung Beetles of the genus *Scarabaeus* from the warmer parts of south-east Europe, North Africa, and central Asia. They are rolling their well-rounded ball of dung along the

Honey Bee and Bumble Bee on a Dahlia ($\times$ 4).

ground in the desert. Of the many kinds of Dung Beetles in the United States, none belongs to the genus *Scarabeus*.

Swarms of small Chafers can be seen in central Europe flying about on summer evenings in July, shortly after dark. These are *Amphimallus solstitialis*, which are hairy, yellowish-brown and little more than half the size of the Cockchafer. They undergo their development in grass-grown clearings, parks and gardens, the larvae living in the ground and feeding on grass roots. The damage caused by them is insignificant as compared with that done by the Cock-chafer, in spite of the fact that they frequently appear in large numbers. A fully-grown larva can be seen below (× 6).

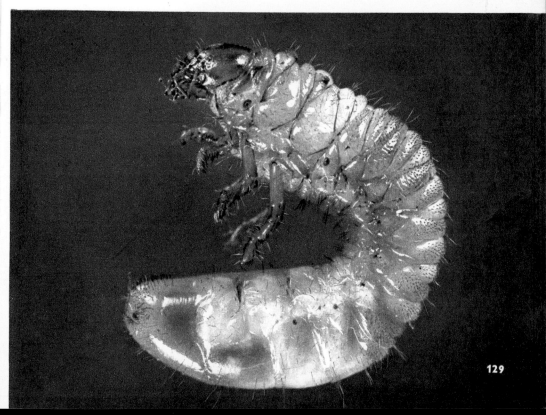

The larvae of the Common Cockchafer (*Melolontha melolontha*) are illustrated above (× ⅓). They take four years to develop, spending this period in the ground where they feed on the roots of plants. Below left are the larvae (× ¼), on the right the pupa of the European Rose Chafer (*Potosia cuprea*) (× 2), found inside a rotting tree-stump on an ant-hill.

On the right is a male Common Cockchafer (× 2$\frac{1}{2}$) photographed just about to take off from the branch.

Below is *Trichius fasciatus* (× $\frac{1}{3}$), a yellow and black Beetle which is one of the most attractive of all the central European species. It is completely harmless, its larvae living in rotting wood.

The extensive Scarabaeid family also includes two sub-families among which are classified some of the most decorative Beetles in the world, both in shape and colouring. The Rose Chafers (Cetonidae) form a large sub-family which is especially well represented in the tropics.

A male *Megalorhina harrisi* (× 3¹⁄₄) from West Equatorial Africa.

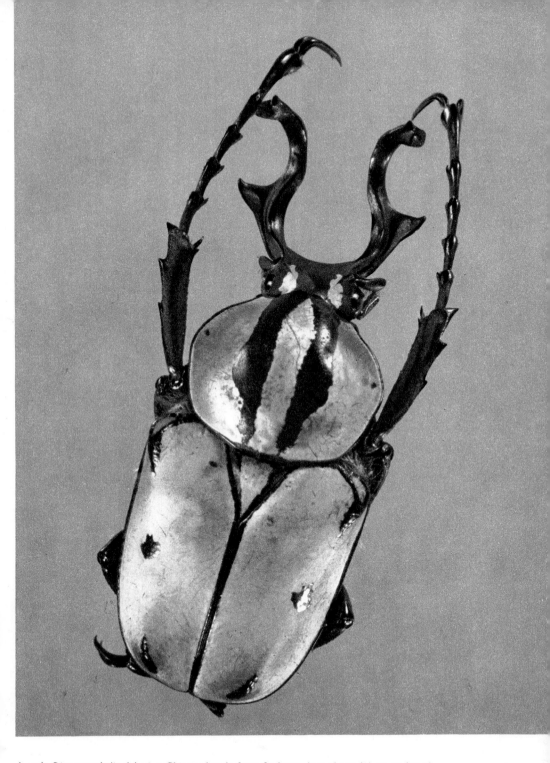

A male *Dicranocephalis dabryi*, a Chinese beetle from Sechuan. It is about $1^1/_5$ in. in length.

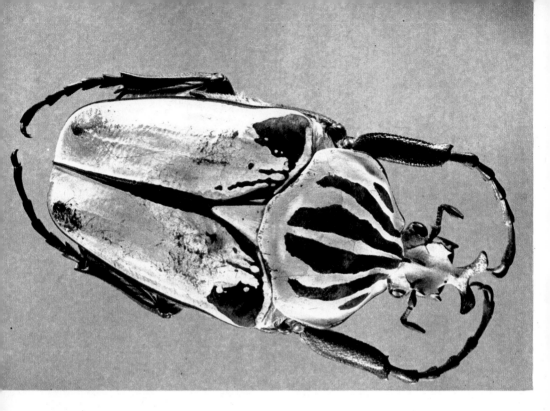

The Goliath Beetles from Equatorial Africa include some of the largest Beetles in the world. Above is *Goliathus caccicus* from West Africa. It is about 3 in. long. Below is the smaller but more beautiful species, *Goliathus kirkianus courtsi*, which is only about $2\frac{1}{2}$ in. long and inhabits East Equatorial Africa.

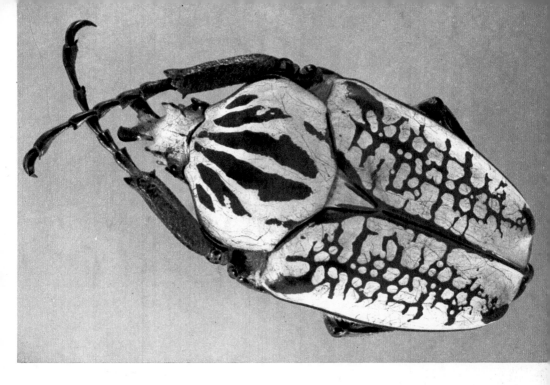

Goliathus meleagris has a mother-of-pearl sheen and lives in Katanga in southern Congo. This male specimen measured $2\frac{1}{2}$ in.

Below is *Goliathus goliathus*, which is widespread throughout most of Equatorial Africa (only $1\frac{1}{5}$ in. larger than actual size). Goliath Beetles fly among the tree tops in the jungle, feeding on the petals and stamens of palm and other flowers. The larvae live in rotting wood.

The Dynastinae are another subfamily of the Scarabaeidae, remarkable for their bizarre shapes and often their size. The males have long, sometimes branched horns on their heads and prothoraces, the purpose of which is not yet known. The European Rhinoceros Beetle *(Oryctes nasicornis) (above, × 3¹/₂)*, is of a rather sober appearance when compared with the more exotic species, but even so it is a handsome insect. Three larvae of *Oryctes nasicornis* (slightly magnified), can be seen on the top of p. 136. They live in forests and gardens, being found in decaying vegetable matter, rotten wood, etc.

The bottom picture shows the pupae of a male *Oryctes nasicornis* (× 2), found in a manure heap.

The tropical Dynastines have curiously-shaped horns on top of their heads and prothoraces. The males use these horns, which are sometimes saw-shaped or pointed on the inside, as a weapon when fighting. Above is *Golofa pizarro* (× 2) from Mexico, which has a rectangular plate, hairy below, at the end of its horn. Below is the Indian and Indonesian *Chalcosoma atlas* (actual size), black in colour with a greenish sheen. The most beautiful specimens live in Celebes, and the largest in Sumatra and Java.

The Hercules Beetle (*Dynastes hercules*) is considered to be the largest Beetle in the world. When making such comparisons, however, it is always a question of what criteria are applied, whether one considers the length or width of the body, or the overall length including the appendages. It is for this reason that there is much inconsistency in these classifications. The Hercules lives in the Antilles, Guatemala, Costa Rica, Nicaragua, and Panama. Its wing-sheaths are a light greenish-blue, irregularly spotted with black. The rest of its body is a shiny colour, the hairy underside of the horn being reddish. The male in the picture is reduced by $1^1/_5$ in. The females are considerably smaller and have no horns. Several species of *Dynastes* live in the United States. Though smaller than the Hercules Beetle, they resemble it closely.

The Long-horned Beetles (Cerambycidae) are another family which includes many of the most bizarre and beautiful species. They vary in size from small insects less than $2/_5$ in. in length to some of the real giants among Beetles. One of the most common in the central European coniferous forests is the *Harpium inquisitor*. What seems to be the same species is widely distributed in North America. It is about $4/_5$ in. long, brownish-grey in colour, with two dark, oblique stripes on its wings. The larvae develop under the bark of dead coniferous trees. Before turning into pupae, they build a kind of cradle out of dry pine needles, in which the pupa lives until the following spring. This is shown in the picture on the left (slightly magnified).

In summer one may find small Longicorns of the genus Leptura crawling about on blossoms in many parts of Europe and North America. They are usually coloured brown or red and develop inside old tree stumps.

Below left is a male *Acanthocinus aedilis* (approx. actual size). It has extraordinarily long antennae. Its larvae live in the wood of pine trees. Several similar-appearing, close relatives in this genus occur in the United States.

Below right is the largest European Longicorn, *Cerambyx cerdo*. It flies about in the woods at the end of May and beginning of June, and its larvae live in old oak trees.

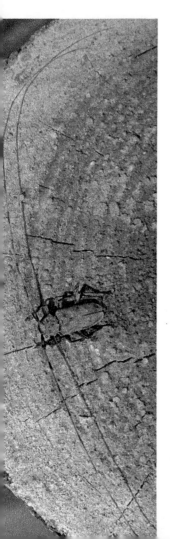

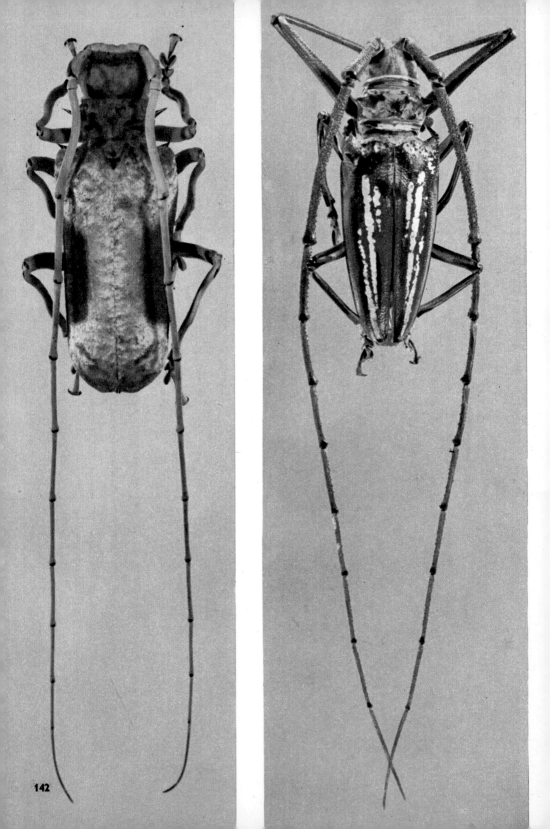

On the opposite page are two large tropical Longicorns. On the left is *Petrognatha gigas* ($\times \frac{1}{3}$), from West Africa, and on the right *Batocera wallacei* (actual size), from New Guinea and the adjacent island of Arru. In some countries certain species of Longicorns are protected, one being the beautiful *Rosalia alpina*, found only in the mountain beech forests of central Europe. It is light greyish blue with black, velvety spots. On the right is a male ($\times \frac{1}{3}$).

Below right is another beautiful Longicorn, species, *Aegosoma scabricorne* (slightly magnified). It lives on deciduous trees.

Below right is another beautiful Longicorn, *Morimus funereus* ($\times \frac{1}{6}$). It is like *Rosalia alpina* in colour, but sturdier in build. Apart from having the same black, velvety spots as the *Rosalia alpina* species, the upper surfaces of its fore-wings are rough grained and wrinkled. This insect is an inhabitant of south-east Europe, being fairly common in some parts.

143

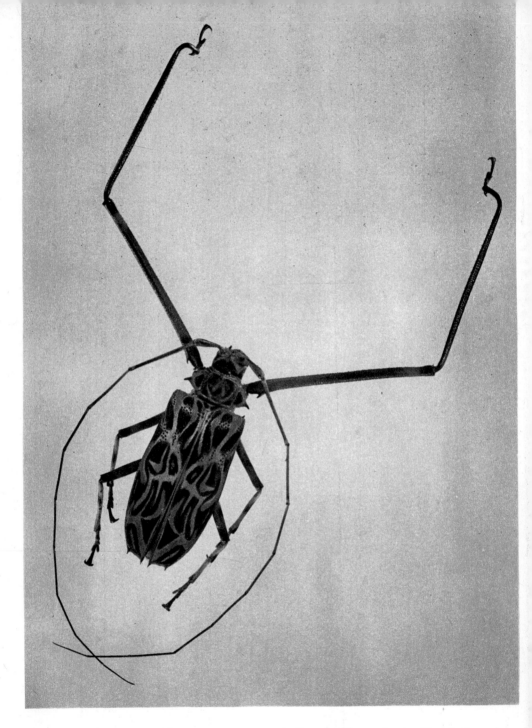

Acrocinus longimanus is a curious-looking Longi-corn from the tropical forests of the Amazon regions.

One of the largest Beetles, *Macrodontia cervicornis*, from southern Brazil, is illustrated on p. 145 (both pictures actual size).

America is the Colorado Beetle (*Leptinotarsa decemlineata*) from North America. It belongs to the family Chrysomelidae, most of whose members are beautiful and harmless. The larvae of the Colorado Beetle are reddish-yellow with black spots. The picture at top left shows three pupae in various positions and one adult larva (× 4). Below is an adult Beetle, crawling over a potato (× 5).

At the top of p. 147 is a pest in North America which attacks lentils, *Laria lentis* (× 6). Its larvae eat their way inside a lentil and there pupate. The adult insect then eats its way out again. The bottom picture shows barley grains damaged by the Granary Weevil (*Sitophilus granaria*) (× 5), a very serious pest in granaries. It has several close relatives of economic importance in the United States.

Other attractive and rare Beetles are pests which must be fought because the damage they do is counted in millions. A well-known pest in North

Common Rhinoceros Beetle (× 3).

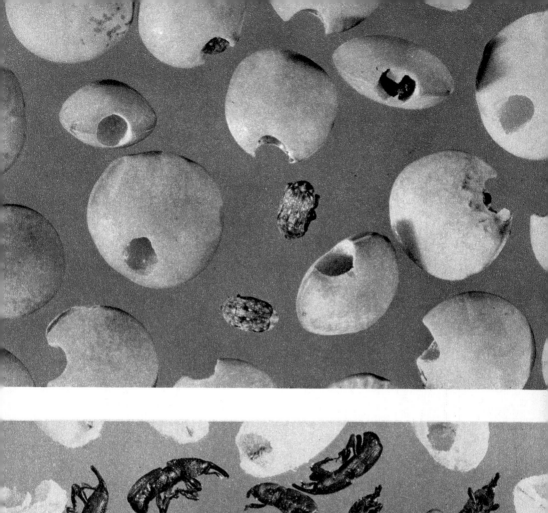

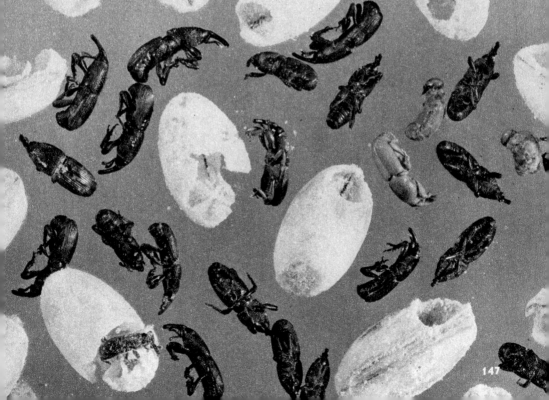

147

growing shoots of young trees as is shown in the picture on the left ($\times$ 5).

Below is a Bark Beetle of the family Scolytidae, *Ips typographus* ($\times$ 20).

Even though this insect attacks only weak or injured firs, it is a serious pest in the forests of central and northern Europe and northern Asia. At swarming time the females bore into the bark, burrowing short vertical corridors, while the males help to excavate the wood dust. Many species of Bark Beetles are adapted for this task by having the rear part of their body appropriately shaped. Blind white larvae are hatched in these corridors out of the twenty or so eggs laid by each female. The larvae then make their own horizontal burrows as they eat their way between the wood and the bark. The picture on the right shows these larva burrows which widen as the larva grows and end with a little 'chamber' where it has changed into a pupa ($\times$ 2). The newly emerged Beetles then make their way out through the bark. Many species of Scolytidae occur in the United States, and engraved tree trunks such as this are a common sight in the forests.

The Weevils (Curculionidae) also include a well-known forest pest – the Pine Weevil *(Hylobius abietis)*. Its larvae bore tunnels inside the roots of pine and spruce-trees and pupate there. The adult insects grow and severely damage the

149

The Neuroptera include several families, one of these being the Snakeflies (Raphidiidae). *Raphidia notata* is the largest central European species. It measures about 1 in., lives in thickets and woods, and is predacious. Typical Raphidiids are also found in the western United States.

Below is the well-known Green Lacewing *(Chrysopa vulgaris)* (× 5). This fragile-looking, bluish-green insect with rainbow-coloured eyes and wings lays eggs on the leaves among colonies of aphids, on which its larvae feed. These larvae have pincer-shaped, sucking mandibles. *Chrysopa vulgaris* hibernates under the bark of trees, in crevices and even in houses, especially in attics and roofs. Numerous *Chrysopa* that look much like this occur in North America.

On p. 151 is the Ant-lion *(Myrmeleon europaeus)* (× 2¼), which can be seen in summer languidly flying among the grasses in dry places and on the fringes of forests with a sandy soil.

The larvae of *Myrmeleon* can be said to be among the most curious of all creatures. Each digs a crater-like pit in the sand by means of rapid movements of its spade-shaped head, revolving as it does so and finally taking up its position at the bottom of its hole. There it burrows into the sand, leaving only its long, open mandibles projecting. Small insects which happen to be crawling past – in particular the smaller species of ant – slip on the smooth slope of the pit and try to crawl out again. The waiting *Myrmeleon* showers them with sand, keeping up its bombardment until they fall right down into its poisonous forceps. After a while the dead body of the ant, which has been sucked dry, is thrown out and the larva lies in wait for the next victim. The picture on the left shows a fully-grown larva (× 6); below can be seen the pits it makes in the sand (half actual size). At the top of p. 153 are the cocoons of *Myrmeleon* (× 2). The bottom picture shows an opened cocoon with a live pupa *(left)*, a pupa taken out of its cocoon *(centre)*, and an adult larva before pupating, seen from the top (× 5). American species of *Myrmeleon* have the same habits and appearance as these.

153

Butterflies and Moths form the order Lepidoptera. Their wings, which are membranous, and body surface, apart from the eyes, are covered with overlapping varicoloured scales which give them their attractive appearance. The mouth – whenever developed – is a proboscis consisting of two maxillae joined into a narrow tube which can be coiled. There are approximately 110,000 known species.

Most Lepidoptera are Moths. The best known of the widely distributed Tortricidae family is the Green Oak-roller (*Tortrix viridana*), above left (× 7). It can often be seen in June on the bark or leaves of oak trees. Its caterpillars eat the newly-opened buds early in spring and defoliate the trees. Many species of Tortricids occur in North America.

Two representatives of the Pyralidae family, subfamily Orneodinae, are shown below. On the left is the *Orneodes zonodactyla*, and on the right, *Orneodes gramodactyla* (both × 6). They live in steppe country, mostly in concealment. *Orneodes hexadactyla* has been reported from the United States.

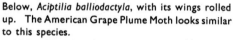

Below, *Aciptilia balliodactyla*, with its wings rolled up. The American Grape Plume Moth looks similar to this species.

Above left, the pupal case of the caterpillar of a male Bagworm Moth *(Pachytelia unicolor)* (× 2).

This is a central European species, but the case is characteristic of many American species.

Above right, one of the numerous species of European Burnet-moths, Zygaenidae, which fly about on dry hillsides in high summer.

In March we can see greyish-brown moths, about $^3/_5$ in. long, on trees and houses near woods. The females have partly stunted wings. In autumn the *Chimabacche fagella* larvae make themselves a 'cocoon' by fastening together twisted leaves, mainly of the oak. On p. 156, a female of this species is shown above and a male below.

The well-known Goat-moth *(Cossus cossus)* has an almost hairless, reddish-coloured caterpillar, which lives in the wood of broad-leaved trees such as chestnut, rowan, willow, poplar and aspen.

The Moth is greyish-brown with a silvery sheen and black markings. (Both pictures × ¼.) Although this species is not found in North America, its relatives attack various trees there.

Two species of the family Tineidae are found in houses.

Above, the Corn-moth *(Tinea granella)* (× 10), whose larvae eat dried fruit, mushrooms and stale bread, as well as grain stored in granaries. It is whitish with dark brown markings.

Below, the cosmopolitan Clothes-moth *(Tineola biselliella)* (× 13), which is straw-yellow in colour. Its larvae destroy woollen fabrics.

Above right, the Flour Moth *(Ephestia kühniella)*, and below right, its larvae and chrysalids (× 6). This species sticks the flour on which it feeds into small lumps. It is known in many countries, including the United States.

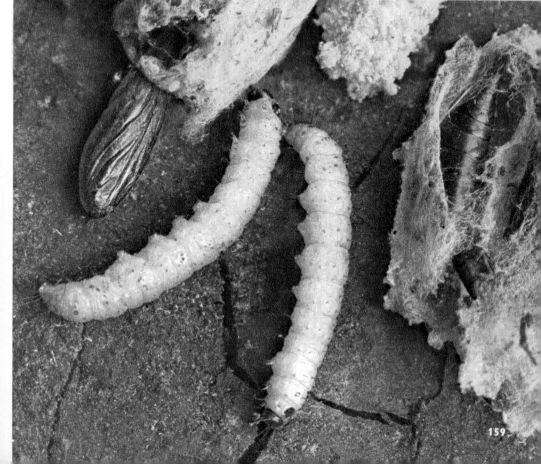

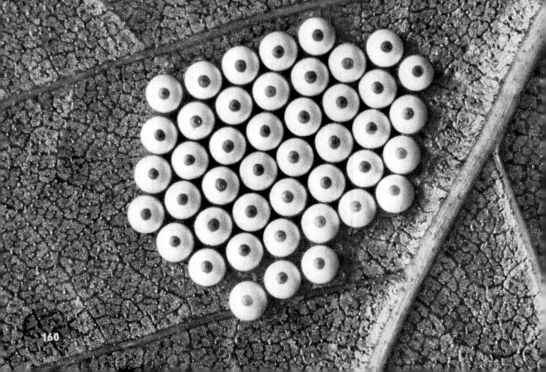

The Hornet Clearwing *(Trochilium crabroniformis)*, belongs to the family of Clearwings – Aegeriidae. Its yellow-and-black colouring and transparent wings make it remarkably like the Hornet, which helps to protect it from its enemies. The caterpillars live in wood, especially in poplar trees. On the left, a pair of Clearwings mating (× 2). Many of the North American members of this family also resemble various species of Wasps.

Butterfly and Moth eggs vary in colour and shape. They are laid both singly and in clusters and sometimes have attractive surface structures. The eggs of the Puss Moth *(Phallera bucephala)* (× 10), of the Notodontidae family have sharply delineated colours; green at the sides, and black and white on top.

Puss Moths have wings which are serrated at the edges. This is well illustrated in the picture of the species *Pterostoma palpina* (× 4), shown on the right.

The caterpillars of Puss Moths are also very interesting. They have tooth-like projections on their backs and adopt curious, contorted attitudes. One of these, the red caterpillar of *Notodonta zicsac*, can be found on young poplar trees (× 3). In North America, the Red-humped Caterpillar *(Schizura concinna)* feeds upon a variety of deciduous trees.

161

The largest European Puss Moth is *Dicranura vinula*. When in danger, the caterpillar, which is green and purple on top, projects two red, motile appendages in the rear part of its body which it raises aloft. This reflex action is usually sufficient to frighten off a possible attacker. The caterpillar is to be

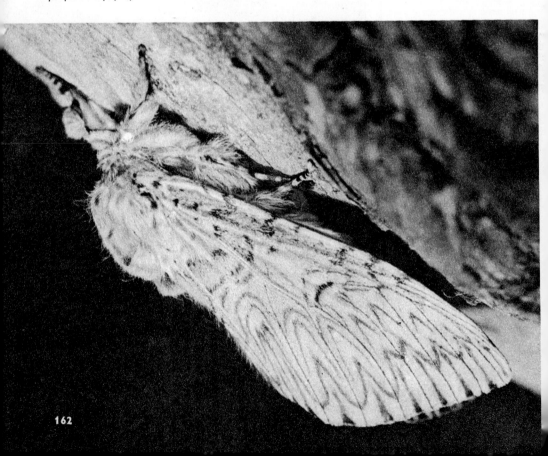

found on willows, poplars and aspens. The greyish Moths emerge from their chrysalids in the following May. The top picture on p. 162 shows a caterpillar and the bottom picture a female Moth of this species ($\times 2^1/_2$).

The Saturniidae family, the Giant Silkworm Moths, includes some of the most beautiful Moths in the world. On the right is a North American *Hyperchiria io* – the male on top, the female below. This is a good example of protective colouring. When sitting with folded wings the Moth resembles a dry leaf; when it opens, it reveals vivid blue eyes against a yellow background on its hind legs. This striking effect intimidates would-be attackers.

Below, two males of the European Emperor Moth *(Saturnia pavonia)* ($\times 2$).

The largest European Moth is *Saturnia pyri*. Some
specimens attain the size of the one in the picture
above.   It is most abundant in the south, but can
also be seen occasionally in the warmer parts of
central Europe.   Its caterpillars live on blackthorn,
ash and fruit trees.   On p. 164 the caterpillars can
be seen above and the chrysalids below.

A Saturnid from North America – a male Polyphaemus Moth *(Telea polyphaemus)* is shown on the
right (approx. × ¹/₅). This species has a transparent patch without scales in the centre of its
wings.

Only a single species of those which have their hind wings protracted into 'tails' is found in Europe. This is the beautiful *Graellsia isabellae*, a pale greenish-blue in colour with reddish-brown nervures in the wings. Its caterpillars are to be found on pine trees in the mountain districts of Spain and in the Near East. The pupa hibernates and the Moth emerges in spring. A female is shown in the picture (× ¼).

The top picture on this page shows a male North American Saturnid, *Platisamia cecropia*. It occurs mainly on the Atlantic coast in places where there are trees of the genus *Cecropia*, on which the caterpillars make their home. However, caterpillars kept in captivity will eat apple or bilberry leaves.

One of the finest Saturnids in the world is the *Tropea (Actias) selene*. The male is illustrated below ($\times \frac{1}{4}$). It is yellowish-green, but the front edges of the front wings are purple. There are several species which are commonly found in areas ranging from the Amur region and Japan in East Asia to Ceylon and Borneo. The 'tails' of the wings are about three times as long in the males as in the females. The large caterpillar is green, with orange-yellow tubercles. It feeds on leaves, chiefly those of *Coryaria*, *Andromeda*, *Salix* and *Hibiscus*. The North American Luna *(Tropea luna)* is a close relative.

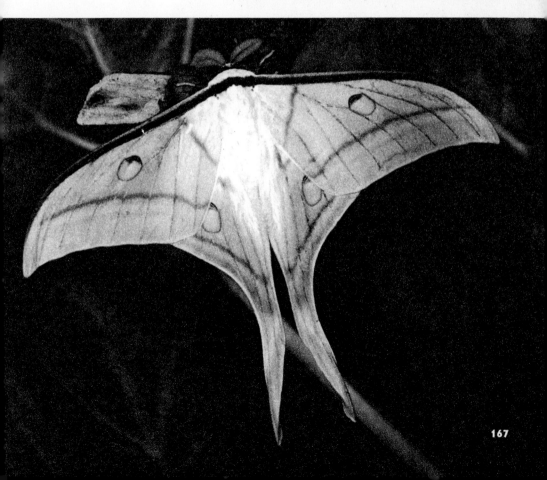

The largest of all the Saturnids with wings protracted into long tails is the lovely Comet Moth (Argema mittrei), which is shown in the picture above. The European Swallowtail Butterfly (Papilio machaon), has been added to enable the reader to estimate its size. If the length of the 'tails' were taken into consideration, Argema mittrei would be the largest Moth in the world. It is a vivid yellow with darker markings, mostly the colour of fired clay. It is found in the southern parts of Madagascar and is one of the most coveted specimens in Butterfly collections.

Philosamia cynthia ($\times$ $^1/_2$), found in China and Japan, is shown on p. 169.

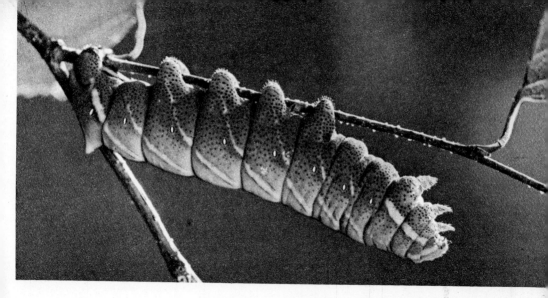

Several different varieties of the famous Atlas Moths, *Attacus atlas*, and the similar A. *edwardsii* are found in India and South-east Asia. These giant Moths measure as much as 10 in. with wings expanded. In each wing there is a transparent triangular patch or 'window'. The top picture on p. 170 shows it from above, and the lower one from the underside.

The pictures on this and the following four pages show the complete metamorphosis of the Kentish Glory *(Endromis versicolor)* – a typical Moth. Eggs are usually laid on a living plant. Caterpillars are hatched out of the eggs and are extremely voracious. They grow quickly and, in temperate regions, change into pupae either the same year or after hibernation. In some species the pupa spins itself a cocoon. Above is a caterpillar of the Kentish Glory (× 2). Below, part of the cocoon and the pupal case, out of which a Moth has just emerged (× 4).

171

The freshly emerged Moth
usually climbs rapidly out of
the chrysalid and on to the
nearest suitable object which
it can grasp with its legs and
where it has adequate space
underneath. See picture at
top left.

At first a Moth's wings are
very small, being unable to
develop fully in the special
wing cases which can be
discerned on the chrysalid.
The fresh wings are soft and
rag-like. The bottom picture
shows the change that has
taken place within a quarter
of a minute.

The Moth breathes intensively, filling the complex system of wing nervures with air. It is an incredibly rapid growth, and the wings can literally be seen growing.

The twisted wings begin to stretch and straighten. Soon they are as long as the Moth's body, as is shown in the picture, above right. Several minutes later, the wings have reached their proper size. They are, however, not yet quite straight and firm. See below right (all the pictures are approx. × 2).

174

The wings of the Moth seen growing on the preceding pages are now fully grown.   However, they are not yet in their final shape, for their upper surfaces are still flat and pressed together, as can be seen in the picture on the left ($\times$ 3$^1/_2$).   Only after resting for many minutes so that the wings can harden, does the Moth expand them into the roof-like shape characteristic of this species.

Some Moths are not remarkable for their beauty but are either interesting because of their queer shapes or important for their usefulness. On the left is a male *Dendrolimus pini* (× 3), which is the same tobacco-brown colour as the bark of the pine trees on which it lives. The caterpillars feed on pine-needles and hibernate in winter. They have caused, especially in earlier times, considerable damage in European pine forests.

Below, a male Silkmoth *(Bombyx mori)* (× 3), which comes from East Asia. There are several varieties which are distinguishable by their colouring. This insect has been bred since time immemorial for the silk fibre which is obtained from the cocoon after the pupa has

been killed. Natural silk is still highly valued in spite of the intervention of various artificial fibres. There are silkworm farms throughout Europe, in particular in the Mediterranean region and in places with an abundance of mulberry trees. Mulberry leaves constitute the silkworms' sole food.

The top picture on this page shows a comparatively rare European Moth, *Odonestis pruni* (× 2). It is orange in colour with white specks in the middle of its head, and is found in summer on lime, alder, birch and blackthorn, as well as other deciduous trees and bushes.

The picture below left shows the Silkworm eggs (× 5), and below right, cocoons of various shapes (slightly magnified).

Above, Silkworm cocoons ($\times$ 3). On the left can be seen an open cocoon with the skin shed by the caterpillar; on the right, a closed cocoon. In the middle is the pupa which has been taken out of the cocoon on the left.

Below, a pair of *Lasiocampa quercus* ($\times \frac{1}{3}$), which live in mountainous areas. The male is on the left and the female on the right. They belong to the same family, Lasiocampidae, as the destructive American Tent Caterpillars, *Malacosoma*.

Above, the Small Eggar Moth (Eriogaster lanestris) (× 2½). The Moth flies in March and April; the caterpillar is found in summer, chiefly on the blackthorn, hawthorn, lime, and birch, living in communal webs.

Below, the eggs of a garden and orchard pest –

the Lackey Moth (Malacosoma neustria) (× 6). The ochre-brown Moths live in summer, their caterpillars hatch out in May from eggs that have wintered. They feed on fruit trees, on blackthorn and hawthorn bushes, and on oak.

A pair of *Cosmotriche potatoria* (× 2). The female is larger, light yellow in colour, the smaller male is brownish-red. This pretty and harmless insect, which is hardly noticed because of its relatively inconspicuous colouring and shape, inhabits central Europe, appearing in damp meadows in June and July. The caterpillar lives there from autumn to spring, feeding on various grasses.

An even better example of protective colouring and shape is provided by the Lappet-moth (*Gastropacha quercifolia*) which looks like a dry leaf, as is shown in the picture on the right (× 5). Its hairy grey caterpillar, illustrated below (actual size), is approximately 4 in. long and feeds on blackthorn bushes, deciduous trees, and in particular fruit trees.

The family Lymantriidae is also made up of Moths that spin cocoons. The picture below shows a caterpillar of the male Scarce Vapourer Moth *(Orgyia gonostigma)* (× 4) which has tufts of fine, feather-like hairs at the sides of its head, a single tuft on the rear portion of its body, and a row of light yellow or ochre brushes on its back. It is found mostly on roses, plum trees, blackthorn, birch and oak.

On the left is a central European species of Moth, the pure white *Stilpnotia (Leucoma) salicis* (× 2). Below it, on the bark of the poplar, can be seen the cocoon from which it has just emerged. Its brightly coloured caterpillar, which has a row of rectangular white or yellow specks on its back, eats the leaves of willow, poplar, lime, elm, aspen and oak. It is mostly found on Italian poplar, where it may occur in very large numbers. This caterpillar resembles that of the Whitemarked Tussock Moth *(Hemerocampa leucostigma)* which is common in North America.

The excessive increase of *Lymantria monacha*, the Nun or Black Archer as it is popularly called, is particularly dangerous, for its greyish hairy caterpillars strip pine and fir forests, and even denude deciduous trees. After such plagues the forest is alive with Moths. Fortunately, today these outbreaks are rare, as with good husbandry the menace can be detected in time and steps taken to avert it. The Nun is illustrated above (× 3). Trees covered with Moths are shown below.

Occasionally fruit-trees are still found completely defoliated by certain kinds of Moth. A plum tree stripped of leaves with only the green fruit remaining is illustrated here. The culprit was the Gypsy Moth *(Lymantria dispar)* which looks rather like the Black Archer. These Moths lay cushions of eggs on the bark, covering them with reddish hairs. The caterpillars are more vividly coloured than those of the Black Archer, having red warts on their back and blue ones behind the head. They are injurious to gardens and orchards, as well as oak forests. Females of this Moth are illustrated below. They remain covering the eggs after they have laid them and slowly die. Each 'cushion' contains up to 400 eggs. This species was introduced into North America many years ago and is a serious pest of eastern forests. The top left picture on the opposite page shows a female Vapourer Moth *(Orgyia antiqua)* (× 3). The female has stunted wings, whereas the male has normally developed wings and is brown with a white spot on each front wing. The strikingly ornamental caterpillars, with their long tufts and brushes, live in late summer on both deciduous and coniferous trees, as well as on such plants as the bilberry, blackthorn and rose. The picture at above right (× 2), shows a male Pale Tussock Moth *(Dasychira pudibunda)*, which flies in May and June, mainly in the forests, and is a light greyish-brown colour. Its beautiful, yellow caterpillar is found in the autumn on various deciduous trees, bushes and weeds.

185

Abrostola triplasia is illustrated in the top inset picture (× 3). Its greyish-black colouring is yet another fine example of mimicry, for the Moth resembles a piece of mud or bird's droppings. Its green or pink caterpillar lives on nettles and is very abundant in central Europe.

One of the world's largest species of Lepidoptera – frequently stated to be *the* largest – the Brazilian *Thysania agrippina*, is illustrated above. This light greyish-brown Moth measures up to 11 in. with its wings expanded.

The caterpillar (× 3) and Moth (× 2) of *Diloba caeruleocephala* are illustrated at the top of p. 187. This is a member of the Owlet-moth family, Noctuidae. It is a very numerous group and includes over 10,000 species throughout the world. Many North American species cause serious damage to crops.

Apatele (Acronycta) psi, a Moth that causes relatively little damage, is illustrated below (× 4). Its protective colouring — dark markings on a light grey background — makes it resemble the bark of the trees on which it lives.

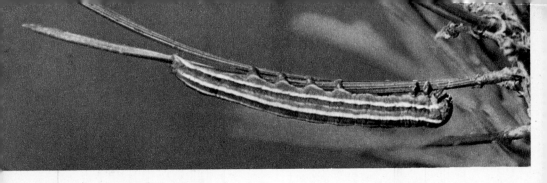

The green caterpillar of *Panolis flamea*, which is very hard to spot among pine-needles, is illustrated above (× 3).

The Red Underwing (*Catocala elocata*), is shown below (× 3). The front wings are protectively coloured, while the red hind wings with their two black bands serve to frighten off attackers when suddenly opened. North America has a large fauna of Underwings.

The top left picture on p. 189 shows the Shark (*Cuculia umbratica*) (× 3). Its grey wings look like decaying wood.

Next to it is the caterpillar of *Cuculia verbasci* (× 3). It is yellow with black spots and lives on mullein. Caterpillars of the American species of *Cuculia* feed mostly on goldenrod and related plants.

The bottom picture on p. 189 is of the well-known Silver Moth (*Plusia gamma*) (× 3), which is widespread in Europe and North America.

Trigonophora (Brotolomia) meticulosa has beautiful combinations of pink, green and brown colours on its wings. It is one of the harmless Moths and it is very beautiful.

On the right, a Garden Tiger Moth (*Arctia caja*) (× 3¹/₂), belonging to the Arctiidae family of Lepidoptera. This species is apparently native to both Europe and North America.

On the left is the Magpie Moth *(Abraxas grossulariata)* — a well-known garden pest. It has white wings with black spots and two yellow stripes on the front pair. Its caterpillars can be seen at the top of p. 193 (× 3). This is one of the large family of Loopers, Geometridae, whose members live both in the tropics and in very cold regions, including those within the Arctic Circle. The caterpillars move by bringing up the rear part of their body to the stationary front part and throwing the body into a large loop — hence their name. In the United States the caterpillars of this family are called inchworms. These caterpillars almost always have the shape and colouring of branches or other parts of plants.

The caterpillars of the species *Boarmia roboraria* are illustrated below (× 2). The one on the left is shown in an erect posture, the one on the right making a loop. At the bottom of p. 193 is a Moth of the same species.

Larva of Spurge Hawk, on a euphorbia plant ($\times$ 3).

193

Hawk-moths, Sphingidae, are among the most beautiful, powerful and perfectly developed Lepidoptera. They can fly astonishingly fast and far, so that they sometimes migrate to distant countries. Two striking visitors from the warm south appear even in Northern Europe. The Death's-head Moth (*Acherontia atropos*), sometimes lays its eggs on potato plants in the summer and the next generation hatches before the autumn. This moth can be seen in the top pictures, while that below shows its pupa.

The Oleander Hawk (*Daphnis nerii*), is a rarer guest in central and western Europe. Its wings have beautiful pink and green colours, the caterpillars feed on oleander. The moth is illustrated in the bottom picture on p. 195 (× 2).

The beautiful *Pterogon proserpina*, illustrated on the left (× 2), is quite small and therefore difficult to see in the open, especially as it is well protected by the green colour of its fore wings and body. Both body and wings have deep indentations. The hind wings are yellow with black fringes. The larvae feed on the evening primrose.

Below is the attractive Spurge Hawk (*Celerio euphorbiae*), a species abundant in central Europe. Its fore wings are olive-brown with pale pink patches, the hind wings bright reddish-pink with black stripes. When the Moth is resting on the grass in the daytime, these hind wings are not seen. If disturbed, it will expand all four wings, bend the rear portion of its body downward and begin bobbing up and down. This strange behaviour usually scares an enemy and often saves the insect's life. Its beautiful, vividly coloured caterpillars are completely harmless, living on euphorbia plants on uncultivated dry hillsides and the verges of fields.

The caterpillars of some of the Hawk-moths raise their heads and twist the front parts of their bodies into a question-mark when resting or when irritated. It is this habit that has earned the genus the name *Sphinx*, as they look a little like ancient sphinxes.

Below is the caterpillar of the Privet Hawk *(Sphinx ligustri)* (× 2^1/$_2$), which is green with violet and white stripes. It lives on privet and lilac bushes. Above the Privet Hawk is the greyish-black Moth with a pink tinge and two pink bands on the hind wings (× ^{1}/$_3$). In the evening it may be seen flying around nectar-bearing flowers.

The grey, delicately-lined wings of the Convolvulus Hawk *(Herse convolvuli)*, blend excellently with the background which this Moth favours when sleeping – the trunks of trees, wooden poles and pillars. When it opens its wings, the bright pink spots on the sides of its body are seen. It migrates from the south, and occasionally its caterpillars and chrysalids are found in western and central Europe. On the left, the Moth can be seen (× ¼), while the chrysalid, which has been dug out of the ground, is illustrated below (× 2). On the bottom side of the head end there is a spiral cover for the future proboscis of the Moth, which in these species is frequently larger than the body.

Only one species of the European Sphingidae is harmful, and then only if its numbers increase excessively. This is the Pine Hawk *(Hyloicus pinastri)*, whose greyish wings match the bark of the pine trees on which it rests during the day. This Moth is illustrated in the picture on the right (× ⅓). The green caterpillars with white or yellow stripes feed on pine-needles, or on the needles of other conifers. Like the larvae of other species of this family, they form their chrysalids on the ground, either in moss or among the needles. The most important economic representatives of the family in North America are the Tomato Hornworm *(Protoparce quinquemaculata)* and the Tobacco Hornworm *(Protoparce sexta)*.

On the left is the Poplar Hawk (*Amorpha populi*), resting on an aspen leaf ($\times$ $^1/_4$). The ochre and blackish-brown colour of the wings, which by their shape perfectly imitate the shape of a dry leaf, makes it hard to see even at extremely close quarters. This Moth lives on poplars and willows throughout the temperate and warm regions of Europe.

The Oak Hawk (*Marumba quercus*), shown above, is light ochre and is another example of protective colouring. Its green caterpillar lives on oaks in southern Europe and South-east Asia, as well as in the warmer parts of central and eastern Europe.

The Lime Hawk *(Mimas tiliae)*, illustrated on the left, is found throughout most of Europe, and is fairly abundant in some parts. Its wings are coloured various shades of pink and green. The green caterpillars live on lime, birch, oak, ash and other deciduous trees.

Butterflies belong to the suborder Rhopalocera, and one of the best-known families is that of the Nymphalidae. This includes an exotic Butterfly with perfect protective colouring and shape – the Dead-leaf Butterfly *(Kallima inachus var. formosana)* from Formosa. The two pictures show it both from above and from the underside. The underside is inconspicuously greyish-, reddish- or greenish-brown, shaded and stippled to form a perfect replica of a dry leaf. When the Butterfly folds its wings, the 'leaf' ends in a short stem – this illusion being created by the tails of the wings. The undersides of the wings are veined in exact imitation of a leaf. The upperside of the wings is a shiny blue with large orange-yellow patches. The contrast achieved by a sudden expansion of the wings helps to drive away pursuers.

Butterflies of the family Pieridae seldom have bright colours, only the European genus *Anthocharis* and some of the exotic genera being conspicuous for their colouring. The Orange Tip (*Anthocharis cardamines*) with orange spots on the top of the fore wings and greenish marbling on the underside of the hind wings is illustrated above left (× 2). It flies early in spring, its caterpillar living towards the end of summer on various cruciferous meadow plants. Four species of Orange Tips, *Anthocharis*, are found in the United States.

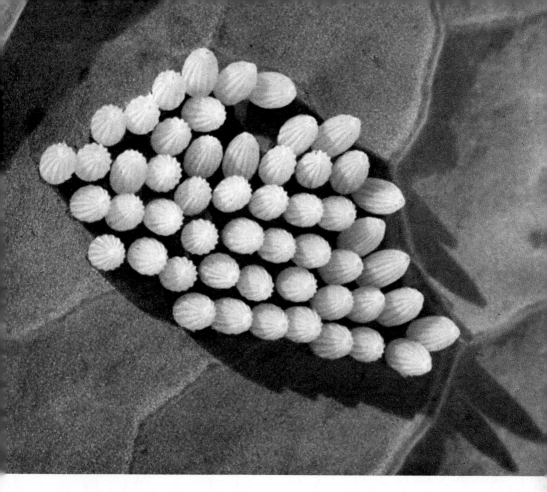

The picture at top right of p. 204 shows the Black-veined White *(Aporia crataegi)* (× 2). This Butterfly is seen in summer. Its caterpillars live in webs on trees from late summer until they pupate in the following May. This species used to be a serious pest when its numbers rapidly increased, but today it is rare in many parts of Europe.

A female Large White *(Pieris brassicae)* (× 3), is illustrated in the lower picture on p. 204. This species is still a great pest, being one of the most abundant Butterflies in Europe. It has two generations in the year, and mainly lives in vegetable gardens and fields. Its eggs (magnified) on a cabbage leaf are shown above. A related species, the Cabbage Butterfly *(Pieris rapae)*, has been introduced into the United States from Europe and is a serious pest.

The chrysalids of the Large White illustrated above (× 3) attach themselves at their rear end and are held by two fibres at the head end which is always uppermost.

The Painted Lady (Pyrameis cardui), illustrated top right ($\times$ $^1/_5$), is very frequently seen in summer, flying on the fringes of woods, in clearings and on hillsides, over fields, paths, and stony ground. It is ubiquitous, being found on the bottom of a dried-up pond as well as near the snowfields in the mountains. Its range covers the whole world, apart from South America and some of the smaller island groups. Flocks of these Butterflies migrate across Europe, from south to north; there the fertilised females lay their eggs on nettles and thistles, and the Butterflies which emerge return to their original home in the south. They are such persistent fliers that they continue their flight even at dusk and have learned to cross high mountain ranges.

Below right, the Camberwell Beauty (Nymphalis antiopa). The chocolate brown wings with yellow rear edge margined with blue spots make it unmistakable. In Europe and North America the Butterfly hibernates, waking early in spring and laying its eggs on willow, poplar and birch.

The Purple Emperor (*Apatura iris*), can be found in deciduous forests, in clearings and especially near brooks. The males have blackish-brown wings, with a purplish sheen. The caterpillars have two small horns on their heads, and hibernate in winter, feeding in spring on sallow. On the left is a chrysalid (× 3), below it the Purple Emperor (× 2). At the top of p. 209 is the chrysalid (× 4) and Butterfly (× 2) of the White Admiral (*Limenitis sibilla*). The strange-looking horned chrysalid is greenish in colour with a golden sheen. The blackish-brown Butterfly has white stripes and spots on its wings, which are ochre and green on the underside. This Butterfly can be seen on forest paths and the fringes of damp deciduous forest patches in July.

At the bottom of p. 209 is the Red Apollo Butterfly (*Parnassius apollo*), belonging to the Papilionidae family (× 2). It is rare and found only in the mountains of central Europe, where it is protected by law. Its red-spotted velvet-black caterpillar also lives in the mountains. North America has four species of *Parnassius*, all of which are montane forms.

The Peacock *(Nymphalis io)* is one of the best-known European members of the family Nyphalidae. It is native to central Europe, where it has two or three generations between March and October. The Butterfly hibernates in crannies, hollow trees and old buildings. The larvae feed on nettles and hop vines (× 2).

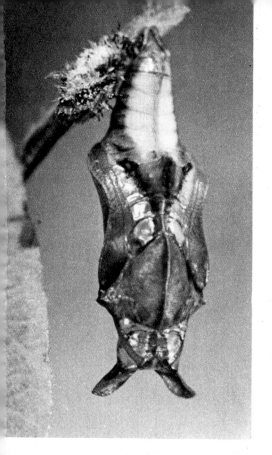

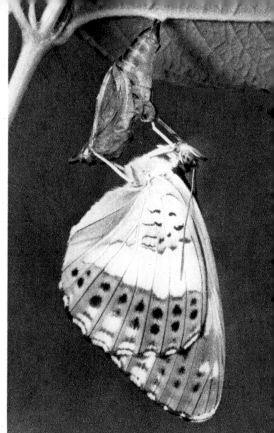

The genus *Papilio* includes the most beautiful Butterflies in the world, and in the tropics they are found in a great variety of shapes and colours. Central and southern Europe, western and central Asia, and North Africa is the home of the Scarce Swallowtail *(Papilio podalirius)*, illustrated above (× 2). It is pale yellow in colour, the bands on its wings being blackish-grey. On the hind wings it has horseshoe-shaped blue patches and a red-fringed eye. The caterpillars live mainly on blackthorn, hawthorn, and plum. In Germany

this species is protected by law. It is found mostly in hilly country.

On the right is the Swallowtail *(Papilio machaon)* (× ⅓). It is similar in colouring to the Scarce Swallowtail but has different markings. It is also found in the same areas. This Butterfly takes the nectar of clover, thistles and viper's bugloss. Its brightly coloured caterpillars live on umbelliferous plants in the meadows. Widespread in Europe and Asia, it is found only in Alaska and Canada and in North America.

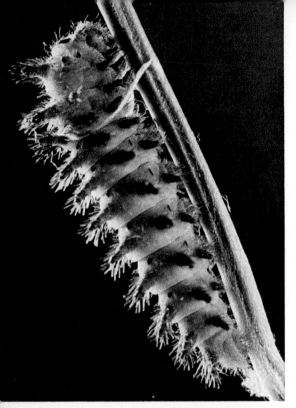

Another genus of the Papilionidae family is *Zerynthia*. One of the many beautiful species, *Zerynthia hypsipyle*, lives in south-eastern Europe. It is yellow-black in colour, with black spots on the underside of both pairs of wings and the top of the hind pair. Its orange-yellow caterpillar has many spines and lives exclusively on clematis, so that the Butterfly is limited to the damp woods, dry sandy lowlands in their vicinity, railway embankments and vineyards where clematis grows. This attractive Butterfly was quite abundant until recent years, but the spraying of insecticides carried out as a measure against mosquitoes has taken heavy toll of a species that should really be protected. Its caterpillar lives in June and July, the chrysalid hibernates, and the Butterfly is seen in April and May.

The upper picture shows a caterpillar ($\times$ 4), shortly before pupating. The threads already woven for attaching the chrysalid to the stem can be clearly seen.

Below is the chrysalid of *Zerynthia hypsipyle*, made inconspicuous by its brownish-grey colouring ($\times$ 4). On the right is the Butterfly on an unfolding fern ($\times$ 2).

Two-winged Flies, order Diptera, are predominantly flying insects of small size; their distribution is worldwide and some 75,000 species are known. For the most part they are parasitic and noxious, only a small proportion being useful – for example those that transform organic matter into humus.

Among the very useful kinds are many Hover-flies, Syrphidae, which feed on blossoms from spring to autumn. They frequently resemble Bees or Wasps. The Currant Hover-fly *(Syrphus ribesii)*, illustrated above (× 3), lays its eggs near groups of aphids. The larvae, in appearance like small leeches, devour these in great numbers; a single larva is capable of sucking as many as a hundred a day. The larva (× 5), is illustrated in the left-hand picture on p. 215. Many similar-appearing Hover-flies are found throughout the world.

On the right is the Bee-fly
(*Bombylius major*) (× 3),
which resembles a small
Bumble-bee. It can be seen
in April and May, visiting the
first spring blossoms and
hovering as it sips nectar
with its long proboscis. The
larvae live as parasites in the
nests of various Hymen-
optera. The species occurs
in Asia, Europe and North
America.

Flies are among the most obnoxious of all insects and several species are associated with human habitations almost throughout the world. The minute, about $\frac{1}{5}$ in. long Fruit-fly *(Drosophila funebris)* is found wherever any sour substance is fermenting. Some species of Fruit-flies, such as *Drosophila melanogaster,* illustrated on p. 216 in. the top left picture, have become important in the study of genetics.

At top right is the Small House-fly, *(Homalomyia canicularis)* (× 9), which in summer flies tirelessly round the lights in houses.

At bottom left is the Common House-fly *(Musca domestica)* (× 7), which is harmful through soiling

and even infecting foodstuffs. Apart from this, its very presence is a nuisance to man.

At bottom right is the Blow-fly *(Calliphora vomitoria)* (× 4). The larvae of the three last-named species develop in refuse, and can, under bad hygienic conditions, penetrate inside the human body and cause serious diseases.

Best-known of the Syrphidae is the Drone-fly *(Eristalis tenax).* This is illustrated above (× 3). It lives in summer on blossoms and the larvae develop in stagnant dirty water. Both larvae and pupae have long 'tails' and are known as rat-tailed maggots. Below are empty pupal cases from which Flies have emerged (× 4).

At the top left of p. 218 is St. Mark's Fly *(Bibio marci)*
(× 5). This black, striking-looking Fly appears early
in spring in gardens and woods along with other similar
species. The larvae take two years to develop in the
ground, and frequently cause damage to plants through
eating their roots. They live gregariously and pupate
together. At the bottom of p. 218 is a clod of earth
with holes from which the adults have emerged; at
top right is a Horse-fly or Cleg *(Haematopota pluvialis)*
(× 5). These insects fly noiselessly round people and
animals on hot, rainy days and inflict painful bites.
Other species of Horse-flies are well-known pests in
North America.

   Some species of Flies are entirely parasitic. The
Green-bottle *(Lucilia silvarum)*, top right of this page
(× 5), lays its eggs in the nostrils of toads. In about
eight days the maggots literally eat the unfortunate
frog alive. After its death they pupate in the ground.
The picture at the bottom of this page shows a toad
shortly before its death. Its head is swollen and
dozens of fly larvae have eaten their way deep inside
the nostrils and eye sockets. American Green-bottle
Flies are *Lucilia cuprina* and *L. sericata*.

The Stomoxyidae include the well-known Tsetse Fly (*Glossina morsitans*) which is illustrated on the left (× 3^1/$_2$). It lives in dry, light forests in tropical Africa, sucking the blood of the larger animals and transferring a malignant disease called Nagana – cattle-disease – to domestic as well as wild animals. This disease, caused by the flagellate *Trypanasoma brucei*, results in the wholesale death of cattle. A similar fly, *Glossina palpalis*, from the damp regions of Africa, carries the dreaded sleeping sickness among human beings.

The Louse-flies, Hippoboscidae, are a species well adapted for a parasitic mode of life. They are flattish, firmly built, and difficult to squash, and have legs which enable them to cling to and quickly move about in the hair or feathers of their involuntary hosts. Many species are wingless, resembling Spiders rather than Flies. Below are two individuals of the Deer Louse-fly (*Lipoptena cervi*) (× 11). Early in spring they are winged and suck the blood of birds. About

June, they seek out animals such as stags and roe-deer, shed their wings and live as parasites in the fur of their hosts. At this period they may also attack humans in alighting on the hair or beard and biting painfully.

Below is the Swallow Louse-fly (Stenopteryx hirundinis) (× 6). It sucks the blood of swallows, mar-tins and swifts, sometimes weakening them so much that they cannot fly. It holds on to the feathers by means of legs similarly equipped to those of the Sheep Ked (Melophagus ovinus), which is illustrated above. It is a closely related parasite which lives among sheep's wool and completes its development there. It is found wherever there are sheep.

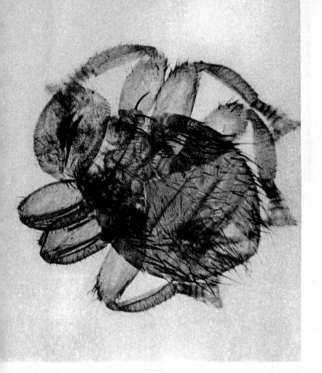

The wingless Bee-louse (*Braula coeca*), belongs to the family Braulidae. It is illustrated on the left (× 35). It lives in beehives, both the imago and its larva feeding on the honey. Adult Flies attach themselves to the Bees and in this way travel about from place to place. They most frequently attack the Queen-bee, which is sometimes infested with as many as a hundred of them. This species is widely distributed and occurs in eastern North America.

Below are the pupae of the Swallow Louse-fly (*Stenopteryx hirundinis*) in a martin's nest (× 10). These pupae hibernate, the Flies emerging in spring after the birds have returned to their nests.

A number of related species spend their entire lives inhabiting various species of birds. Thus, for instance, the Common Louse-fly *(Ornithomyia avicularia)*, torments small songbirds in summer. The females of all these parasitic flies do not lay eggs. The larva develops in the mother's body, pupating immediately after being deposited. The photograph shows three female Flies with adult larvae in their abdomens and two larvae at top right (× 7).

The wingless parasitic Flies of the Nycteribiidae family are found on bats. They are reddish-brown in colour and move about among the fine hairs with such speed and assurance that they are difficult to detect even when the bat is examined at close quarters. One of these Flies is illustrated on the left (× 15).

Below are two Sheep Keds (*Melophagus ovinus*). They have no wings and live in the wool of sheep, sucking blood from the skin. The pupae also remain close to the sheep's skin, so that the Flies multiply on the host's body and never leave it.

One of the most terrible of the Oestridae, whose larvae live in the bodies of ungulates, is the Deer Bot Fly (*Cephenomyia stimulator*), a hairy, black-and-yellow Fly resembling a small Bumblebee. These Flies deposit their small larvae inside the nostrils of roe deer. The larvae then crawl into the animal's throat and bite into its soft palate and root of the tongue. If they do not cause the deer's death, they will be sneezed out in summer and will pupate in the ground. Right is a pupa and an adult Fly (× 4). Below are the larvae in the throat of a shot deer. The related *Cephenomyia pratti* attacks deer in North America.

225

The order of Fleas, Aphaniptera, are to-day placed at the very end of the insect system. This is not because they are the most perfect, but simply because it is difficult to determine their exact standing and relation to the other orders. Various authorities give them a common ancestry with Flies, others with Beetles or the Neuroptera, but no definite decision has been made. Over a hundred different species are known, living on mammals and birds all over the world. The top picture shows a female of the cosmopolitan Human Flea *(Pulex irritans)*, which is approximately $\frac{1}{8}$ in. long. This species is found on dogs, cats, and human beings living in poor hygienic conditions. As they are also found on rats, they can easily spread bubonic plague in some countries.

A typical flea which spreads plague is the Indian Rat Flea *(Xenopsylla cheopis)*. Although under $\frac{1}{10}$ in. size it spreads the infection among rats and can also transfer it to humans. The bottom picture shows a male specimen. In the Middle Ages there was a catastrophic spread of the plague and the "Black Death" which raged in 1348–50 took a toll of twenty-five million people in Europe alone. Even in the period from 1898 to 1918 more than ten million human beings perished in India from the same cause.

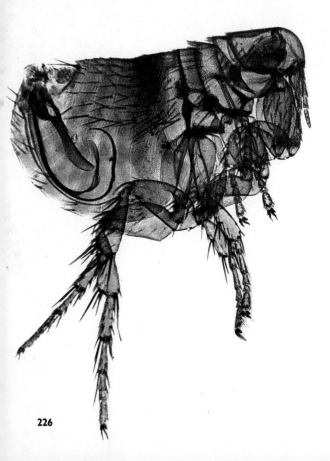

SEA AND FRESHWATER ANIMALS

Some marine and freshwater animals make up a small remnant of groups which were at the apex of their development in early geological periods. Known as the Bryozoa or Moss Animals, they have survived to the present day; some 3,800 species are known, most of them marine, though about ten species inhabit the fresh waters of central Europe. The are minute aquatic animals living in colonies rather as corals do.

Colonies of *Plumatella fungosa* can be seen on reed stalks at the bottom of ponds after they have been drained. They consist of concentric tubes in which are the individual, oblong-shaped animals. At the top of the colony, individuals spread their tentacles and grasp their food. They feed on free-floating weeds, protozoa, and other microscopic organic matter.

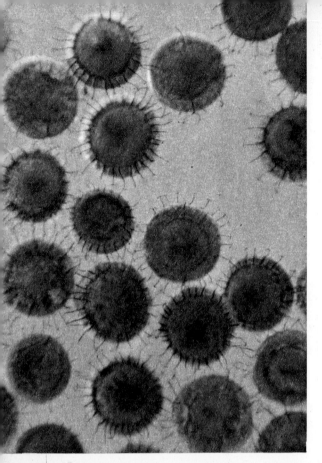

In countries with changing seasons, these colonies of Bryozoa die off in winter, surviving in the form of winter spores or statoblasts. These floating formations, in which the Bryozoa are in a resting state, are frequently able to fasten themselves. They are of various shapes and sizes, usually less than $1/20$ in. In spring, each statoblast forms a new, growing colony.

Pectinatella magnifica has in recent years been discovered in the ponds, rivers and river dams of central Europe. On the left (× 2), are magnified statoblasts; below, part of a colony. This interesting organism, brought to Europe accidentally from North America, forms jelly-like growths which sometimes measure as much as 3 ft. 3 in. in diameter and weigh many pounds.

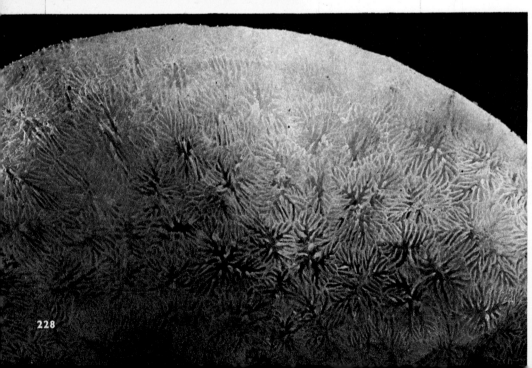

The phylum Echinodermata is a uniform one. The Common Starfish *(Asterias rubens)*, belongs to the class of Starfish – Asteroidea. It is abundant everywhere in the North Sea and the Atlantic. A live Common Starfish is illustrated top right (actual size). *Valvaster striatus* from the Pacific, viewed from the underside, is shown below. With this side it enfolds its prey – sea-snails and bivalves – which it forces open with its tube-feet before devouring the soft parts with its extensile mouth.

Most adult Echinoderms are characterised by a radial symmetry of structure. In their larval, floating stage, however, they are usually bilaterally symmetrical, suggesting that radial symmetry is a secondary development due to the animal's sedentary way of life on the ocean-bed. Most of them have tough, calcareous plates embedded in the thin skin, so that they retain their original size and shape after dehydration. The picture at the top of this page shows the dehydrated 'skeleton' of the Sunstar (*Solaster papposus*), viewed from above. When alive it is a beautiful brownish-red colour with bright yellow lateral bands across the arms. It lives in the sea along the coasts of the Northern Hemisphere.

The bottom picture is of *Heliaster helianthus* from the coasts of Chile. These Echinoderms have separate sexes and reproduce by means of eggs which are fertilised in the water. Starfish are predators and cause considerable damage in oyster-beds.

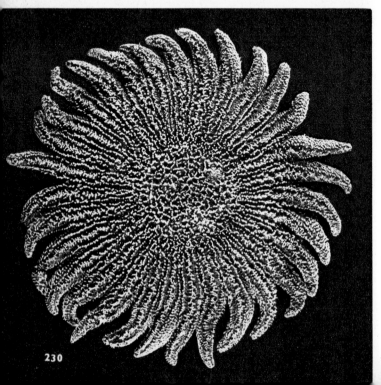

The Sea-urchins, Echinoidea, likewise inhabit the sea bottom. They move about freely with the aid of their spines or cling to rocks, sometimes living in hollows they have excavated. Some species burrow into the sand. The top picture, taken from the side, shows the Sea-urchin, *Centrostephanus rodgersi*, from the shores of South Australia.

Below is the calcareous 'skeleton' of another Sea-urchin, *Strongylocentrotus franciscanus*, from the California coast. Spines and skin have been removed and the underside is shown. In the centre is the anus, on the opposite side to which is the mouth equipped with strong teeth. The semi-spherical formations on the surface are the tubercles which, in the live animal, carry the spines.

Various species of Sea-urchin are only bilaterally symmetrical, having oval, heart, or horseshoe shapes. These are Irregular Sea-urchins, Irregularia. They usually have short spines, sometimes so short that they form a velvet-like covering. They live in the sand, and their only link with the surface is a narrow chimney-like aperture. The teeth in the mouth on the bottom of the flat body are usually weak, sufficient only to eat dead organisms which have sunk to the ocean-bed, or for shredding sea-weed. In some species the teeth are not developed at all – these swallow sand and mud, digesting the organic contents. Above is *Meoma ventricosa*, which is found in the Bahamas (actual size).

A Sea-urchin of the species *Encope grandis* from the ocean near the Antilles is shown above (× 2).

This, too, is only the shield-shaped skeleton with spines removed.

Many Echinoderms are adapted in various ways for life in the surf or in rough water. Using their many tube-feet they attach themselves firmly to the rocks, and their spines are reinforced so that they form thick, cigar-like formations or are shortened and rounded. At the top of p. 234 ($\times$ 2) is *Prionocidaris baculosa*, which comes from Mauritius. It has strong rugged spines.

Below it can be seen the purple-coloured *Colobocentrotus atratus* from Peru. It is shown from the underside. On top it is quite smooth. In the centre is the mouth with five strong, chisel-shaped teeth. The greater part of the teeth are concealed in the musculature, where they are continued as calcareous rods into a special formation known as 'Aristotle's lantern'. The inner structure of the calcareous spines is extremely complex, to give them added firmness. The above picture shows thin cross-sections of the spines of various Sea-urchins ($\times$ 24).

The Phylum Chordata includes all the vertebrates, together with all those marine creatures which form a transition between the invertebrates and the vertebrates. These are animals which instead of having a developed backbone and vertebrae have only a notochord that gives support to the body and presages. One such animal standing on the threshold of the large group of vertebrates is the Lancelet or Amphioxus (*Branchiostoma lanceolatum*). It is classified among the Acrania and the subphylum Cephalochordata. The above picture clearly shows the heads pointing to the right, with the sensory papillae around the mouths. On the left can be seen the median fold ending in a small tail-fin. The Lancelet is very like a small fish, differing from all true vertebrates, however, in that it has neither skull nor heart in the normal sense of the words. It possesses only a pulsating tube like that of some insect larvae. The spinal cord is developed, but not the brain. Instead of eyes there are only pigment dots which react to light and darkness. On the sides of the body can be seen the segmented muscles – Myotomes ($\times$ 2). The Lancelet spends most of its time buried in the sand, only the anterior part of its body protruding, the cilia agitating the water to bring into its mouth small infusoria and sea-weed. The species shown lives in European seas, and lays eggs.

FISHES

Somewhat less than 20,000 species of Fishes, Pisces, are known. The class Chondrichthyes (Cartilagnous Fishes) includes the Tope *(Galeus canis)*, illustrated above, which measures about 6½ ft. This Shark lives in almost every sea, feeding on the smaller marine creatures. It is viviparous, having as many as thirty young at a time.

Below is the Thornback Ray *(Raja clavata)*. It reaches up to about 10 ft. in length and inhabits the coastal areas of European seas, preying on small crabs and fish. Several related species occur in American coastal waters. Some Rays attain a width of about 17 ft.

237

The upper picture shows a young Ray, viewed from the underside. On the right can be seen two dark eggs of the Ray, with four tendrils by means of which they are attached to sea-weed. Also in the picture is a newly-hatched Ray.

One of the more primitive sub-divisions of the class Osteichthyes (Bony Fishes) is the order Polypteriformes. The species shown above, p. 239, is *Polypterus ornatipinnis*. It is strikingly coloured in black, white and yellow and lives in the fresh waters of the central Congo. Members of the order Acipenseriformes, which have skeletons that are only partly ossified, belong here. The Sterlet (*Acipenser ruthenus*), illustrated at the bottom of p. 239, attains a maximum length of 3 ft. It lives in the Black and Azov Seas and in the rivers which flow into them. With its shark-like mouth on the underside it feeds on various small aquatic creatures on the sea or river bottom. About seven species of Sturgeons are found in North America.

The Gars, order Semionotiformes, family Lepisosteidae, which are found in lakes and rivers of the southern parts of North America, might be termed living fossils. They lead a predatory existence in fresh waters and are not at present in danger of extinction because, fortunately, their flesh is not valued for food. Above is the olive-green Long-nosed Gar Pike (Lepisosteus osseus), which has a long, narrow, tapering beak. This species is up to 6 ft. in length.

Below is the Short-nosed Gar (Lepisosteus platystomus), about 2 ft. long.

The Great or Alligator Gar (*Lepisosteus spatula*), from southern U.S., Central America, Mexico and Cuba. It grows to about 11½ ft. and it is olive-green above and whitish below.

The family Cyprinidae, of the order Cyriniformes, is one of the largest freshwater fish families. There are about 200 species in North America alone. At top left is the Bleak *(Blicca björkna)*, a freshwater European species, European in range, extending north of the Alps as far as southern Scandinavia. It is usually only about 8–12 in. long.

At bottom left is *Squalius cephalus* from the rivers of southern and central Europe. It is only about 2 ft. in length and extremely voracious, with a special fondness for cherries and cockchafers. Its breeding season is from April to June.

Above is the Gudgeon *(Gobio gobio)* a Carp-like fish between 4 and 6 in. long. It lives throughout most of Europe and Asia in shoals, in running water which has a hard bottom and muddy patches. It is much favoured as food in some countries: for example, in France.

Below, the Barbel *(Barbus barbus)* which likewise lives throughout central Europe in shoals, in clear running water with a sandy or stony bed. Its maximum size is about 3 ft. but this is exceptional. The roe and liver are poisonous to man and, indeed, the flesh on many species of fish is inedible during the spawning season.

One of the smallest of the European Cyprinids is *Leucaspius delineatus*. As a rule it is no more than 2 in. or at most 4 in. long. It lives in shoals, in small ponds or gently flowing streams.

Below is the Rapfen *(Aspius aspius)*, an inhabitant of eastern European rivers which may also occasion-ally be found in brackish waters. It achieves a maximum length of about 3 ft. As a rule it lives in the same way as the other Cyprinids, but the larger individuals are extremely wary and shy, and prey on other fish.

The Loach, shown above, *(Cobitis taenis)* is a member of the family Cobitidae, which is found only in the Euro-Asian region and in North Africa. There are many subspecies, none of them more than 4½ in. in length. They have three pairs of barbels on the mouth and movable spikes under the eyes.

Below is another, larger member of this family — the Pond Loach *(Misgurnus fossilis)*. It inhabits the rivers and ponds of central and eastern Europe. Like the preceding species, it is a nocturnal fish. It attains lengths of up to 1 ft. Both these fishes have auxiliary intestinal breathing. If held in the hand, they can be heard to emit a whistling sound as the air is expelled. A related species, *Misgurnus anguillicaudatus*, was recently introduced into the United States.

The Tench *(Tinca tinca)*, is the second most important Cyprinid fish of Europe. It mainly inhabits pools and other stagnant waters overgrown with vegetation. It feeds on aquatic insects and plants. Its maximum size is about 2 ft. 8 in., but it is usually much smaller than this. Its flesh is tasty. The Tench has been introduced into the United States.

Below is *Abramis vimba*, one of the Breams, an interesting Cyprinid found in quiet waters in Europe. Although as a rule only 8–12 in. long, it may grow to 1 ft. 8 in. Its mouth is well adapted for collecting its food – small water animals – on the river bed. This species too, is considered very edible.

Above is the Veiltail, an artificially bred variety of the Goldfish, *Carassius auratus* (actual size). It took over a thousand years of artificial selection to produce this interesting variety. It comes from China, but is today no rarity in European aquariums.

The original Goldfish was first brought to Europe in the 17th century.

The Catfish, also of the order Cypriniformes, sub-order Siluroidei, include the Bull-head (*Ictalurus nebulosus*). This interesting species comes from the eastern parts of the United States, where it reaches up to 1 ft. 4 in. It was brought to Europe by aquarium keepers and later inadvertently introduced into the ponds; here, however, it remains stunted and never weighs more than about a pound. It is extremely voracious, feeding on fish-roe and spawn.

Below is the Wels or Danubian Catfish (*Silurus glanis*). This is a freshwater fish living in the rivers and estuaries of central and eastern Europe and western Asia. It is the largest central European freshwater fish, attaining a maximum length of 10 ft. It makes very good eating. It preys on fish, aquatic birds and any small vertebrates it encounters on the surface, and it has also been known to attack small children bathing in rivers.

The brown Trout *(Salmo trutta)*, order Clupeiformes, family Salmonidae, lives in mountain streams in Europe and Asia Minor. Its flesh is considered a delicacy everywhere.

Osteoglossum bicirrhosum, order Clupeiformes, from the Guianas and the Amazon region, is up to 1 ft. 8 in. long. Mainly silver grey, with red on the throat, it shines with all the colours of the rainbow.

The Pike *(Esox lucius)*, order Clupeiformes, is found over most of Europe, Asia and North America. It is a predator in fresh and brackish waters and attains a maximum size of 4–5 ft.

A member of the family Umbridae is the Hungarian 'Hundfisch' *(Umbra krameri)*, which is closely related to the Pikes. It is a rare European species with a range limited to Hungary and southern Slovakia. Three other related species live in a similarly limited area on the eastern coast of North America.

Below is the only European freshwater representative of the order Gadiformes, *Lota lota*, the Burbot, which is related to the marine Cod-fish. It inhabits Europe and central Asia, ranging as far as India and northern North America, and is found in rivers and lakes, as well as the sea. In European waters it is usually only up to 1 ft. 8 in. in length, but the larger individuals may weigh as much as 33 lb. It is a predator, and will eat even large fish, frogs and crayfish. It has excellent flesh.

The family Scorpaenidae, order Perciformes, includes one of the most bizarre of all fish, *Pterois volitans*, the Dragon Fish. Its pectoral and dorsal fins have extraordinarily long rays, and the fish is coloured, red, brown and white. Some of its spines have poison glands. Despite the Latin name of the species, it does not fly, but swims gracefully among the sea-weed and coral reefs of the tropical seas of the Indo-Pacific (approx. actual size).

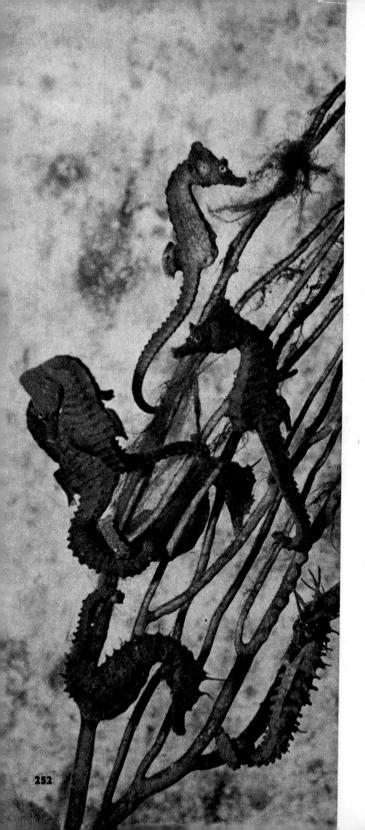

The suborder Thoracostei, order Gasterosteiformes, family Syngnathidae, includes the popular Sea-Horse *(Hippocampus guttulatus)*. The species shown here lives chiefly in the Mediterranean and along the coast of the Atlantic in western Europe. Sea-Horses are perhaps the most attractive of all sea creatures. They move about with the aid of their small dorsal fin which waves incessantly. There is no caudal fin. The vertical position in which they swim lends them a special attraction of their own, making them resemble the so-called 'Carthusian Devils', little toy figures in fluid-filled cylinders. Their heads and arched necks make another remarkable feature which gives them a strong resemblance to horses. They use their prehensile tails to grasp sea-weed and corals, sometimes allowing themselves to be carried considerable distances on floating sea-weed; otherwise, they are weak and slow swimmers. Sea-Horses feed on various small marine animals which they mainly pick off the sea-weed. At the mating season pairs of these charming creatures can be seen standing face to face and repeatedly touching one another with their mouths – literally kissing each other. In reproduction the eggs are transferred to a pouch on the male's abdomen and remain there until they hatch. Sea-Horses dry easily and retain their shape, for which reason they are much in favour as souvenirs of the seaside (approx. actual size).

A species sometimes said to be related to the Sea-Horses is the Three-spined Stickleback (*Gasterosteus aculeatus*), the adult of which usually measures about 2 or 3 in. It lives in small stagnant or brackish waters near the estuaries of large rivers flowing into the sea. It has a wide range practically throughout the temperate zone of the Northern Hemisphere. The Stickleback is a very agile, pugnacious and voracious little fish. In the spring mating season the male acquires beautiful green and red colours and builds a fine nest out of aquatic plants, into which it then proceeds to chase the females to fertilise them and keep watch over large quantities of spawn.

The family Percidae, order Perciformes, includes the Pope (*Acerina cernua*), which may attain a length of 10 in. but is usually smaller. It is therefore considered useless from the economic point of view. Its range includes central and northern Europe, where it is found in deeper, calm, fresh and brackish waters.

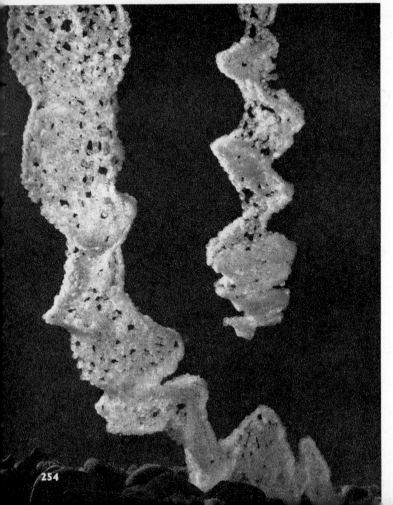

The Perch (Perca fluviatilis) lives in Europe and North Asia. A related species, Perca flavascens, is found in North America. It may be as long as 20 in.; the usual size, however, is only about 10 in., and in cold waters only 6 in. It is gregarious, but is so voracious that individuals occasionally prey on their own kind. The spawn, laid early in spring, is suspended in ribbons on aquatic plants. The picture on the left shows this in the actual size.

The largest member of the Perch family is the Pike-Perch (*Stizostedion lucioperca*), which inhabits fresh and brackish waters in central and northern Europe. As a rule it is about 20 in. in length, though it may grow to over 3 ft. Except in fry stage, it lives exclusively on fish. It is one of the best fish for the table because its flesh is white, soft and fairly fat without small bones *(above)*. It is a very close relative of the American Walleye, Blue Pike, and Sauger.

The bizarre 'Miller's Thumb' *(Cottus gobio)*, order Perciformes, also has spiny fins, but is of the family Cottidae, most of whose members are marine fish. They are characterised by the large flattened head, large, spiky fins, and by the fact that they have no bladder. *Cottus gobio* is a freshwater species inhabiting most of Europe, Siberia and Asia Minor, being particularly abundant in mountain streams where, if too plentiful, it may become a menace to trout spawn. It is also found in brackish waters *(below, actual size)*. Many members of the genus *Cottus* live in North America.

The family Centrarchidae includes the Freshwater Bass and Sun-fishes. The above picture shows the Black Bass (*Micropterus salmoides*) from the large lakes, rivers and brackish waters of the eastern United States. It is an attractive olive-green colour with dark specks, reaching up to 18 in. in its native habitat. It has been introduced to the southern parts of central Europe, where it has successfully bred, especially in ponds and river dams.

Below, the attractive Sun-fish (*Lepomis gibbosus*) which comes from the same North American waters. The Sun-fish, too, has been brought to the warmer parts of Europe, but here it only attains a length

of 4 to 6 in. It is green in colour, sometimes with a golden tinge, with rainbow-coloured sheen and red spots.

On the right can be seen the Argus Fish (*Scatophagus argus*) from tropical Asia. They live mainly in the Pacific and Indian Oceans, as well as in the fresh waters of adjacent rivers, where they reach a maximum length of a foot. These fishes are closely related to the Coral Fishes of the tropics. Of interesting appearance and lively behaviour, they are imported to Europe as aquarium fishes. They are fond of earthworms and other live food, but will also eat lettuce and similar green plants which they eagerly tear up and swallow.

The Perciformes also include a large group of attractive freshwater fish of the family Cichlidae. They inhabit sluggish streams or brackish waters in the warm areas of Central and South America and most of Africa. Some species at first carry their spawn in the mouth and are known as Mouth-breeders, while with others the parents carefully look after the fry.

Above, the Jack Dempsey (Cichlasoma biocellatum) from the Amazon river basin and the Rio Negro. In its native waters this species is up to 8 in. long. It is brownish with shiny dots on almost every scale and on parts of the fins. The dorsal fin is bordered with black.

Below, the Festive Cichlid (Cichlasoma festivum), which grows to only about 6 in., and comes from the same region as the above. It is usually yellowish-green in colour with a metallic sheen, but it frequently changes its colouring according to environment and mood. A black transverse stripe extends obliquely along its body, its hue becoming more or less intense, again according to circumstances. This species also does well in aquaria, when given aerated water at the right temperature.

The Cichlidae also include well-known aquarium fishes with flattened bodies decorated with vertical black stripes. Both shape and colouring have a protective value as the fish swim among the thick tangle of aquatic plants. The top picture on this page shows the Pompadour *(Symphysodon discus)* from the tributaries of the Amazon. It was first exported to Europe in 1921 and since then has become popular with aquarists. Its colouring is yellowish-brown with dark vertical stripes, the fins and the areas near them being reddish with shiny blue wavy lines and spots. In its native waters it is about 8 in. in length. It can be bred in well-tended aquaria.

The Angel Fish *(Pterophyllum eimekei)* is a popular species from the same habitat as the preceding one. It is a beautiful fish of delicate appearance which can also be bred by careful and experienced aquarists *(bottom*, actual size).

259

The Labyrinth Fishes of the family Anabantidae, order Perciformes, include interesting tropical species, some of which can live a long time out of water. They have a special labyrinth organ in a cavity above the gills, in which they store and then use atmospheric air; these fish come to the surface at intervals varying with their activity to replenish their fresh air supply, otherwise they would quickly drown. They can, on the other hand, spend as much as a day out of the water if they are, for instance, among damp vegetation. The ventral fins are placed far forward and often protracted into thin sensory fibres. At top left, the Blue Gourami (*Trichogaster trichopterus*) – a freshwater species from the Malayan Peninsula and Indonesia. Its colouring is light bluish-grey and it attains a size of up to 6 in. The specimens kept in aquaria, however, are usually only about half this size.

On the left is the beautiful Lace Gourami *(Tricho-gaster leeri)*, which comes from the same region. Its colouring is most attractive – orange, reddish or purple – and changes constantly. The males' colours are brightest at mating time (× ¹/₃).

Above, the largest of all these fishes, the Gourami *(Osphronemus gourami)* from Indonesia. It attains a size of 2 ft. and is kept as a table fish in many eastern countries, especially in the irrigation ditches of rice paddies.

The most fantastic-looking and beautiful Coral Fishes of the tropical seas belong to the suborder Percoidei, order Perciformes. They often have very vivid colours, one of the few exceptions being the Sea Bat (*Platax orbicularis*) from the Indo-Malayan seas, the Red Sea, and the eastern coast of Africa. This species is grey, a soiled yellow-white, brownish, and greyish-black. Its vertical stripes serve to conceal the fish among the marine vegetation.

The order Tetraodontiformes also includes various species of bizarre and vividly-coloured Coral Fish. The environment in which they live suggests the reason for their strange shapes and bright colours — the corals, anemones and other inhabitants of the reefs among which they swim are so brightly coloured that only similarly ornamented creatures can remain inconspicuous. The Trigger Fish *(Rhinecanthus aculeatus)* has pastel colours in pink, yellow and blue. It is a member of the family Balistidae, fishes living among coral reefs and having large heads and prominent mouths equipped with strong teeth; the name comes from the spiny dorsal fin which can be locked erect or folded back.

The above picture shows the anterior part of the body of the African Lung Fish *(Protopterus dolloi)* from the Congo basin. This strange fish is Eel-like in appearance and reaches a length of nearly 3 ft. Two pairs of its fins are filamentous and rope-like. It inhabits muddy swamps which dry out periodically. In the dry season it burrows into the ground, makes a chamber for itself, and may spend as much as half the year asleep. At such times its auxiliary lungs, derived from its air bladder, are supplied with atmospheric air through a small tunnel it has made in the dry mud. This is one of the several Lung Fish belonging to the order Dipteriformes in the subclass Sarcopterygii. Thus *Protopterus* is closely related to the Crossopterygian fishes from which, some three hundred million years ago in the Devonian period, the first amphibians evolved.

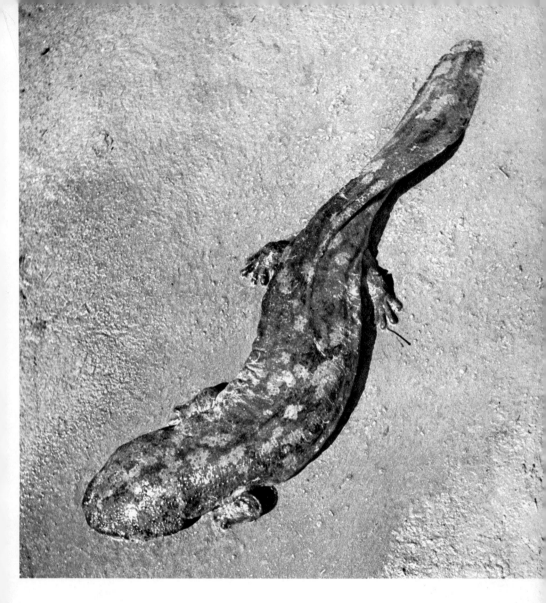

AMPHIBIANS

The superclass Tetrapoda includes vertebrates originally equipped with four paired limbs, adapted according to their function. These fall into the following classes: Amphibians – Amphibia, Reptiles – Reptilia, Birds – Aves, and Mammals – Mammalia. The Amphibia are the oldest and most primitive. These vertebrates usually breathe through gills in the larval stage and mostly through lungs when adult; only a few retain the gills throughout their life. These are chiefly small animals, but they also include the Giant Salamander (*Megalobatrachus maximus*), largest of the Amphibia, which may measure nearly 6 ft. It lives in deep mountain streams in Japan. The variety *Megalobatrachus maximus davidianus* lives in certain parts of China. It is illustrated here. The Giant Salamander is a sluggish creature which comes up only now and again for a breath of air. It subsists on fish and frogs, lays eggs and may live up to the age of fifty.

Many species of Newts and Salamanders are known; their larvae usually develop in the water and emerge only after the disappearance of the ramified external gills. American Axolotls, however, can live in water for years as larvae, laying fertile eggs while still in the non-adult (neotenic) condition. The best known of these is the Mexican *Amblystoma mexicanum*.

These axolotls are bred in biological research laboratories all over the world. Above, a normally coloured neotenic larva; below, an albino variety with pink gills.

Top right, the central and southern European Spotted or Fire Salamander *(Salamandra maculosa)*. It lives on worms, arthropods and molluscs. It is viviparous. Bottom right, the Alpine Salamander *(Salamandra atra)* from the Alps and the Balkan countries. This species produces from two to four young which are able to live out of water at once. (Both pictures actual size.)

The family Salamandridae (about 150 species) of the subclass Urodela (or Caudata) includes, apart from the Salamanders living on land, Newts which live mostly in water. These are brightly coloured amphibians with laterally flattened tails. They remain in the water throughout the pairing and breeding season, the male growing broad cutaneous folds on the tail, back, and sometimes also on the limbs. At the same time they acquire vivid colours. Their tadpoles develop in ponds, usually taking from two to four months. In summer the Newts leave the water and live in a moist environment on land. They feed mostly on worms, but when in the water they also take small insects, etc. Above, a female of the commonest European species, the Smooth Newt *(Triturus vulgaris)*: below a male of the same species. Its range extends as far as the Arctic Circle in the North and to Asia in the warmer regions (× 2).

Above right is a male of the Alpine Newt *(Triturus alpestris)*, which lives in central Europe and various southern European countries, especially in mountainous areas. The tadpoles sometimes stay permanently in the water and reproduce while immature (× 2).

Below right is a male of the largest central European species, the Crested or Warty Newt *(Triturus cristatus)*. It inhabits ponds, pools and large ditches.

269

The subclass Anura (Tailless Amphibia) consists of amphibians whose larval stages are found mostly in fresh water as tadpoles. These are similar to fish in their adaptation to aquatic life, for they breathe through gills and propel themselves largely by their broad tails. The head and body together have an oval, sometimes almost spherical shape. Tadpoles at first eat algae, then a range of plant and animal food. As the tadpoles grow, the gills disappear and are replaced by lungs. They also develop first the hind and later the fore limbs. The little Frogs then leave the water and the long tail is gradually absorbed. The picture on the left shows tadpoles of the *Rana dalmatina* shortly before leaving the water.

Above right is a tadpole of the same species, viewed from the side with the broad tail-fin well in evidence. At the root of the tail can be seen the hind pair of legs, which develops first. At the bottom of page 271 is an older tadpole of the same species with all four limbs, in the stage just before the absorption of the tail ($\times$ 3). The body gradually acquires the characteristic frog shape.

Below, an amphibian which has some of the toes of the hind legs equipped with claws. It is the Clawed Toad (*Xenopus laevis*), an interesting species from the warm regions of Africa. It spends its entire life in the water, where it feeds on small aquatic animals and insects which have fallen on to the surface. Its tadpoles have a pair

of sensory tentacles or feelers sprouting from the mouth, thus giving them a resemblance to Catfish. They soon begin to breathe with the lungs and at first feed on plankton. This species of Frog is a sensitive indicator of hormones and for that reason is kept in medical laboratories (actual size).

The Common Toad (Bufo bufo) inhabits central and northern Europe and adjacent parts of Asia, ranging as far as central Asia. The related species in the United States is Bufo americanus. It lives in woods, gardens and fields. During the day it remains hidden among stones and in cellars, coming out to hunt at night. It catches various insects, snails and worms, occasionally also smaller vertebrates such as baby mice. The female of the central European variety attains the size shown in the above picture; the Mediterranean variety is even larger.

At top left of p. 273 is the Green Toad (Bufo viridis), found in Europe except for the western and northern parts), in North Africa, and throughout temperate Asia, far to the East. It is yellowish-grey with olive-green spots.

At top right is the Natterjack (Bufo calamita), recognisable by the light stripe along its back. This lives in northern and western Europe, the eastern limits of its habitat extending as far as central Europe. These Toads feed on insects, worms and snails. They hide in daytime among stones and in holes. They only enter the water early in the spring to lay their eggs.

At the bottom of p. 273 is a picture of the Spade-foot Toad (Pelobates fuscus). This is a smaller species than the two preceding ones. It lives in the north-eastern parts of central Europe and throughout central Asia, keeping to low altitudes. It is rarely seen, as it stays hidden in the sand all day. Its tadpoles are comparatively large, being as much as 7 in. in length.

One of the largest among the approximately 1,700 known species of Frogs and Toads is the Giant Toad *(Bufo marinus)*, which attains a maximum size of some 10 in. Behind each eye it has developed a conspicuous gland which exudes an unpleasant substance. It inhabits Central and South America. The males make a loud barking noise. It the hot season these Frogs remain in hiding, coming out, often in large numbers, during cooler and wet weather. They subsist on small vertebrates; in all other respects their way of life is similar to that of other European Toads.

The best-known member of the Hylidae (Tree-frogs) family is *Hyla arborea* – the southern European Tree-frog. This is a beautiful little Frog, usually a bright green, which is active during the day. It is an excellent climber and jumper, keeping mostly to trees and bushes. Its range covers the whole of central Europe, extending south to Italy and east to central Asia. Tree-frogs can be heard in daytime and at dusk making series of rapidly-repeated croaking notes. They seize their insect prey with their sticky tongues, usually as it moves.

Many species of Tree-frogs are found in the exotic parts of the world, often being conspicuous by their shape and colouring. The Australian Tree-frog *(Hyla coerulea)* has a tendency to obesity, which combined with its great appetite for food leads, in captive specimens, to their acquiring strangely bloated shapes (both pictures × 2)

The female of the Pouched Frog (*Nototrema mar-supiatum*), from the forests of Ecuador and Peru, has a pouch on its back which is filled with eggs at breeding time. The eggs develop in this receptacle and finally the female discharges the newly-hatched tadpoles into the water. The eggs are probably inserted in the pouch by the male during the mating season ($\times \frac{1}{3}$).

The Horned Toads (family Leptodactylidae, genus *Ceratophrys*) live in South America. They are very vividly-coloured Frogs with horn-like protuberances above the eyes. They usually remain hidden in sand or mud, with only the head showing. Their protective colouring makes them just about invisible as they lie in wait for their prey. Some Horned Toads attain sizes up to 10 in. and can puff themselves up to a great width. *Ceratophrys varia*, patterned light green, dark red and dark brown can swallow a comparatively large prey.

Frogs leading a terrestrial existence for a time. These Frogs feed on insects and small vertebrates. They hibernate in mud on the bottom, breathing only through the surface of their bodies (*left*, slightly magnified).

Below, a pair of the species *Rana arvalis* (× 2), which inhabits central and northern Europe, and the northern parts of Asia, ranging as far as the Arctic Circle. They are nocturnal animals, preferring moist meadows and fields and peat-bogs to actual water. They are extremely agile jumpers.

The most accomplished jumpers among Frogs are those of the genus *Rana*. They catch their prey with their extensile, forked tongue. At mating-time they, especially the males, make loud croaking noises, their 'concert' being heard for miles around. The Edible Frog *(Rana esculenta)* is common in shallow waters throughout central Europe as far south as Italy.

Its whole life is spent in or near water, only the very small

The Common Frog *(Rana temporaria)* has an even more northerly distribution than that preceding, extending southwards as far as Bulgaria and eastwards to Japan. It is mainly a nocturnal Frog, only the younger individuals being seen in the daytime. These Frogs often live considerable distances from water, in woods and gullies, in moist meadows, gardens, and so on. They are relatively poor jumpers (picture slightly magnified).

Below, the agile *Rana dalmatina* (× 2), an excellent jumper which can cover more than 6 ft.

It inhabits the southern parts of central Europe, southern Europe, and the warm regions of western Asia. The more common species in the United States are the Leopard Frog *(Rana pipiens)*, the Bullfrog *(Rana catesbiana)*, and the Pickerel Frog *(Rana palustris)*.

279

REPTILES

develop. The reptiles were at the height of their development in the long distant past and today only a little over 4,000 species are known.

The order Chelonia (Testudinata) includes both terrestrial and aquatic Tortoises and Turtles, without teeth but with sharp, horny jaws. They have a firm, partly horny carapace. They lay eggs with hard shells, and breathe through lungs as do all reptiles. The upper picture shows a Hawksbill (*Eretmochelys imbricata*) from the warm seas. It is a little over 3 ft. in length. It is seldom found in temperate or cold waters.

Below, the Green or Edible Turtle (*Chelonia mydas*), another inhabitant of warm seas, which reaches sizes of more than 5 ft. These Sea Turtles have limbs transformed into paddle-shaped flippers. They eat both animal and vegetable food. Their eggs — 150 to 200 at a laying — are buried in the sand on the beach.

Just as the amphibians are similar to fishes, so do reptiles have many affinities with the higher vertebrates, the birds and the mammals. These classes — mammals, birds and reptiles — form the group called Amniota, this name deriving from the special membrane covering the embryo and filled with embryonic fluid, in which the embryo is cushioned. This arrangement replaces the water environment in which the larvae of the fishes and amphibians

The Snapping Turtle (*Chelydra serpentina*) lives in the rivers and marshes of North America, east of the Rockies, and southwards to northern South America. It grows to a length of some 2 ft. 'Snappers' inflict dangerous bites. They eat fishes and other small vertebrates and lay clutches of about 60 eggs on river banks.

Below, the Alligator Snapping Turtle (*Macroclemys temmincki*) a distinctly larger species than the preceding one, inhabiting the same geographical region and environment. Its main food is fish, which it catches by attracting them into its gaping mouth with a motile, worm-shaped structure on the tongue. The Turtles are often covered with green algae and are thus rendered almost invisible among the vegetation.

Some kinds of Tortoises – Testudinidae – are imported to other countries from the Mediterranean and the neighbouring regions. One of these species is the Greek Tortoise (*Testudo graeca*), which is up to a foot long. It is herbivorous and frugivorous, but also eats worms, caterpillars, snails and the like.

In captivity it will become accustomed to food such as bread dipped in milk. Its habitat includes the south-eastern parts of Europe and south-west Asia (*left*).

The Giant Tortoises are well named: there are several different species, but some are now extinct. The length of the shell in some individuals is as much as 25 ft. over the curve, and they may weigh several hundred-weight. The age of such giants has been estimated at three hundred years, though this is not fully proved. They are herbivorous and frugivorous. In past centuries these Tortoises were killed in large numbers for food by sailors whose voyages took them past the Galapagos (*galapago* is the Spanish word for tortoise) or Aldabra Islands where they were mostly to be found. Like all reptiles, they can go a long time without a meal. Below, one of the Giant Tortoises from Aldabra – *Testudo gigantica*.

Above, the Margined Tortoise *(Testudo marginata)* from south-east Europe and Asia Minor which grows to a length of about 12 in.

Below, the Spurred Tortoise *(Testudo sulcata),* of Africa, which attains a size of 20 in.

The range of the Four-toed Tortoise *(Testudo horsfieldi)* extends from the western Caspian region across the whole of central Asia as far as western Pakistan. This species is distinguished from its relatives by having four claws on the forelimbs, and by its flat, rounded carapace.

The Red-footed Tortoise *(Testudo carbonaria)* has a carapace that is black with yellow markings, and is a South American species which sometimes attains a length of over a foot.

The strange Forest Hinged Tortoise *(Kinyxis erosa)* with a shell more than a foot long is a native of tropical West Africa. Its carapace is divided, being bell-shaped in front.

The Radiated Tortoise *(Testudo radiata)* of Madagascar, is one of the most decorative species. It feeds chiefly on shoots and the fruits of succulent plants. It is a very attractive creature which can reach a length of 18 in. It is now protected by the government of the new Malagasy Republic.

Many different species of carnivorous Turtles live in the fresh waters of the tropical and temperate zones of various continents. Most northerly of the European Turtles (extending as far as Holland and Lithuania) is the European Pond Turtle *(Emys orbicularis)*. It is from 8 to 10 in. long and may live a hundred years *(left)*.

Below, the Eastern Box Turtle *(Terrapene carolina)* from the United States. Though in appearance it would seem to be an aquatic Turtle, it is, in fact, almost

entirely terrestrial. It is one of the species which are able to withdraw entirely into their carapaces and close the folding bottom parts of the shell over themselves.

At the top of this page is the False Map Turtle (*Graptemys pseudogeographica*) an aquatic form from the United States. At the bottom of the page, the head of an interesting carnivorous Tortoise called Matamata (*Chelys fimbriata*) which inhabits the swamps of Brazil and the Guianas (actual size).

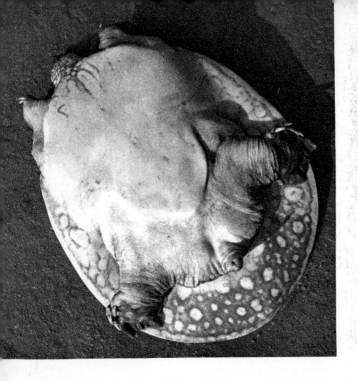

used to be revered as a sacred animal.

The subclass Archosauria is represented in our present-day fauna only by the order of Crocodiles — Crocodylia. The best known of these is the Nile Crocodile (Crocodylus niloticus) which lives in the rivers of northern and central Africa and on Madagascar. It attains a maximum length of 16 ft. or more (right).

The Broad-fronted Crocodile (Osteolaemus tetraspis) from equatorial West Africa is seen at the bottom of p. 289. It reaches a length of only 5 or 6 ft. and is mostly found in small forest streams. In contrast to the Nile Crocodile, it does not attack human beings.

The African Soft-shelled Turtle (Trionyx triunguis) belongs to the suborder Trionychoidea. It inhabits the swamps of equatorial Africa, ranging northwards to Egypt and Syria. It may measure over 24 in. in length (left, viewed from the underside).

Below is a related species from China (Trionyx sinensis) which

On the left, the head of a young Spectacled Caiman (*Caiman crocodilus*), from the basin of the Amazon and Orinoco rivers. It attains a maximum length of 8 ft.

The American Alligator (*Alligator mississippiensis*) inhabits the Mississippi river in the south-eastern part of North America. It has a broad, flattened snout and in the past grew to a length of 19 ft. It will usually flee at the approach of man, but it may drown cattle by pulling them into the water. It is sometimes bred in 'Alligator farms' (*below*).

The Broad-nosed Caiman *(Caiman latirostris)* is found in the rivers of eastern Brazil. It is only a little over 6 ft. in length. The picture on the right shows the head of a young specimen of this species.

The Indian rivers, Ganges, Indus and Brahmaputra are the home of the interesting Gharial (or Gavial) *(Gavialis gangeticus)*. This Crocodile's head is extended into a long, narrow, toothed beak. It lives chiefly on fish, but will also eat any other vertebrates within its reach. It attains a maximum length of 23 ft. and was once regarded by the Hindus as sacred *(below)*.

Another subclass of the reptiles is Lepidosauria, of which all except one species belong to the order Squamata of the Lizards and Snakes. This in turn is divided into two suborders, Lacertilia, the Lizards, and Ophidia, the Snakes. The Geckos (Gekkonidae) are in the main small Lizards of climbing habits, possessing a flattened body and a relatively large head. They eat insects or small vertebrates. About three hundred species are known, belonging to some seventy genera.

The largest species, the Tokay (*Gekko gecko*) is abundant in Southeast Asia. Up to 14 in. long, they are usually a light greyish-purple colour with orange or reddish spots. They are frequently found in houses, climbing the walls in pursuit of insects. Their strange toe pads enable them to cling even to the smoothest surface. The Gecko at top left has been photographed through a vertical pane of glass to show the structure of these pads; the one at the bottom of the page on the bark of a tree, where it is difficult to discern.

The Indian Bloodsucker (*Calotes versicolor*) is chiefly to be found in the forests of India, Ceylon, the Malay Peninsula and Indochina (*right*). It belongs to the family Agamidae and measures some 16 in. It is a shy creature but will bite if captured. It is able to change its colour, for which reason it is sometimes mistaken for a Chameleon. The colour change occurs especially at the mating season when the males fight each other ferociously, adopting various comic poses. Their throats swell and redden on such occasions.

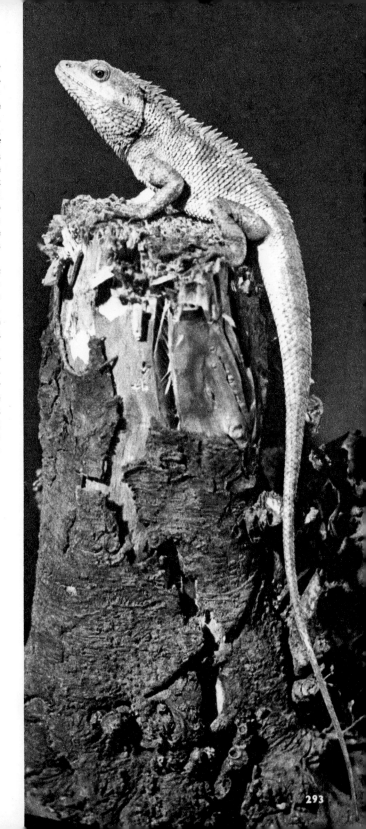

The Spiny-tailed Lizard *(Uromastix acanthinurus)* from North Africa is also an Agamid. It lives in the stony deserts of Algeria, Egypt, Arabia and Palestine. When young, it catches the larger insects, later it is exclusively herbivorous. Its spiked tail serves it in good stead as a weapon with which it can deal painful blows *(on the left,* the head; *below,* the whole Lizard).

The steppes of central Asia are inhabited by the Agama (*Agama sanguinolenta*), which is about a foot long. Its colouring varies, according to the animal's mood, in much the same way as that of the Chameleon, from brownish-grey to reddish or bluish. This Lizard hides in holes in the ground, feeding on insects and partly also on vegetable matter (*above*).

On the right can be seen the vividly-coloured Butterfly Agama (*Leiolepis belliana*). The male may be as long as 3 ft. The colouring of this species is blackish-blue, yellow, and a vivid orange. It is a ground Lizard inhabiting the tropical parts of Southeast Asia. It feeds on both insects and plants.

The Australian Bearded Lizard (*Amphibolurus barbatus*) lives in the dry regions of Australia. It is a ground Lizard, about $19\frac{1}{2}$ in. in length. Its diet consists chiefly of insects. When annoyed, the males change colour and puff up the spiny 'collar' under their throat to an astonishing degree (*above*).

On the right, the Green Iguana (*Iguana iguana*) belonging to the family Iguanidae. This is a beautiful, green-coloured arboreal Lizard from the tropical regions of America. It attains a length of 6 ft. or more. Iguanas feed on insects when young, later on leaves, shoots and fruits of plants. They are fond of the water and are accomplished swimmers. Their eggs are hidden in the sand on the banks of rivers. The natives hunt the Iguana for its tasty flesh.

The family of Girdle-tailed Lizards (Cordylidae) includes the Armadillo Lizard (Cordylus cataphractus), one of a number of related species inhabiting Central and South Africa. These Lizards have large scales arranged in transverse rows, and frequently have spiky protuberances at the back of the head. The species shown here attains a length of 10 in. It lives in deserts, where it preys on the larger insects. When in danger, it sometimes curls up like an Armadillo; it can, however, also defend

(*Sauromalus obesus*). This is a Lizard up to some 16 in. long, which clambers about the bushes, eating leaves, flowers and fruit. It hides in rock crevices, and if in danger will puff itself up to such an extent that it cannot be extricated (*left*).

Below is another member of this group, the American Basilisk (*Basiliscus americanus*). Together with a few other similar species it inhabits the forests of tropical America, feeding chiefly on insects. It is a brisk climber and swims excellently. Together with the tail it measures about 31 in. In the Middle Ages the Basilisk was considered to be a cross between a cock, a frog, and a serpent, because it has certain external features of all these animals.

itself by lashing out with its spiky tail (*picture at top of the page 298*).

At the bottom of p. 298 can be seen the Texas Horned Lizard (*Phrynosoma cornutum*). It is an Iguanid Lizard with a flattened, spiked body which lives with a number of other species in the southern parts of North America. It is found in arid deserts, its diet consisting of small insects, ants in particular. It can very quickly hide itself in the sand (approximately actual size).

In the deserts of Arizona and in the south-west of the United States lives the Iguanid Chuckwalla

Some of the Lizards have no visible limbs and consequently are often taken for Snakes. The best known of this family – Anguidae – is the European Slow-worm or Blind-worm *(Anguis fragilis)*, said to live over 50 years. A length of 21 in. has been recorded but they are usually only about 1 ft. long. In populated areas this harmless creature is frequently killed because of its resemblance to Snakes. It differs from them by having eyes with movable lids and a hard, firm body which does not coil and twist but merely swings from side to side. Under each of its scales is a bony plate which lends it firmness. The Slow-worm's colour varies, the most usual being greyish-brown, frequently with a copper sheen. It inhabits most of Europe, a part of North Africa, and extends as far as Southeast Asia. Its favourite habitat is wooded country,

bush-covered hillsides, swamps and other places that are not too dry. It feeds on snails, worms and small insects. The female gives birth to as many as twenty-five young, though usually fewer. In captivity it has been known to live to between 30 and 50 years *(left pictures)*.

The largest member of this group is the European Glass-Snake or Scheltopusik *(Ophisaurus apodus)* which may be as long as 4 ft. It lives in broken rocky country covered by grass and scrub in southeastern Europe and south-western and central Asia. It likes to be near water and feeds on insects and smaller vertebrates. It is very tame when in contact with humans and does not usually even attempt to bite. It will soon learn to eat out of the hand – in captivity its diet usually consists of mice, birds and raw meat *(above)*.

It used to be a widespread belief that all Lizards were poisonous. Science has disproved this superstition, except in the case of the two species which make up the family Helodermatidae and live in the deserts of the southern United States and Mexico. The Gila Monster (*Heloderma suspectum*) measures about 20 in. On a dull-black body it has variously-shaped reddish-orange markings. The Gila is a very slow-moving creature and it is surprising that it manages to find sufficient prey for its sustenance. This consists mainly of fledgling birds, the larger and slower insects, and all kinds of eggs. These Lizards have poison fangs in their lower jaws, and their bite is similar to a Snake's, but though it is fatal to small vertebrates, human beings usually suffer only painful swellings.

Above and on the right is the most common Lizard of central Europe, the Sand-Lizard (*Lacerta agilis*). Its range extends from England eastward as far as the temperate region of western Asia. It is up to 8 in. long and found mainly on warm hillsides, field boundaries and the fringes of forests, and in gardens, parks and clearings. It feeds on insects, molluscs and worms. It lays eggs with a parchment-like shell. Each clutch contains up to fourteen eggs.

Below, the head of the large, carnivorous South American Lizard known as the Golden Tegu (*Tupinambis nigropunctatus*). It is black and yellowish in colour and grows to about 3 ft. Its diet is made up of small animals and eggs of every kind, though it sometimes also eats fruit.

Another Tegu – *Tupinambis teguixin* – is larger still, reaching a maximum length of some $4^1/_2$ ft. It is an inhabitant of the same dry regions of South America, but is also found in the islands of the West Indies. Apart from large insects it feeds on the smaller vertebrates. It is frequently hunted, as much for its tasty flesh as for the damage it does by invading hen-houses.

The Monitors – family Varanidae – are exclusively carnivorous.

Below, the head of the Yellow Monitor of the species *Varanus flavescens*, which comes from India (actual size).

At the top of p. 305 is the head of the Grey Monitor *(Varanus griseus)*, from central Asia. Other subspecies are found in North Africa,

The Texas Horned Lizard in its natural surroundings.

Arabia, Iran and eastwards as far as western India. It attains a length of over 3 ft.

Below, a Desert or Bosc's Monitor (*Varanus exanthematicus*), a smaller species than the preceding one. It usually reaches a length of only about 3 ft. but occasionally as much as 6 ft. It does not climb trees in search of birds' nests as the foregoing. It digs holes in the dry country where it lives and retreats to them if threatened.

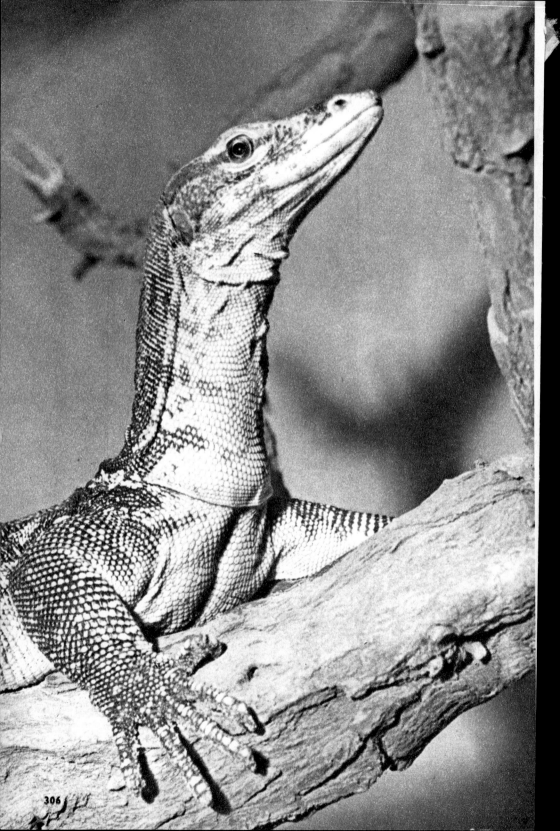

Left is one of the largest living Monitors, the Water Monitor *(Varanus salvator)* of south-eastern Asia. Its maximum size is 8 to 9 ft. A much larger Monitor inhabits the island of Komodo, and its discovery was a great sensation. The Water Monitor lives near the sea-coast or rivers and is a very good swimmer. It preys on other reptiles, climbs trees to lie in wait for birds, and will even steal poultry: in fact it will eat almost anything it can catch. Though it tends to run away from man, it will fight powerfully if attacked.

Above is a member of the Skink family — Scin-cidae — of the species *Ablepharus kitaibelii fitzingeri* (often called the Snake-eyed Sheik) found in the south-eastern parts of central Europe. It lives in scrub country, hiding under stones (× ¹/₃).

Below, the curious Stump-tailed Lizard *(Trachysaurus rugosus)* from the littoral deserts of Australia. It is about a foot long, omnivorous, and resembles in appearance a large black and yellow fircone. It has a short, broad, stump-like tail in which it carries fat reserves. It does well in captivity, feeding largely on eggs.

The Common Chameleon (*Chamaeleo chamaeleon*) is the only European representative of the Chameleon family – Chameleontidae. It is found in the south of Spain and on some of the Mediterranean islands, North Africa, Arabia, Syria and Asia Minor. Other species live in various parts of Africa and on Madagascar, and just one species in India and Ceylon. The Chameleon shown above is from Spain. Chameleons are arboreal climbing Lizards, feeding on insects which they seize with their long, sticky tongues. They can change the colour of their skin quickly and their eyes are independent so that they can look in two different directions simultaneously. The large, spherical eyeballs are hidden beneath fused eyelids and the Chameleon looks through a small central opening. The species shown here reproduces by means of eggs; some other species are viviparous.

The second suborder of Scaly Reptiles (Ophidia) contains the snakes, of which there are some 2,300 species. They are limbless creatures with elongated bodies, their size ranging from 4 in. in length and the thickness of knitting wool to huge monsters as thick as the human body and over 30 ft. long. The well-known Boa Constrictor (Constrictor constrictor) lives in the damp forests of Brazil, Venezuela and north-east Peru. It is usually not more than about 13 ft. long. Its diet consists of mammals and birds, varying according to the snake's size. It gives birth to live young.

The beautiful Emerald Tree Boa *(Corallus caninus)* is another of the Boas. It has white markings on its green body, which is strongly compressed laterally. The Snake is about 6 ft. long. It lives among the branches of trees in the forests of tropical South America, feeding on birds.

Top right is the beautiful Central and South American Rainbow Boa *(Epicrates cenchria)* which is not much more than a yard long. It has a shiny body coloured with all the hues of the rainbow.

In the Old World are various Boas which have adapted themselves to life in a sandy environment. The Indian Sand Boa *(Eryx johnii),* less than 3 ft. long, looks as though it has had its tail amputated. It feeds on the small desert birds and mammals, constricting them in the same way as do its larger relatives *(bottom, right).*

311

The largest of the true Boas is the Anaconda *(Eunectes murinus)*. Living in the inaccessible forests and swamps of the northern regions of South America, it usually reaches about 20 ft., though individuals are on record which attained more than 30 ft., with enormous girth. The age of such huge Snakes is estimated at fifty years.

The Boas and Pythons form a group of Snakes with a very old ancestry, their anatomic features suggesting that all Snakes originally developed from reptiles with limbs. Experts believe that the present-day Monitors are the most closely related to these huge Snakes. The best known of the Pythons is the Indian species *(Python molurus)* which is frequently seen in menageries and zoological gardens. It is a little over 13 ft. long on the average and inhabits India, Ceylon, and, a somewhat larger and darker variety, the Malay-Indonesian region. In contrast to the Boas, Pythons lay eggs.

In central Europe the non-poisonous Snakes are represented by the family Colubridae. The best known representative here is the common Grass-Snake *(Natrix natrix)*. This is characterised by a yellow mark on either side of the head. It ranges through most of Europe, to western Asia. Its favourite habitat is grassy marshland in the neighbourhood of water. It hides in the banks of rivers and ponds, among stones, as well as in the masonry of inhabited houses. Its usual length is less than 3 ft., but old Snakes may reach almost 5 ft. It hunts by day for frogs, tadpoles, newts and small fish. The Grass-Snake lays leathery-shelled eggs *(left)*.

The bottom picture shows the head of the harmless European Smooth Snake *(Coronella austriaca)* which is frequently mistaken for the venomous Viper. It has on its back a series of dark spots which give it this unfortunate resemblance, and when danger threatens, it even adopts the same fighting attitude as the Viper. A reliable distinctive feature, however, is the round pupil of the eye, possessed by all the Colubridae, as distinguished from the vertical, slit-like pupil of the Vipers. The Smooth Snake is not an aquatic species like the common Grass-Snake, preferring dry places and forests. It lives on lizards, snakes and small mice, which it hunts in the daytime. It is rarely more than 20 in. long. Its range extends over most of temperate and southern Europe east to the borders of Asia. It is viviparous.

At the top of p. 315 is a common Grass-Snake swimming. In the middle, a Tessellated Snake *(Natrix tessellata)* with its eggs. It inhabits central and south-east Europe, being usually less than a yard in length.

At the foot of page 315 is the Dice Snake *(Natrix piscator)*, an attractive snake from South-east Asia which is, however, given to biting.

The Malayan and Indo-Australian forests are inhabited by so-called 'Golden' or 'Flying' Snakes; it was once believed that they could fly from tree to tree; they have, in fact, some ability to glide. These Snakes with poison fangs towards the rear of their upper jaw belong to the genus *Chrysopelea*. Top left is *Chrysopelea ornata* ($\times \frac{1}{3}$). At top right is the head of the European Whip Snake *(Coluber gemonensis)*, which lives in southern Europe and western Asia. Some forms attain 9 ft. in length, this species thus being the largest European Snake. Though not venomous, some individuals are extremely aggressive and much given to biting.

Below, an inhabitant of the Californian desert, the Shovel-nose Snake *(Chionactis occipitalis annulata)*. It is vividly coloured white, black and orange, its scales are shiny, and it measures only about a foot. It lives in the sand, the shape of its head allowing it to 'swim' through it.

The Mountain King Snake *(Lampropeltis zonata)* from the western states of the United States is even more vivid in colouring than the preceding species. These beautiful, pastel-coloured and extremely active Snakes grow to be as much as 5 ft. long. They feed on small vertebrates and often on other Snakes. They attack their prey in the same way as the Boas and Pythons, coiling themselves round it, and only when it is weakened by strangulation do they start to swallow it. They lay eggs, about ten at a time.

Heterodon platyrhinos, the Eastern Hog-nose Snake, is a brightly coloured snake from Florida and regions to the west as far as Texas. It is less than a yard in length, makes burrows in the sand, and feeds on toads. Harmless to human beings, it has an interesting way of defending itself: it spreads its neck like a Cobra, hisses, rolls about convulsively on the ground, or feigns death. The 'Opistoglyph' group of the Colubridae is made up of Snakes which, while possessing poison fangs, do not as a rule use them in self-defence. These fangs are situated in the rear of the upper jaw, so that the prey is only bitten after it has been seized.

The Long-nose Tree Snake *(Ahaetulla nasuta)* from the jungles of Malaya and the East Indies region is a member of this group. Its green body and head are elongated to such an extent that it is almost indistinguishable from the lianas and other vegetation among which it lies in wait for small lizards and frogs. Although quite slender, it can open its mouth very wide and swallow large prey (× 2).

The picture *(left)* shows the Vine Snake *(Oxybelis acuminatus)* which has the greyish-brown colouring of the twigs and aerial roots among which it lives, preying on small lizards, in the tropical regions of America. This also is a rear-fanged snake (× 2).

The largest of all the harmless Snakes is the non-poisonous Oriental Rat Snake *(Ptyas mucosus),* which is usually between 6 and 9 ft. long, though exceptionally large individuals have been known to grow to as much as 13 ft. It is found in the greater part of central and southern Asia, and as far east as China. Its most usual colouring is yellowish or brownish, with a beautiful sheen. The Rat Snake subsists mainly on rodents and toads.

Snakes with poison fangs fixed in the front part of the upper jaw make up the family Elapidae. They include some of the most venomous of all Snakes – the Cobras. Various species of Cobras inhabit the warm regions of Asia and Africa, but they are similar both in behaviour and general way of life. When angry or alarmed they can form the characteristic 'hood' by spreading some of the anterior ribs which are larger than the others. When the Cobra bites, its short teeth inject an extremely potent venom into its prey, which affects the nervous system and finally causes paralysis. A Cobra may have sufficient poison to kill ten or fifteen people. What is more, the Cobra has the habit of holding its victim with its teeth, chewing at the wound and all the time injecting more and more of the deadly venom. Best known of the Cobras is the Indian or Spectacled Cobra (Naja naja). It attains a length of about 6 ft. and hunts small rodents, amphibians, lizards and fish, as well as eating birds' eggs. One form of this species lives in the western part of central Asia. It reproduces by means of leathery shelled eggs about the size of pigeons' eggs. A frightened or angry Cobra will erect the front part of its body, lowering the head into a horizontal position. In some varieties a distinct pattern shows on the expanded skin behind the head. In the case of the Indian Cobra this frequently takes the shape of a pair of 'spectacles' (top right).

The Monocled Cobra *(Naja naja kaouthia)* from the more eastern parts of south Asia and the Malay Peninsula, has only a single, circular or heart-shaped mark with several dark spots inside it *(left)*.

The largest of the Cobras and, indeed, the largest of all venomous Snakes is the King Cobra or Hamadryad *(Ophiophagus hannah)*. It attains a maximum length of about 18 ft. and is usually yellowish-green with black bands. This is the most aggressive species of Cobra, which inhabits South China, Vietnam, Burma, Malaya and the Philippines. It feeds chiefly on other Snakes. At the breeding season a pair of King Cobras will build a nest out of dry plants and keep careful watch over the eggs which the female lays in it *(below)*.

The poison fangs of a Snake grow in the upper jaw, being linked with the poison-gland. In the Elapids these fangs are rather short and always erect. In the Viperids (Vipers and Rattlesnakes) they are much longer and stand erect only when the Snake opens its jaws. When these are closed, the fangs lie back against the palate, resting against the mucous membrane. In both of these groups, if the teeth are extracted or worn away, reserve teeth soon replace them, and this process is repeated indefinitely. Occasionally a Snake has two functional teeth together on one or both sides. Such a case is illustrated at left, in the picture showing the open mouth of a Common Viper (× 4).

The Elapids also include the ornamental but deadly Banded Krait *(Bungarus fasciatus)*. It has bands of black and yellow and measures some 5 ft. An inhabitant of South-east Asia and the Malayan Archipelago, it comes out at night to hunt small mammals and frogs *(below)*.

To the west of India lives the central Asian Cobra *(Naja naja oxiana)*, a yellowish-grey Snake with no markings except bands across the neck of a darker shade than the body *(above)*. Its usual length is about a yard, and it is less ferocious than the Spectacled Cobra.

The legendary 'Asp' or Egyptian Cobra *(Naja haje)* grows to a length of nearly 6 ft. Its usual colour is yellowish-brown with bars on the underside. It is as poisonous and dangerous as the Indian Cobra and, length for length, is much heavier. Four different forms are found. It ranges over most of the semi-desert country of Africa, often spending the day in the burrows of rodents. Like all the Cobras, it can swim, though most of its habitats are almost waterless *(below)*.

The Asp Viper *(Vipera aspis)* is found in many parts of south-west Europe, reaching about as far north as Paris. An extremely venomous snake, much given to biting, it can be distinguished from the Common Viper by the slightly upturned snout and by the head markings. Adult males attain a length of 2½ ft. *(left).*

The Levantine Viper *(Vipera lebetina)* measures up to 5 ft. It inhabits North Africa (with the exception of Egypt), and ranges from Greece almost to India. Its colour is grey, with brown or olive *(below).*

The best-known European venomous Snake is the Common Viper *(Vipera berus),* which extends from 67° N. down to parts of southern Europe, as well as over the entire temperate zone of Asia. Females are larger

than males, growing to a length of about 34 in.   The average size of a Viper, however, is about 20 in.
Young Vipers eat lizards;   the adult Snakes also hunt mice, voles and shrews *(above)*.

Southern Europe is the home of the small Orsini's, or Desert Viper (*Vipera ursinii*). Its maximum length is about a foot, and its food chiefly lizards, the young of various small mammals, and large insects. It hides in rodents' burrows, and has a docile reputation.

Also an inhabitant of south-east Europe, the attractive European Long-nosed or Sand Viper (*Vipera ammodytes*), has a small, cone-shaped 'horn' on its nose. The male is usually larger than the female, attaining as much as a yard in length. It actually lives on stony ground and in old walls, never in sand. It feeds chiefly on mice and lizards.

The semi-deserts from West Africa through to western India are the habitat of the dangerous Carpet or Saw-scaled Viper *(Echis carinatus)*. It is slightly longer than the Common Viper, but not so stout *(above)*.

The Daboia, Tic-Polonga, or Russell's Viper *(Vipera russelli)* is a deadly venomous Snake from eastern India, Ceylon, Burma and Thailand. It measures up to 5 ft. *(below)*.

The stoutest of the Vipers is the Gaboon Viper *(Bitis gabonica)* which lives in the forests of equatorial Africa. It often reaches a length of over 5 ft. It is sluggish and placid, normally using its poison fangs only to kill its prey, and not striking a human unless seriously molested *(opposite)*.

At the top of p. 332 is the Puff Adder *(Bitis arietans)* from the open country south of the Sahara. Its bite is often fatal. It may reach a length of slightly over 3 ft.

The dangerous Water Moccasin or Cottonmouth *(Agkistrodon piscivorus)* is one of the Pit-vipers (Crotalinae): it inhabits the swamps of Florida and the neighbouring regions of North America. It grows to about 5 ft. and feeds mainly on fish *(above)*.

On the left is the Copper-head Snake *(Agkistrodon contortrix)*. Its colouring is copper-reddish and its maximum length is about 4 ft.; it lives in the forests of the eastern part of the United States other than Florida.

Above is the venomous Siberian Moccasin (*Agkistro-don halys caraganus*) from the steppes of central Asia (actual size).

Below, the Fer-de-Lance (*Bothrops atrox*) which inhabits Central and South America (× ¹/₉).

On the following page is a picture of the Urutu (*Bothrops alternatus*) from the jungles of the central part of South America. The bite of all the Snakes of this group is extremely dangerous.

Rattlesnakes are perhaps the best known members of the Crotalinae and they are found only on the American continent. About fifteen species of these poisonous Snakes are known while many species include a large number of local races. Rattlesnakes have well-developed curved poison fangs, measuring in some species as much as an inch long. Their tails are equipped with a rattle composed of loosely jointed dried skin, which they erect and shake rapidly when irritated, emitting a dry, ratting sound. Cattle grazing or running about in the wilderness are alarmed by this warning noise and do not tread on the Snakes which might otherwise be killed by the hooves. Rattlesnakes feed on the smaller mammals and birds, some species also hunting frogs and fish. They give birth to a large number of living young.

Head of an Indian Cobra (× 2).

The Prairie Rattlesnake *(Crotalus viridis helleri)* inhabits south-west California. It is at most 5 ft. long *(picture on p. 336)*.

The Horned Rattlesnake or Sidewinder *(Crotalus cerastes)* is found in the deserts of Arizona, California and Nevada *(above)*. It rarely reaches 30 in. in length and has small, triangular, horn-like protuberances above the eyes. It moves in the strange manner common to Snakes living in sand – by throwing loops of its body sideways and travelling obliquely.

BIRDS

The class of Birds – Aves – is made up of oviparous vertebrates possessing a cloaca and covered, when adult, with feathers. From the point of view of development they stand near the Reptiles, transitional forms being known from fossil finds. Our present-day birds fly, swim or run, the last being true of those species which have lost the ability to fly. The superorder Paleognathae (Walking Birds) includes the North African Ostrich *(Struthio camelus camelus)*, which lived originally only in the open grasslands and semideserts of Africa, but has been farmed, and sometimes liberated, in other parts of the world, such as North Africa, Australia and South America.

The cock Ostrich may stand 5 ft. high to its back (about 7 ft. to its head) and it moves by running, being unable to fly. It feeds on plants and small animals *(top left).*

The Common Rhea or Nandu *(Res americana)* inhabits the pampas of Argentina, Brazil and Uruguay. Smaller in size than the North African Ostrich, its diet consists of small plants and insects. The males have the care of the nest and eggs. A male Rhea brooding a nestful of eggs can be seen bottom left, another with a family of well-grown youngsters is above. At first the young birds are striped but as they grow they assume the grey plumage.

Darwin's Rhea *(Pterocnemia pennata)* lives in Patagonia and in the mountains of western South America *(left)*.

An altogether sturdier bird is the Common Emu *(Dromiceius novaehollandiae)* whose flocks are to be found in the grassy plains and dry open forests of Australia. This bird, too, feeds on low-growing plants and small animals *(below)*.

Cassowaries *(Casuarius casuarius)* belong to the same order as the Emu. They stand about 4 ft. high and, like all the family, have stunted wings which are incapable of flight. Their neck wattles are blue and red in colour. This species lives in Northern Australia and nearby islands: other Cassowaries inhabit the forests of New Guinea and other islands in that region *(right)*.

Below is one of the three species of Kiwis, nocturnal, flightless birds with poor eyesight, compensated for by an exceptionally good sense of smell, unusual in birds, which helps them find their food, consisting in the main of worms and insect larvae. They have nostrils at the very tips of their sensitive beaks. Natives of New Zealand, Kiwis lay a single, rel- atively large egg. (The specimen in the picture, which belongs to the species *Apteryx oweni*, is about the size of a domestic cock.)

The Great Crested Grebe *(Colymbus cristatus)* inhabits lakes and vegetation-covered waters almost everywhere in Europe except in the extreme North. It also occurs in Asia and Northwest Africa. With the approach of winter it migrates to the south. It feeds on aquatic insects and the smaller aquatic vertebrates. Above, it can be seen sitting on its nest; on the right, removing the vegetable debris with which it covers the eggs while away from the nest. Various other species of Grebes are found in both North and South America.

A Fulmar *(Fulmarus glacialis)* winging its way above the waters of the Atlantic. It is one of the birds of the order Procellariiformes which spend all their lives at sea, sailing in the sky above the waves by day and by night, effortlessly and almost without moving their wings, and coming to land only at nesting-time. The Fulmar is a northern bird but it has been moving noticeably southwards in recent years. Fulmars nest on steep cliffsides, frequently forming large colonies with other birds.

The Penguins — order Sphenisciformes — are flightless birds which are exceedingly well adapted for life in the water, where they can swim as well as the fish on which many of them feed. Penguins live on the coasts of seas in the Southern Hemisphere. Though most species live in the far south, some species are found near the Equator in the Galapagos Islands.

Top right, a Humboldt's Penguin *(Spheniscus humboldti)* from the coast of South Africa. Below, Cape or Jackass Penguins *(Spheniscus demersus)* from the coast of South-west Africa.

The Gannets and Boobies, Sulidae, belong to the order Pelecaniformes. All the nine known species are marine birds and excellent flyers with long, tapering wings and wedge-shaped tail. The Northern Gannet or Solan Goose (Sula bassana) is a bird the size of a Goose. It lives in the Atlantic, breeding on the coasts of western England, Scotland, Ireland, the Faroe Islands, Norway, Iceland and Canada. In winter Gannets migrate southwards to the Mediterranean and the Gulf of Mexico. They hunt fish, diving head first into the sea to catch them. Their nests are high up on the coastal cliffs. They nest in colonies, each pair having only one young. On the left, two adults in flight; above, the young of two different pairs with one adult.

The Pelecaniformes also include the Cormorants and the true Pelicans. On the left, a view of a colony of nesting Cormorants (*Phalacrocorax carbo*). There are eight subspecies on the sea coasts and river banks of north-eastern North America, central and eastern Europe, Africa, Australia and Asia. Colonies of Cormorants make their nests on either rocks or tall trees in the vicinity of water. Their sole food is fish, which they seize by diving into the water.

The bottom picture is of a Dalmatian Pelican (*Pelecanus crispus*) which is a whitish-grey colour. It breeds in the waters of south-east Europe and some parts of central Asia, spending the winter months in north-east Africa or in southern Asia. Its diet consists of fish. Some Pelicans reach a total length of 6 ft. and a wing span of 10 ft.

The European White Pelican (*Pelecanus onocrotalus*) has pinkish feathers, which are especially attractive at nesting-time. It has approximately the same range as the Dalmatian Pelican. Despite their large, heavy bodies Pelicans are excellent flyers, but except for the American Brown Pelican (*Pelecanus occidentalis*), they cannot dive under the water as do the Cormorants. They therefore hunt their fish in shallow water, whole flocks combining to 'drag' the river or pond, by advancing in a semi-circle to force the fish towards the banks, sometimes beating the surface with their wings. In the shallows they then easily fish out their prey, using the pouches under their beaks as drag-nets. Pelicans are among the largest flying birds. The American White Pelican (*Pelecanus americanus*) is found from western Canada to California and Texas.

The family Ardeidae of the Stork order – Ciconii-formes – includes the Night-Herons. Several species live in the warmer parts of every continent. These birds nest colonially in bushes near swamps. The species Black-crowned Night Heron (*Nycticorax nycticorax*) inhabits North and South America, Europe, Asia and Africa. It flies and hunts even at dusk feeding on aquatic insects and small vertebrates. The birds from colder areas move south to spend the winter nearer the Equator (about half actual size).

he Bittern (*Botaurus stellaris*) lives solitary and ncealed in thick reedbeds in Europe, Asia and orth America. In the nesting season the males' deep booming call can be heard a mile away. Its brown mottled and barred plumage serves as camouflage.

The Little Bittern (*Ixobrychus minutus*) is about half the size of its larger relative. It occurs in central and southern Europe, central and southern Asia, and North Africa, being frequently found near even quite small ponds or mere pools of water with thick vegetation round them. It makes its nest in the reeds above the surface of the water and, like the Bittern, hunts vertebrates, large insects and worms, though it also eats molluscs. It is an adroit climber, demonstrating its skill on the reeds. The tiny Least Bittern (*Ixobrychus exilis*) is a similar but even smaller bird.

The Buff-backed Heron or Cattle Egret *(Bubulcus ibis)* lives in Africa and South-east Asia. In the breeding season the feathers on its head, neck and back acquire a rufous tinge. It nests in colonies, either in trees or in the villages, where it is a welcome guest: it is in the habit of perching on the heads and backs of cattle and picking off parasitic insects and from time to time it also catches small water creatures. These birds also accompany large wild animals such as elephants and buffaloes, warning them of approaching danger by taking flight. This species nas become established in both North and South America in recent years.

Among the most beautiful of the Heron family is the Little Egret *(Egretta garzetta garzetta)*. It is snowy white in colour with a black beak and, in summer, lace-like plumes some 10 in. long on its back. These were very popular as an ornament up to the beginning of this century and this bird, as well as the American Egret *(Casmerodius albus egretta)* and Snowy Egret *(Leucophoyx thula thula)* of southern North America and South America, were consequently massacred in great numbers. Egrets build colonies of nests in trees in marshy areas, inhabiting suitable parts in the southern United States, tropical South America, southern Europe, the temperate and warm parts of Asia, as far east as India and Japan, and much of Africa. They leave the colder areas and migrate towards the Equator in winter.

The Common Heron (*Ardea cinerea*) is the most
abundant member of the Heron tribe in central
Europe. It is also found in some countries of
northern Europe, in the south across Asia to China,
and in some parts of Africa. It favours quiet spots
near water, both inland and on the coast. In
central Europe it most frequently nests in high
trees, sometimes also among reeds on the ground.
Its food consists of aquatic animals, mostly vertebrates. The Heron is almost as large as a Stork
Above, it can be seen with its brood of offspring
in a nest at the top of a 98-ft.-high poplar. The
Great Blue Heron (*Ardea herodias*), of which severa
races are found in North America, is a similar bu
larger species.

Right, the slightly smaller Purple Heron (*Arde
purpurea*) nesting on the ground among reeds
This species has its home in Europe, Asia and Africa

The extremely shy Shoe-bill *(Balaeniceps rex)* is found only in tropical Africa, mainly in the marshes of the Upper Nile. It is a little over 3 ft. in height, and its beak is adapted for the catching of slippery fish.

The Black Stork *(Ciconia nigra)*, a rare relation of the common White Stork, occurs in a few European, Asian and African countries. It nests chiefly in forests.

The Stork has an equally well known cousin in the hot parts of Africa. This is the Marabou (*Leptoptilus crumeniferus*) a bird standing about 5 ft., with slate-grey and white feathers. Under the throat it has a distensible, naked pouch. It feeds on refuse and carion; it will also hunt small animals, both on the ground and in the water. It nests in the trees and is a strong flyer (left).

Bottom right is the Jabiru (*Jabiru mycteria*) from the jungle swamps of Central and South America. Slightly larger than the Marabou, it is white with a bare black head and neck. It also makes its nest high up in the trees.

Below left, the Saddle-billed Stork (*Ephippiorhynchus senegalensis*) is about the same size as the American Jabiru, coloured black and white. Its bill is red at the root and tip, the bare patch under the eyes being deep yellow. It lives on the banks of large African rivers and feeds on fish, amphibians and insects. Like its relatives, it nests in trees.

Right, the largest of the Marabou tribe, the Indian Adjutant or Argala (*Leptoptilus dubius*). Similar in colouring to the African species, it differs from it in having no throat pouch. The beak itself has a somewhat different shape. It lives in warm parts of Asia, leading an existence similar to that of the African Marabou.

359

The African Open-bill *(Anastomus lamelligerus)* has a curiously shaped beak. When closed, it has an obvious gap roughly in the middle. It feeds chiefly on molluscs and the gap enables it to crack open the shells and thus get at the contents. It lives in swamps and on sandy river banks in East Africa and nests in colonies *(left)*.

The Wood Ibis or Yellowbill Stork *(Ibis ibis)* has pink-coloured plumage, a yellow beak, and purplish-red bare spots on the head. It is found near water in central Africa, living on small animals. It nests in colonies in the trees *(below)*.

The White Stork (Ciconia ciconia) inhabits practically the whole of central and southern Europe, Asia Minor and partly also central Asia, as well as North and North-west Africa; it migrates south for the winter, sometimes reaching as far as South Africa. It frequently makes its nests on trees and buildings in villages and even in towns in the Orient. In moist lowland forests it chooses fairly tall trees among dense vegetation. The above picture shows a White Stork nesting on top of a poplar, the crown of which has been struck by lightning. The White Stork measures about 3 ft. and feeds on a wide range of small animals up to the size of a mole (below).

The Glossy Ibis *(Plegadis falcinellus)* is about 22 in. long, with dark-brown feathers, which at close quarters are seen to have a greenish and reddish gloss. Two subspecies are known, in southern Europe, the warm regions of Asia, Oceania, Africa, Madagascar, and in southern North America. Its home is in swamps and on muddy river banks, where it makes its nests in the reeds, together with other Heron-like birds. It leaves the colder countries for the winter, migrating nearer to the Equator *(above).*

The best known of the Ibis family is the Sacred Ibis *(Threskiornis aethiopica).* It is white, but the adult birds have a bare black head and neck. Its home is in central Africa, from where it used to fly in ancient times along the Nile to Egypt. As this migration took place at the period of the river's inundation, the ancient Egyptians associated them with the life-giving irrigation of their arid land and worshipped them. That is why Ibis figures are to be seen on ancient Egyptian stone tablets, while thousands of embalmed Ibises have been found. Ibises live on grasshoppers and other insects, as well as various small animals. They nest in the trees in swamp regions *(right).*

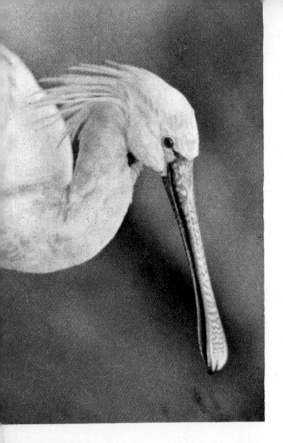

The Spoonbill (*Platalea leucorodia*) is also classified among the Ibises. It is slightly smaller than a Stork, white in colour, with yellow feathers on the neck in the breeding season. Its flat, curiously broadened bill is used to extract from mud and shallow water the small animals on which it lives. Two forms of the Spoonbill are found in various parts of Europe and Asia, another on the coasts of the Red Sea. The European Spoonbills winter in central Africa. Other species live in south Asia, extending as far as Australia, while the beautiful Roseate Spoonbill (*Ajaia ajaja*) is found from the southern United States to Chile. The European Spoonbill nests gregariously in reed-beds, and occasionally in trees and bushes. It lays from two to four eggs (*left*).

The Phoenicopteridae family contains six important and characteristic birds. These are the Flamingoes, of which the Common Flamingo (*Phoenicopterus ruber roseus*) lives in Europe, chiefly in the Mediterranean area; its range outside Europe includes central Asia, and both North and Central Africa. Its body measures about 50 in. Like all Flamingoes, it has long, slender legs and a long, snake-like neck. Young Flamingoes are a dirty greyish-brown, the adult birds rose-tinged white. The wings are scarlet with black fringes. Flamingoes live in huge flocks in quiet, shallow waters — fresh, sea, as well as brackish. They lay a single egg in mud nests, up to 18 in. high, which they build on the banks. Flamingoes have specially adapted beaks with which they explore and sift water and mud in search of their food — algae and various small aquatic animals (*right*).

The Horned Screamer (*Anhima cornuta*) is a strange-looking bird, about 30 in. long, from the forests of equatorial and warm South America. It belongs to the Anhimidae family of the order Anseriformes. The Horned Screamer is mostly slate-coloured and has two strong spurs, up to an inch long, on the front edge of each wing, which are most effective weapons. The forehead has a slender, quill-like horn. A good flyer and swimmer, it lives in flocks near water. Its main food is grass. Only two eggs are laid (*bottom left*).

The largest of the order Anseriformes are the Swans, both the large European species being more than 5 ft. long. Both are also white in colour. The Whooper Swan (Cygnus cygnus) has the basal half of its black bill lemon-yellow; the Mute Swan (Cygnus olor, right) has the root of the bill black with a distinct black knob, the rest of the bill being orange. The Whooper spends the summer

in the Arctic regions of the Old World, chiefly to the north of the Arctic Circle, wintering in Africa, Palestine and Turkestan. The Mute Swan makes its nests on the lakes and swamps of parts of northern and central Europe and Asia. Once a year it produces a brood of about six cygnets. It is a partial migrant, passing the winter in the south, mainly in the Mediterranean. Both these Swans feed on water plants, but they also eat aquatic animals.

On the opposite page a pair of Mute Swans can be seen nesting among reeds. Nearer to the camera is the brooding female, behind her the male, which spends most of the time swimming about in the vicinity of the nest, greeting intruders with the fighting posture illustrated on the preceding page.

Above, a pair of Black Swans *(Cygnus atratus)*. They are black all over, with the exception of the white tips of the wing feathers. The red bill is also white-tipped. They live on the lakes and rivers of Australia, and are the official emblem of West Australia.

370

The White-fronted Goose *(Anser albifrons)* is one of the wild Geese which winter on the waters of central Europe; many also visit England, southern Scandinavia, Italy and Greece. It nests in treeless tundras in the far North. It is a little smaller than the Grey Lag Goose, and differs from it in having a bold white forehead, pink bill, orange legs, and broad black bars on the belly *(left)*.

The Swan Goose *(Cygnopsis cygnoides)* inhabits parts of Siberia, the Altai and Mongolia, where it also nests. The birds roost in trees and are extremely shy. At bottom left is an individual of the original wild form, on the right the head of a gander of the domestic variety first bred by the Chinese and known now as the Chinese Goose. It has certain characteristics which make it more suitable for domestication than its European relative – it is larger and heavier and does less damage in gardens.

The largest European wild Goose *(left)*, the Grey Lag Goose *(Anser anser)* lives in northern and central Europe, its range extending through central Asia as far as Kamchatka, and southwards to north-west India and China. It is the original form from which were bred the European domestic Geese.

On the right, two individuals belonging to different varieties of Snow Goose *(Anser hyperboreus)*. It lives and nests near the Arctic Circle.

Below, the Barnacle Goose *(Branta leucopsis)*, which nests gregariously in the far North, in the Arctic region, wintering in southern Scandinavia, England, and sometimes even as far south as Spain and Italy.

The Canada Goose (*Branta canadensis canadensis*) is more heavily built than the European wild Goose and has a much longer neck. It lives wild in North America, where it is often domesticated. It occasionally turns up in Europe: in some parts of England it has become established as a regular breeder. A family of this species can be seen at the bottom of p. 374.

Similar to it but only about half the size is the Richardson's Canada Goose (*Branta canadensis hutchinsi*) (*right*). It inhabits the Arctic swamps of Alaska.

Below, the Tibetan or Bar-headed Goose (*Anser indicus*). It is slightly smaller than the European domestic varieties and nests on the steep rock-sides above the mountain lakes of Tibet. It migrates to the large Indian rivers for the winter.

The Andean Goose (*Chloëphaga melanoptera*) shown top left, is from the mountain ranges of South America. Its predominant colours are black and white. In the nesting season it is extremely aggressive and will even stand up to humans.

The Cape Barren Goose *(Cereopsis novae-hollandiae)* is slighter in build than our domestic Goose and greyish-brown in colour, the bill mostly greenish-yellow. It inhabits the forests of South Australia, Tasmania and New Zealand, keeping to dry land and avoiding the water *(left)*.

Above, a pair of Ruddy Shelduck *(Tadorna ferruginea)*. A native of the steppe country of central Asia, it also occurs in the south of Greece and Spain. It prefers drier localities, and nests in hollow trees or in the ground.

On the right, a drake Common Shelduck *(Tadorna tadorna)*, in breeding plumage. The colours are white, black and chestnut, the bill is blood-red. This Goose-like Duck inhabits the coasts of the colder European seas and the cold lakes of Asia. It usually nests in rabbit holes.

The waters of South America are the home of the so-called Coscoroba Swan (*Coscoroba coscoroba*). It is white with black wing tips and only slightly smaller than the Swans. Its bill and legs are pink (*top left*).

The Mallard (*Anas platyrhynchos*) is the most cosmopolitan of the Duck family and at the same time the most abundant in Europe, inhabiting the entire continent, as well as Africa, Asia and North America. It can be found on a variety of inland waters and on the sea-coast. It nests in the undergrowth, chiefly on the ground near water. Shy when living in the open, it becomes tame on rivers and in town parks. Bottom left, are Mallard drakes in summer (eclipse) plumage; and above, on the ice in breeding plumage which they moult at the end of April.

The genus *Anas* is represented in Europe and Asia by numerous species. The Japanese or Formosan Teal *(Anas formosa)* is one of the most attractive. The drake in breeding plumage has interesting combinations of brown, red and green. This species nests in eastern Siberia, on the Kuril islands, Sakhalin, and in Japan. It winters in Japan, China and Korea.

Below, a pair of Pintail *(Anas acuta)* from northern and eastern Europe and the adjacent parts of Asia. Both the sexes have their tail-feathers extended into conspicuous needle points. They winter on the sea-coast and nest in swamps, on islands and in peat-bogs.

Two species of attractively coloured Ducks are often seen on European ponds. Above is a drake of the Green-winged Teal *(Anas crecca)*, the smallest of the European varieties. It occurs as far north as the Arctic Circle, in North America, and northern and central Asia. It often winters on the sea-coast, particularly in the estuaries of large rivers.

Below, a drake of the Garganey *(Anas querquedula)*. It prefers freshwater localities, nesting in high grass, and is a summer visitor to most of Europe.

The European Widgeon (Anas penelope) is distinctly smaller than the well-known Mallard. The drakes can easily be recognised by the reddish-brown head with the light ochre-coloured stripe on top. Widgeons nest in various places in northern Europe and Asia, mostly in Scandinavian countries, favouring peat-bogs and marshes. They fly to southern Europe and North Africa for the winter. The males have a high whistling call. The American Widgeon (Anas americana) is extremely similar in appearance and habits.

The Pochard (Aythya ferina) is a handsome diving Duck, very abundant in central Europe. The drakes have a chestnut-coloured head, dark breast and pale-grey body. Other Pochards are also found in eastern Asia and North America. They keep almost exclusively to the water, nesting in the reeds. Some examples are the Canvasback (A. vallisneria), Redhead (A. americana), and Greater Scaup (A. marila).

The Egyptian Goose (Alopochen aegyptiacus) is a beautiful Duck which lives in North Africa and almost everywhere throughout the tropical part of that continent, and also in Syria. It nests on the banks of lakes and rivers, mostly in trees, in which it builds open nests.

The Shoveler (Anas clypeata) is easily recognised by the large, spoon-shaped bill. The drakes are very brightly coloured. This species has a wide distribution over the entire Northern Hemisphere, wintering in Central Africa, South Asia and Central America (top right).

The Muscovy Duck (Cairina moschata), of which a drake is seen below, comes originally from tropical America. It has been domesticated and taken to many other parts of the world. In the wild state it nests in hollow trees.

The North American Wood or Carolina Duck
(*Aix sponsa*) inhabits most of North America, from
Mexico as far as the southern parts of Canada,
nesting in tree hollows on the banks of lakes and
rivers. The drake's colouring and shape is most
striking (*above*).

The drakes of the Mandarin Duck (*Aix galericulata*)
also have remarkably coloured plumage. This
species lives in eastern Asia, ranging from south-
east Siberia down to China and Japan. It has
similar habits to those of the Carolina Duck
(*picture on p. 385*).

The King Vulture – the most vividly coloured vulture in the world.

Above is a drake of the rare Red-Crested Pochard (Netta rufina). It has a vivid red bill, a crested, rufous-coloured head, and white flanks. It nests on the sea-coasts and freshwater lakes of southern Europe, in southern Scandinavia, southern Moravia, and central Asia. In winter it migrates southward.

Below, two ducks and three drakes of the Tufted Duck (Aythya fuligula) wintering on a central European river. (In front of them is a Black-headed Gull.) This Duck is chiefly found in the north of Europe and Asia, but it also nests in many places in central Europe, near lakes and ponds.

Above, the Scaup Duck (Aythya marila), two hens in the middle, the drakes at the side, which can be distinguished from the Tufted Duck by the lighter back of the drakes, and the lack of a crest. In summer they live in the north of Scandinavia and in Iceland, northern Asia and North America, nesting gregariously on lake islands. They are rare winter visitors to central European rivers, normally wintering on the coast.

Below is a drake of the Golden-eye (Bucephala clangula) wintering on a large central European river. It has a similar range to that of the Scaup. It nests on islands in rivers or forest lakes, choosing either hollow trees or holes in the ground.

The genus *Mergus* is recognisable by its narrow, saw-like bill, the tip of which is hooked, making it very effective for fishing. On the left is a female Goosander or Common Merganser *(Mergus merganser)*, the largest of the seven European species, which can measure over 1 ft. It lives and nests in northern Scandinavia, Iceland and northern Scotland; it has also been seen in Roumania and ranges across Asia, and most of North America. Its nests are built in hollow trees and holes in the ground. For the winter it migrates south to the sea-coasts and the larger rivers. When fishing, it dives below the surface like the Cormorant.

The Common Eider *(Somateria mollissima)* is a wholly maritime species inhabiting the coasts of northern Britain, Scandinavia and Iceland, the southern limits of its

range being the south-west coast of France. It is also found in northern Asia and North America. It migrates to the Mediterranean region for the winter. The Eider Duck nests on rocky coasts, lining the nest more liberally with fine down than any other species. For centuries this eider-down has been collected, and sold at a high price, being the best quality down obtainable. Bottom left, a hen Eider in the water; above, a nest of the Eider on the shores of Iceland.

The order Falconiformes consists of a large number of birds with strong, hooked bills adapted for the tearing of flesh. They are mostly excellent flyers and, with but a few exceptions, are carnivorous. The New World Vultures – Cathartidae – includes the Andean Condor (Vultur gryphus). It is the largest flying bird, having a wing span of up to 12 ft. The males have a high, fleshy wattle which forms a crest extending from forehead to crown. This bird, known as 'King of the Andes', lives in the South American Cordilleras, where it sails majestically at altitudes of between 9,000 and 16,000 ft. It nests in cliffs and feeds chiefly on carrion, but will take young goats and lambs (above).

Another important member of this family is the King Vulture (Sarcoramphus papa). Vividly coloured, its plumage is black and pink, the head red, yellow and orange. It lives in the forests and wooded plains of warm parts of Central and South America. Like the Condor, it is a scavenger, feeding on carrion and the remnants of jaguars' prey. Its spread wings reach a span of 6½ ft. (left).

The largest of the European Vultures is the Black or Hooded Vulture (Aegypius monachus), inhabiting southern Europe, North Africa, Asia Minor and central Asia. It is occasionally seen even in the northern parts of Europe, but only in migration. Its wing span is about 8½ ft. The plumage is brown. It favours mountainous areas, nesting mainly in trees, and feeds on carrion (below).

The Rough-legged Buzzard *(Buteo lagopus)*, shown at top left, is a bird of prey up to 2 ft. long, an inhabitant of the northern tundra. Its legs are feathered down to the toes. It occurs in the north of Europe, Asia and America, migrating southwards in winter. Its main food is rodents, but it will also attack weak or injured game.

The Carancho or Crested Caracara *(Caracara cheriway)* belongs to the subfamily of Carrion Hawks. It lives in Central America and the warmer parts of South America, feeding on carrion and small live vertebrates *(below, page 392)*.

The second largest Vulture in Europe is the Griffon Vulture *(Gyps fulvus)*. It is of a lightish sandy-brown colour and has a wing span of about 8 ft. It inhabits southern Europe, North Africa and western Asia, and very occasionally wanders as far as the Scandinavian countries. Though it prefers rocky localities, it is also found in the plains *(above)*.

The Bearded Vulture or Lämmergeier *(Gypaëtus barbatus)* is now rare in Europe, where it is found only in a few mountain areas of the south, but it inhabits Africa and Asia as far as western China. It measures about up to 9 ft. with expanded wings. It is tawny-coloured with a cluster of dark, stiff bristles under the bill. It is found in large mountain ranges and feeds both on carrion and live prey, such as tortoises, which it smashes by dropping them on to rocks *(left)*.

Two species of Kite are known in Europe. The Red Kite *(Milvus milvus)* is reddish-brown and about 2 ft. in length with a long, deeply-forked tail. It lives in southern and eastern Europe, throughout central Europe with the exception of the western regions, in one part of Britain, in southern Scandinavia, North-west Africa and western Asia. It leaves its more northerly habitats and winters in the south. Its food consists of small vertebrates, large insects, worms, etc. *(bottom left)*.

Slightly smaller – about 22 in. long – is the Black Kite *(Milvus migrans)*, distinguishable by its darker colour and less forked tail. It occurs over all Europe except the northern parts, and various subspecies inhabit the whole of Asia, Australia and Africa. It migrates from the colder regions towards the Equator for the winter. Similar in feeding habits to the Red Kite, it sometimes robs other birds. Top left, a Black Kite with fledglings in its nest on a high oak in central Europe; above, in flight.

Of the many species of Eagle the largest European one is the White-tailed Eagle or Grey Sea Eagle *(Haliaeetus albicilla)*. Dark-brown in colour, the adult birds have lighter-coloured heads, huge yellow beaks and white, wedge-shaped tails. Right, is a young Sea Eagle in juvenile plumage. Fully-grown it may measure up to 36 in., with a maximum wing span of $7^1/_2$ ft. It is distinguishable from the

Golden Eagle by its unfeathered toes and much shorter tail. It lives chiefly on the coasts of European seas and is found in eastern Europe, Asia and North America, reaching northwards as far as Greenland, Scandinavia and Iceland. Occasionally it nests inland on high trees. On the coast it chooses inaccessible cliffs, in more deserted localities it sometimes nests on the ground. The winter migration takes it from the more northerly countries to the Mediterranean region.

The Goshawk *(Accipiter gentilis)*. This 'Gentle Falcon' of olden times is a notorious and much-persecuted bird of prey, up to 2 ft. long (the hen being much larger than the cock) and with a wing span of over 3 ft. It lives in North-west Africa, throughout Europe with the exception of Britain, Iceland and Portugal, in Asia and North America. Above is the European variety *(Accipiter gentilis gallinarum)*. It preys on birds up to the size of domestic fowl. In the colder and temperate regions it prefers coniferous forests, nesting in the more densely wooded parts.

The Common Buzzard *(Buteo buteo)* feeds chiefly on mice and other small vertebrates and insects. Frequently mistaken for the Goshawk, it pays for this resemblance with its life. It differs from the adult Goshawk chiefly in being browner and lacking the bars on the underside of the body, but a reliable mark of distinction is the eyes – dark brown in the Buzzard, whereas the Goshawk has a sulphur-yellow iris. The two birds are of similar size. The Buzzard has several subspecies throughout Europe and Asia, as well as in North-west Africa, being partly migratory. Its New World counterpart is the Red-tailed Hawk *(Buteo jamaicensis)*, which resembles it closely.

The Short-toed Eagle (*Circaëtus gallicus*) is larger than both the preceding birds. Its relatively large head is reminiscent of an Owl's. The underside of the body is white with brown streaks, the eyes are yellow. It nests in southern and eastern Europe, throughout most of warmer Asia, on migration passing as far north as Finland and Sweden. It likes desolate areas, with old woods and rocky slopes. Its food consists mainly of snakes, including poisonous ones, also lizards, frogs and insects. Its winter migration takes it southwards to the warm parts of Africa or southern Arabia. It nests in trees and as a rule has only one young at a time.

The Osprey *(Pandion haliaëtus)* measures up to 23 in. long. It is dark-brown above, almost white below, with a darker band across the breast and dark spots on the underside of the wings and tail. Its whitish head has a small crest and there is a dark eye stripe. Five different races of the Osprey are known in Africa, the Indo-Australian region, and America. In Europe it occurs throughout the Mediterranean region, also nesting in small numbers in various parts of Europe and western Asia; its range extends as far north as Scandinavia, its migrations taking it through Britain and Iceland. It builds its nest on a tall, preferably solitary tree. Ospreys live on fish, catching even quite heavy ones, which sometimes pull the bird under and drown it *(top right)*.

The Kestrel *(Falco tinnunculus)* is perhaps the most widespread European bird of prey, with more than ten different forms covering practically the whole of Europe, Asia and Africa. Some migrate to warmer parts for the winter. It is some 13 in. in length, has a long tail, tawny plumage on top and lighter below, with dark streaks and spots. It has the typical moustachial streak of the Falcons. It preys chiefly on mice of various kinds but if these are short it will eat lizards, slow-worms, frogs and insects. It hovers in the air, head to wind, searching the ground for its prey. Then it swoops down suddenly and pounces on the unsuspecting victim. It nests on cliffs and in trees, often in the nests of other birds. Other parts of the world also have species of Kestrel, all with habits and appearance in common. The North and Central American Kestrels are known as Sparrow Hawks *(Falco spaverius)*. In towns it will also make its nest on buildings, in particular in church steeples *(bottom right)*.

The Hobby *(Falco subbuteo)* is about the same size as the Kestrel. It is almost black above and whitish below, with reddish-brown streaks. The head is blackish, the thighs tawny-red. This fast-flying bird of prey, considered the fastest of all European species, able to take a swift or swallow in flight, lives in open forests and country with commons, fields and coverts. Its range takes in all of Europe except the northern countries, parts of Asia as far as North-east India and North-west Africa. In winter it migrates south.

The Peregrine Falcon *(Falco peregrinus)* greatly resembles the Hobby, but it is appreciably larger, reaching a length of up to 1 ft. 7 in. It is almost cosmopolitan, its various forms covering most parts of the world. In the more northerly parts of its range it is migratory. Its prey, which it

seizes in flight, usually consists of birds the size of a pigeon, though it will not hesitate to tackle even wild ducks. Because of its hunting prowess this Falcon was, and still is, in great demand for falconry. Falcons make their nests on sheer cliffs, in the ruins of castles, and, in forest regions, in trees; *(bottom left)* young Falcons in their nest; *above*, a Falcon with its prey – a pigeon).

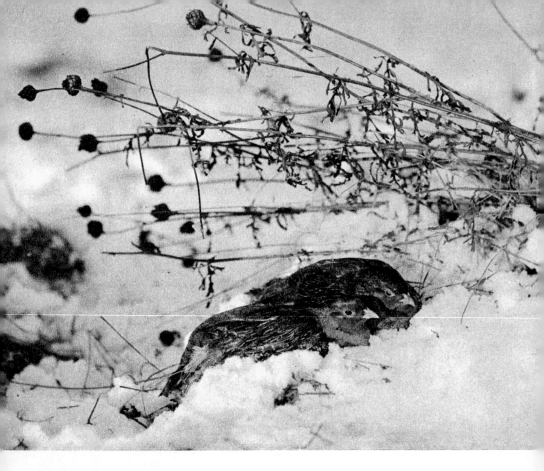

The order Galliformes – the Game Birds – is made up of some two hundred species, mostly medium-sized, adapted for life on land. Their distribution includes every part of the world except Polynesia and the Arctic region. The most common central European member of this order is the Partridge (*Perdix perdix*). It is about 1 ft. long, of an inconspicuous brown colour which makes it look like a lump of earth in the fields where it lives. Three races inhabit Europe with the exception of most of the Iberian Peninsula, the Balkans, and a large part of Scandinavia. It is also found in Asia and has been introduced to America and New Zealand. Its food consists of plants, seeds and insects. It can fly only for short distances, but will swim. In winter it remains in its home locality even though it has to put up with great hardship in really cold weather, when the snow prevents it from finding its normal food. The Partridge is carefully protected and also reared artificially.

The Alps and the countries to the south-east, including Italy, Greece and Asia Minor all the way to India, are the home of the handsome Rock Partridge *(Alectoris graeca)*. This is a larger species, some 1 ft. 2 in. in length, strikingly coloured yellow, black, grey and rufous. It lives at fairly high altitudes, nesting on the ground. It seeks the lowlands in winter *(above)*.

Six species of the genus *Excalfactoria*, the smallest game birds, live in China, India, Africa, Indonesia, New Guinea and Australia. The small Chinese Painted Quail *(Excalfactoria chinensis)* is one of the smallest Galliformes. The picture below shows *(left)* a hen of this species, and *(right)* a cock.

The Helmet Guinea-Fowl (Numido meleagris) has slate-grey, white-spotted plumage and a bare red and light-blue head with bony protuberances. It measures about 1 ft. 9½ in. in length. Several other species are found in Morocco and other African countries south of the Sahara. Guinea-Fowl live in families of about twenty, while sometimes several such families join together to form larger flocks which make their home in the bushy undergrowth on the forest edge. Domesticated birds were once common, but today they are usually kept as ornamental rather than table birds.

A cock Lady Amherst's Pheasant (Chrysolophus amherstiae) in breeding plumage. It has a collar of black and white feathers which it spreads fanwise on both sides. The rest of its body is coloured yellow, red, metallic green and blue. The tail-feathers, up to nearly 4 ft. long, are white with black bars. It is one of the most magnificently coloured of all birds. It originated in Tibet, China and North Burma, but is now widely kept in captivity.

Some species of Pheasant have been introduced into woods and open country in various parts of the world, and in many places they have become naturalised. The Common Pheasant (Phasianus colchicus) is the species most frequently seen in Europe. Originally a native of the Caspian region, it has been bred as a game bird in various European and Asian countries since the 11th century and perhaps much earlier. The cock is up to 3 ft. long, the hen up to 2 ft. 1 in. An excessive increase of Pheasants gradually reduces the larger species of insects which form the birds' diet in summer.

A cock Californian Quail *(Lophortyx californicus)*, a brightly coloured bird about $9\frac{1}{2}$ in. long which lives in the United States, from the east across to California.

Another and larger genus of Guinea-Fowl lives in the dry grassland and coastal areas of East Africa. This is the Vulturine Guinea-Fowl *(Acryllium vulturinum)*, which has a splendid plumage of blackish-brown, reddish-brown, ultramarine and shining white.

Below, the Grey Eared Pheasant *(Crossoptilon auritum)* from Tibet and certain mountainous regions of China.

Above, Wild Turkeys *(Meleagris gallopavo).* Below, the head of a Turkey. These birds, about the size of Geese, have their home in the forests of the eastern United States and Central America, where they live in flocks. They feed on vegetable matter and small animals. Domesticated Turkeys are now kept throughout the world; the hens were used to hatch eggs prior to the invention of the electric incubator.

In the mating season the cock Turkey seems to be a different bird as it displays all its feathers and gives the impression of being nearly round, struts about with fluttering wings, and spreads its tail-feathers into a fan. The wattle above its bill fills with blood and becomes elongated. At the same time the bird emits strange gobbling noises.

The Domestic Fowl (*Gallus gallus domestica*) is one of the most important of all domestic animals and has

been bred by man for more than four thousand years. Today it is completely cosmopolitan, providing man with eggs wherever he leads a settled existence.

Under favourable conditions a single Hen may lay as many as three hundred eggs a year; some varieties, bred for their meat, weigh as much as 12 lb. Bottom left, is the head of a 'broody' Hen sitting on her eggs; below, White Leghorns on a chicken farm; right, a chick of the same variety.

The ancestor of all the present Domestic Fowls is considered to be the Red Jungle Fowl (*Gallus gallus [bankiva]*). This has a small, slender form and is brightly coloured, not unlike some of the domestic breeds, the Italian, for instance. With his tail-feathers, the cock measures about 2 ft. 4 in. This species lives in the undergrowth of jungles from India to Indonesia *(top left)*.

The Peacock (*Pavo cristatus*) is found in both mountain forests and lowland jungles in India and Ceylon. One of the most decorative of all birds, it is frequently kept as an ornamental species. A male Peacock in his full plumage is some 7 ft. long, his tail (actually his tail coverts) resplendent with golden-green and 'peacock' blue and its 'eyes'. Peacocks breed everywhere without difficulty and they stand up well to the colder climate of the more northerly countries, even in winter. Left, a male Peacock at the end of winter; above, the same bird displaying in the spring.

Below, the hen of a curious breed of the Domestic Fowl, the so-called Chinese Silk-fowl or Silkie. Its feathers are hair-like and frayed, and make it quite impossible for this variety to fly.

The Urumutum Curassow (Nothocrax urumutum) from British Guiana belongs to the Curassow family (Cracidae) of which about forty species are found in Central and South America. The Urumutum is glossy black in colour. The bare patches on its head are vivid red and the ends of the head-feathers are 'curled'. It lives in groups, mostly in the trees, where pairs of them build their nests. They feed chiefly on fruit and berries (above).

Right, the Crowned Crane (Balearica pavonina) belonging to the suborder of Cranes. It lives in large flocks in the marshes and grassy flats near the rivers and lakes of central Africa. It reaches a length of about 3 ft.

Of the other Cranes the best known in Europe is the Common Crane *(Grus grus)*, some 3 ft. 9 in. long, greyish black in colour with a curved white stripe from each eye along the side of the head. Before the draining of European swamps it was very common, but it has survived only in the north-east and south-east, and in the central part of northern Asia. As winter approaches migrating Cranes can be seen flying in regular V-formations, heading for the Mediterranean and north-east Africa. These Cranes live on vegetable food and small animals such as mice, amphibians, worms and insects. They nest in swamps (*right*, a male Common Crane in the mating season).

Both the pictures above show the Demoiselle Crane *(Anthropoides virgo)*. This is smaller than the Common Crane (about 3 ft. 2 in.) and prefers open lowland and mountain plateaux for its home. It nests on dry land and only goes near the water at times of drought. It inhabits central and southern Asia, North Africa, and breeds in a few places in southern Europe. Locusts form a large part of its diet.

Left, the Sarus Crane *(Grus antigone)* from Southeast Asia. It reaches a length of 4 ft. 4 in. Different species of Cranes live in practically all the habitable parts of the world, except South America.

415

The Crane order also includes the family of Rails (Rallidae). These are medium-sized and smallish birds, which look somewhat like fowls. While they swim very well, they are poor flyers. They are most frequently found in overgrown swamps. The Water Rail *(Rallus aquaticus)* is one of the best-known European species, living all over Europe and Asia, with the exception of northern Scandinavia and Finland. It leaves Europe before winter, migrating to the Mediterranean, the Asian varieties wintering in India. Some 11 in. long, it is streaked brown on top and grey below with distinctly barred flanks. Its long bill is reddish. The Water Rail makes its home in swamps, frequently nesting under small piles of old sedge. (In the picture at left the reeds have been parted, otherwise the nest would be quite invisible.) In the nesting season the Water Rails make loud squeaking and groaning noises, which do not sound at all like bird calls.

Right, the Spotted Crake *(Porzana porzana).* It is olive-brown, white speckled, and has green legs and a yellow bill with a red base. It is adept at concealing itself in the marshy vegetation. When walking through the reeds it extends its neck, becoming long and thin. Its range is similar to that of the Water Rail, but it is not found in Iceland, in the north-east and west of Britain, nor in the southernmost parts of Europe on the Mediterranean.

The Spotted Crake lays between nine and fourteen relatively large, light-green eggs, dappled with dark-brown and violet-grey spots. Its nest is a neat basket made of sedge stalks. There are many species of *Porzana* scattered over most of the world exclusive of polar regions. The North American representative is the Sora Rail *(Porzana carolina)*.

One of the commonest European Rallidae is the Coot *(Fulica atra)*. About 1 ft. 3 in. long, slate black, with a white bill and white patch on the head, it is found even on small ponds which have vegetation growing on the banks. The European Coot is found in nearly all the Old World Northern Hemisphere other than the far North, and India to South-east Asia *(right)*. The similar American Coot *(Fulica americana)* is an abundant bird in North American marshes.

Many Coots move south for the winter, which they spend on lakes and rivers or along the sea-coast, often in company with other birds. Above, a Coot on an ice-floe in a central European river, with two Black-headed Gulls in the foreground.

The Bustards – family Otididae – contain several genera and some twenty-five species, mostly of large-sized birds. The cock Great Bustard (Otis tarda) is up to 3 ft. 9 in. long, with a wing span of about 8 ft., and a weight of 30 lb. The hens are much smaller. It is an inhabitant of steppes and open plains, but in cultivated areas it now also lives in the fields.

In Europe it is found in Spain, Roumania, Hungary, Germany, Czechoslovakia and Poland, as well as in western Asia as far as the Altai mountain range. Its colouring is rufous-brown and greyish-yellow. During the mating season the cocks perform their celebrated 'dance', strutting, puffing themselves out, spreading and drooping their wings, and spreading the tail into a fan. At such times the males are extremely pugnacious and frequently fight each other. In Europe this occurs in April. Left, an almost adult cock with the 'moustaches' as yet undeveloped.

The family Burhinidae (Stone-Curlews) belonging to the order Charadriiformes, includes three genera and thirteen species, inhabiting warm dry regions where the soil is naturally barren and sandy. In Europe, with its dense population and high degree of cultivation, the only native species is becoming increasingly rarer. The Stone-Curlew *(Burhinus oedicnemus)* is about 1 ft. 4 in. long, being about the size of a Wood Pigeon. Its plumage is pale brown with darker streaks. Its legs are yellow and fairly long. It has very striking eyes, large and yellow, rather like those of the Owl. It is a nocturnal bird which only becomes active at dusk. It nests on the ground, and feeds on large insects, molluscs, worms and small vertebrates. An inhabitant of the warmer regions of central and southern Europe, the adjacent parts of south-west Asia, and North Africa, it winters chiefly in East Africa.

The family Haematopodidae (Oyster-catchers) belongs, like the Burhinidae, to the suborder Limicolae. The Oyster-catcher *(Haematopus ostralegus)* is 1 ft. 5 in. long, black and white with pink legs and a long orange bill. Found on almost all the coasts of Europe except those of southern Spain, Italy and Greece, it also has seventeen subspecies throughout Asia, Australia, the Americas and South Africa. It lives and nests on the sea-shore, less often on inland lakes or rivers. Its diet is made up of worms, molluscs, small crustaceans and insects. Its name may come from its habit of decorating its nest – a little hollow on the shore –

with fragments of sea-shells *(above,* an Oyster-catcher from the Faroe Islands).

Best known European member of the family Charadriidae, the Lapwing *(Vanellus vanellus)* is a foot long with blackish-green, glossy plumage, white underneath, and a prominent crest on top of the head. It favours moist meadows near ponds and rivers, nesting on the ground. The Lapwing's range covers the whole of Europe except for the most northern and southern areas; it also occurs in central and northern Asia, migrating south for the winter. Many Lapwings winter in Britain. They feed on insects, worms and molluscs *(right).*

The Ringed Plover (*Charadrius hiaticula*) is a lively, active little bird to be met with on the shores of Britain, Scandinavia, Iceland and Greenland. It winters on the sea-coasts of the western regions of southern Europe. It also lives in the north of Asia and North America. About $7^1/_2$ in. long, it is larger than the Little Ringed Plover of central Europe and Asia. The Ringed Plover feeds on insects and worms, finding its food on the shore, where it also nests on the sand. The nest is formed by making a little hollow, which is then lined with small bits of sea-shell and other objects found near by. Sometimes the eggs are easily seen against their white background, in contrast to those of the Little Ringed Plover, whose nest and eggs are well camouflaged among the surrounding pebbles (both pictures from the coast of Iceland).

The Common Sandpiper *(Actitis hypoleucos)* is an active greyish-brown bird, less than 8 in. long, which is easily recognised by its habit of continually bobbing its head and tail. It lives on the banks of ponds and rivers almost everywhere in Europe and Asia. It winters in the south *(top left)*.

The Redshank *(Tringa totanus)* has approximately the same range as the Common Sandpiper, but lives in wet meadows and in marshy areas near rivers and lakes. It measures 11 in. and is a mottled greyish-black with white back and rump, red legs and a long reddish bill with black tip. Redshanks are partial migrants *(bottom left)*.

Right, the Black-tailed Godwit *(Limosa limosa)*, one of the finest European waders. About 1 ft. 4 in. long, blackish-brown with long legs (head and breast chestnut in summer), it has an unusually long, straight bill. The Godwit nests in the eastern parts of central Europe, in eastern Europe and western Asia. It also occurs in some countries in northern Europe, for instance in south-western Iceland. It favours marshy ground in the vicinity of swamps and ponds. The winter is spent in the south. A closely related species, the Hudsonian Godwit *(Limosa haemastica)* breeds in northern Canada and migrates to the United States, but is now becoming rare.

The best known of the Sandpiper family is the Woodcock *(Scolopax rusticola)*. About 1 ft. 1½ in. long and heavily built, its dappled brownish and buff colouring gives it good protection on the forest floor where it lives, in contrast to most of the Charadriiformes. It feeds chiefly on earthworms, insect larvae and small molluscs. It is sparsely distributed over central Europe and temperate Asia as far as Japan. Woodcock-hunting used to be a fashionable sport which resulted in the killing of large numbers of these birds and the related Snipe (*left*, a nesting Woodcock). When flushed, both this and the American Woodcock *(Philohela minor)* fly an erratic, zigzag pattern, making a difficult target for the hunter.

The Snipe (*Gallinago galli-nago*) is some 10½ in. long, its range being somewhat wider than that of the Wood-cock. In the Northern Hemi-sphere it extends across Europe, Asia and the Ameri-can continent. In the nesting season the males make strange bleating sounds, by vibrating their side tail-feathers which are spread sideways when the bird is diving in its display flight. (*Right*, a pair of Snipe at their nest on a central European pond).

Bottom left, the Whimbrel or Hudsonian Curlew (*Nu-menius phaeopus*) on its nest on the shores of a small Icelandic lake. This species nests in the far north of Europe, Asia and America, frequenting bogs and tundra regions, and migrating south in winter. It is about 1 ft. 4 in. long, its colour being a dappled greyish-brown. The bill is thin and slightly curved.

The Avocet *(Recurvirostra avosetta)* is one of the most graceful wading birds. It is about 1 ft. 5 in. in length, black and white with a long, thin upturned bill which is glossy black in colour. It stands in the shallows of lakes, particularly those with salt water, or beaches and river estuaries, where it nests in the sand or mud. Occasionally it also nests on the muddy banks of inland ponds. In Europe it is found around the North and Baltic Seas, and the Mediterranean, as well as in Austria and Roumania, in parts of Asia and on the salt lakes of Africa. Some winter in Britain but most go to the south of France and the African continent. Its food consists of the larger plankton and the larvae of aquatic insects. The North American species, nearly identical, is *Recurvirostra americana*.

The family of Gulls (Laridae) includes aquatic birds which are equally good swimmers and flyers and are basically carnivorous. The majority are marine. Top right is a Herring Gull *(Larus argentatus)* in flight. This species is grey and white with black and white wing-tips and a yellow bill. It reaches some 1 ft. 10 in. in length and a wing span of about $4^1/_2$ ft. Abundant on the coasts of Europe, Asia and America, it moves south in winter. It eats whatever is provided by the sea.

Bottom right is the smaller Kittiwake *(Rissa tridactyla)*, only about 1 ft. 4 in. long. It lives on the open seas around the north of Europe and Asia and the entire Arctic circle, and never normally comes inland. Its food consists mainly of fish. Colonies of Kittiwakes make their nests on the cliff faces of 'bird islands'.

The Great Black-backed Gull (*Larus marinus*) reaches a length of some 2 ft. 5 in. and a wing span of 5 ft. It is white with black on top of the wings and body. The head and tail are white. It lives around the sea-coast and on the estuaries of large rivers in northern Europe, Asia and North America, nesting on the cliffs or on the ground *(below)*.

The Black-headed Gull (*Larus ridibundus*) is the species most frequently seen inland in Europe. Its colouring is white and grey with black wing-tips and chocolate-coloured hood in summer. In winter even the head is white, with a few dark spots. The bill, feet and eye-ring

The Hoopoe on its nest.

are red. It measures 1 ft. 3 in., with a wing span of over 3 ft. It is widespread in central, and to a certain extent also in northern Europe and the adjacent parts of Asia. It breeds near the coast and in large colonies on inland ponds and lakes and by the larger rivers, nesting on the ground in reed-beds or on islands or mud-flats, sometimes even in low trees. Apart from the usual food of the Gulls – insects, larvae and various small animals up to the size of mice – it also eats vegetable matter, sometimes feeding its young with cherries. In winter it leaves the more northerly areas, occasionally ranging as far as Africa, and at this season it accepts food scraps from humans (photograph, top of page 432). The very similar Sabine's Gull occupies the same niche in North America.

Above is a Common Tern or Sea-swallow (Sterna hirundo) nesting on a floating island in the middle of a lake. Somewhat similar to the Gulls in appearance, it has a glossy black crown and no red eye-ring. It inhabits most of central Europe, Asia and North America, migrating south for the winter. It measures about 1 ft. 2 in. Like some gulls it is a colonial breeder, but it selects inaccessible spots such as floating islets and swamps. Its chief food is small fish which it catches by swooping down from a height.

The family of Auks *(Alcidae)* consists of twelve genera and about twenty-two species of medium-sized aquatic birds. They are weak flyers, their bodies being adapted for swimming and diving; the feet are placed right at the back, so that they walk upright in much the same way as Penguins. They live at sea, coming to land only to nest in colonies on the coastal cliffs. The females lay one or at most two eggs.

The Razorbill *(Alca torda)* is 1 ft. 4 in. long, and black-and-white with a laterally flattened bill. It inhabits the shores of north-western and Arctic Europe, its winter migrations, however, taking it as far south as the Mediterranean. The picture at left was taken at its nesting-grounds in Iceland.

The Bridled Guillemot or Common Murre (*Uria aalge*) has about the same range as the Razorbill. It is slightly longer – about 1 ft. 4½ in. – and its bill is slenderer. The eye has a white ring and a streak of white behind it. Bottom left, a nesting colony, with several young birds, photographed in Iceland.

Above, two mounted specimens of the extinct Great Auk or Garefowl (*Pinguinis impennis*): left one, an adult bird; next to it an almost fully-grown youngster which, however, still lacks the large white patch in front of the eye. In the foreground can be seen a replica of the Great Auk's egg. These birds attained a length of up to 3 ft. and bred on the shores of the North Sea, North Atlantic and Arctic Ocean. They seem to have been most abundant and survived longest in Iceland, around Greenland and in Newfoundland. Defenceless and unable to fly, they were exterminated by man within about 300 years of being discovered, the last Great Auks being killed on a little island on the west coast of Iceland in 1844.

Another interesting Auk, typical of the northern waters, is the Atlantic Puffin *(Fratercula arctica)*. It is about a foot long. In summer it has a red, yellow and blue beak, very deep and flat, and bright red feet. It nests on the shores of Iceland, the Faroes, Britain, north-western Norway and north-western France, and is found also in the northern regions of eastern America. The nests are made in holes, often rabbits' burrows, in the grassy slopes of the high coastal cliffs. Its food consists mainly of fish no larger than earthworms, of the genus *Ammodytes*. Thousands are taken annually for the table, but it is to be hoped that this slaughter will be regulated before the Atlantic Puffin follows the Great Auk and becomes an extinct species to be seen only in museums *(left)*.

The Pigeon family *(Columbidae)* of the order Columbiformes covers some three hundred bird species with a cosmopolitan range excluding only the Arctic and Antarctic regions. One of the largest and most attractive is the Crowned Pigeon *(Goura coronata)*, 2 ft. 6 in. long, bluish-grey in colour, and with a tall head-crest of feathers, which inhabits north-western New Guinea and some of the neighbouring islands. Like most Pigeons, it feeds on seeds. During the day it keeps to the ground and only perches in trees for the night *(top right)*.

A number of species of wild pigeons live in Europe, one of these – the Rock Dove *(Columba livia)* – being the species from which all domestic forms are descended. Of these, there are some 125 basic forms, the picture below, right, showing

one which differs most from the original type, which resembles the popular carrier-pigeon. This is the Fantail Pigeon, white in colour, with a short bill and a fan-shaped tail.

Other European wild species include one of the common spring and summer visitors to the forests, the Turtle-Dove *(Streptopelia turtur)* which is seen top left. It measures about 11 in. and can easily be recognised in flight by the white edging on the dark tail and the oblique stripes on either side of the neck. Turtle-Doves nest in bushes and reveal themselves by their characteristic soft cooing. In the past few decades the equally large Collared Turtle-Dove *(Streptopelia decaocto)*, illustrated top right, has colonised in south-eastern,

central and north-western Europe, reaching Great Britain. It is reddish-grey in colour with a black collar band. All the year round it stays near houses, being seen as much in towns as in the country, nesting on trees and buildings. Its call is 'boo-booo-coo'. The Ring-Dove or Wood-Pigeon *(Columba palumbus)* illustrated below, left, is a partial migrant found everywhere in Europe except the most northerly parts. It is about 1 ft. 4 in. long, nests in trees, and its characteristic cooing sound is 'coo-coo-roo-coo-coo'. The smaller Stock-Dove *(Columba oenas)* is only 1 ft. 1 in. long and has the same range as the former. It nests in various hollows and its cry is 'hoo-roo-oo'. In winter it moves southwards *(below, right)*.

The order of Parrots (Psittaciformes) contains over 600 species of birds in about 100 genera. They inhabit tropical and sub-tropical regions, keeping chiefly to the forests and jungles, where they eat fruit and other vegetable food. Parrots are noted for their longevity and in captivity may live as long as their owners. These pets accustom themselves to cooked food, including meat, but experienced breeders advise against such unnatural feeding, the parrots' digestive organs not being adapted for such food. What is more, it may result in starting bad habits, such as biting and plucking their feathers.

At the top of this page are several Australian Cockatiels (Nymphicus hollandicus). These are slender birds about 1 ft. 1 in. long, light greyish-brown, with an orange spot behind the eye and a pale yellow crest. They are found all over Australia, living in large flocks and nesting in hollows. Young Cockatiels can be tamed, becoming very affectionate and often learning to repeat words.

The so-called Love-birds of the genus Agapornis are the size of sparrows or a little larger, and have the habit of sitting in rows. Some fourteen varieties of six species are known. The most popular pet is Fischer's Lovebird (Agapornis fischeri) with its coral red bill, orange head, green body, reddish-brown wings, and green, blue-topped tail. It has a white ring round the eye. Its habitat is in the forests of northwest Tanganyika (right).

The White-crested Cockatoo (*Cacatua alba*) is 1 ft. 6 in. long, white all over except for the pale yellow underside of the wings and tail. The white cockade is composed of broad feathers arranged in a row one behind the other. The length of these feathers startles the onlooker when the crest is suddenly erected. The White-crested Cockatoo inhabits the jungles of the Molucca Islands.

Below, the Lesser Sulphur-crested Cockatoo (*Cacatua sulphurea*) which is only about 1 ft. 1 in. long, white, with a sulphur-yellow crest. It inhabits Celebes and neighbouring islands and is a popular pet in Europe. In captivity it can be gentle and learns to repeat words.

Most popular of the Parrots kept in Europe and America as pets is the Budgerigar (*Melopsittacus undulatus*). Budgerigars are now up to about 1 ft. in length, but the wild form is only $7\frac{1}{2}$ in. long, greenish-yellow with black bars and striations, and dark blue patches on each cheek. Many different colour forms have been developed all over the world, some of them being very valuable. The Budgerigar inhabits the dry plains of Australia (*left*).

The Blue-and-yellow Macaw (*Ara ararauna*) is one of the largest of the Parrot family, achieving a length of over 2 ft. 6 in. (measured with the tail-feathers). It is a glossy blue above, deep yellow below, the bare patches on the cheeks are white and lined with rows of small black feathers. Its home is in the jungles of equatorial America. It becomes very tame in captivity and learns to repeat whole sentences (*below*).

The Owls (order Strigiformes) contain some 220 species of interesting birds with a range covering just about the whole world. Their bodies are well adapted for their way of life – they fly at night in search of the rodents and other small vertebrates which make up most of their food. Perfect eye-sight, the faculty of soundless flight, the ability to turn their head through 270 degrees, the strong and sharp claws – all these are of great advantage, making the Owl an excellent hunter under even the most adverse conditions. In past centuries the Owl was regarded as a symbol of death, being linked with the idea of ghosts and every kind of misfortune; for this reason it was killed in large numbers. Today all Owls are protected in every civilised country.

The Tawny, Brown, or Wood Owl *(Strix aluco)* lives in woods, overgrown gardens and old parks through most of central and southern Europe, and Asia, being quite abundant in some localities. It measures about 1 ft. 3 in.; the plumage is brown, grey, or tawny, with dark mottling and streaks. It is distinguished from similar species by its black eyes *(above)*.

The similar but much larger Ural Owl *(Strix uralensis)* is rare in central Europe, living in deciduous forests in parts of south-eastern and especially north-eastern Europe and the adjacent regions of central and eastern Asia, ranging as far as the Pacific. It is about 2 ft. long. Nesting in tree hollows, it hunts mammals up to the size of a hare and birds as large as the black grouse *(left)*.

The Little Owl *(Athene noctua)* is common in many parts of central and southern Europe. It is also found in neighbouring Asian territories and in North Africa. It is a small species, a little over 8 in. long, with bright yellow eyes, often seen flying about in daytime. It nests in hollow trees, old buildings and walls, occasionally also in holes in the ground. Its main food is mice and insects.

The largest European Owl is the well-known Eagle-Owl (*Bubo bubo*) which measures up to 2 ft. 4 in. and has a wing span of about 5 ft. It is tawny with broad dark streaks, and it has conspicuous tufts over the eyes. The eyes themselves are large and orange-coloured, the feet feathered right down to the claws. The Eagle-Owl is found all over Europe except for Iceland and parts of Scandinavia, France and Great Britain. Eastwards it extends far into Asia, and the related Great Horned Owl (*Bubo virginianus*) is found in North Africa. It nests in the hollows of very old trees, or among rocks and, in barren country, sometimes just on the ground. Occasionally it takes over abandoned nests of large birds of prey. It preys on mammals, from mice to hares and martens, as well as on birds as large as goshawks (*top left*).

The Snowy Owl (*Nyctea scandiaca*) is rare and found only in the extreme north of Europe, Asia and America. It measures up to 2 ft. 2 in. long and is white with irregular brown bars which, however, sometimes almost disappear, in particular in older birds. Its eyes are sulphur-yellow, and its feet are feathered to the claws. The Snowy Owl nests in the tundras and hunts mammals as large as the Snow Hare and birds as large as the Eider. When migrating south it sometimes turns up in central Europe (*bottom left*).

Both the pictures at the top of p. 445 show the Barn Owl (*Tyto alba*). About 1 ft. 1$^1/_2$ in. long, it is whitish-beige with fine speckling. It has black eyes, relatively long legs, and no ear tufts. It is fairly cosmopolitan, being absent only from the polar and other cold regions. There are many subspecies and geographical races. The Barn Owl nests in old houses and feeds chiefly on mice.

The Long-eared Owl (*Asio otus*), shown at bottom left of p. 445, has colouring similar to the Eagle-Owl but is much smaller, measuring only some 1 ft. 2 in. It is found almost all over Europe, Asia and America, living mostly in coniferous forests and using nests abandoned by other birds. In open country it nests on the ground. It hunts small mammals, birds and insects.

The Short-eared Owl (*Asio flammeus*) has ear tufts that are scarcely visible but the same yellow eyes as the Long-eared Owl. The Short-eared Owl is about 1 ft. 3 in. long, It flies by day as well as night and its prey includes small mammals, birds, frogs and insects. It nests in peat-bogs, sand dunes, swamps, reed-beds, and similar localities. It is found over much of Europe, Asia and North America, but not in Spain, the Balkans and the south of England. It is a partial migrant (*p. 445, bottom right*).

445

The Cuckoo family (Cuculidae) includes over one hundred species in some forty genera. The Cuckoo (*Cuculus canorus*) is found over most of Europe and Asia, migrating for the winter to the tropics of Africa. It measures about 1 ft. 1 in. long. Cock and hen are alike, grey, paler below, with fine dark barring. The female is sometimes rufous with fine barring all over, which resembles the juvenile plumage. The Cuckoo mostly lives in woods, where the males are heard making their characteristic call. It feeds on every kind of caterpillar including the hairy varieties. Cuckoos lay a single egg in nests of other birds, chiefly of the small passerines. When hatched, the young Cuckoo throws out all the original eggs or fledglings and is fed by the parents. The female Cuckoo deposits some twenty eggs in this way, being fertilised by various males. Above is a young Cuckoo in its first plumage. The North American Cuckoos are very different from their Old World relatives and do not lay their eggs in the nests of other birds.

The order Caprimulgiformes includes night or dusk-flying birds with a very broad, short bill lined with stiff bristles. It has extremely short legs, and soft 'owl's' feathers. In some species the wing or tail-feathers are extended into pennants. These birds sleep during the day, hunting insects at night. The Nightjar or Goatsucker (*Caprimulgus europaeus*) is about 10$^{1}/_{2}$ in. long, and it is mottled brown and buff, like the bark of some trees. Several forms range throughout most of Europe and Asia, as well as north-west Africa. It prefers dry woods and commons, where it spends the day either on the ground or perched on a branch, facing along it. Its nest is usually on bare ground, with only two eggs. The males emit a continuous purring sound at the nesting season. The Whip-poor-will (*Caprimulgus carolinensis*) is widespread in North America.

The order Micropodiformes includes the Humming-birds and Swifts. The Humming-bird family – Trochilidae – contains over 300 species and almost twice as many local races. Their average length is 4 in. The smallest is $2^1/_4$ in. long, the body only an inch, and these minute birds weigh 14 to the ounce, so they are the smallest birds in the world. They live in both Americas and on neighbouring islands, their range extending from the coastal areas up to an altitude of 16,000 ft. They feed on the nectar of flowers, and on small insects and spiders, either caught in flight or picked off plants. Humming-birds have specially adapted bills, sometimes curved like forceps, the long, forked, extensile tongue being rolled into a tube with which they suck nectar. Their wing beat is extremely rapid and it produces the characteristic humming noise. They can hover in the air and change course with astonishing speed. With their beautifully coloured plumage, metallic sheen and ornamental patterns, Humming-birds are among the most magnificent of all living creatures. They build little basket-shaped nests, either in the trees or among plants, usually rearing two chicks from eggs that are frequently no larger than a pea. Many species are migratory and can travel very long distances.

At top left of this page is the Small Humming-Bird (*Mellisuga minima*). It is glossy dark green in colour and only $2^1/_4$ in. long, inhabiting the Great Antilles.

The Grey-throated Humming-Bird (*Phaethornis griseogularis*) measures 4 in. and has a tapering, wedge-shaped tail *(bottom left)*.

The Swifts (family Apodidae) include the well-known Common Swift (*Apus apus*) a black bird, about $6^1/_2$ in. long with long, sickle-shaped wings and a short, forked tail. The feet are so formed that these birds can only cling to vertical surfaces, there being four toes on each foot, all of them turned forwards. There is a white spot under the chin. In summer Swifts are to be found throughout Europe except in the extreme north. They also inhabit Asia and north-west Africa. As a rule the nest is built under the eaves of houses, but sometimes on rocky cliffs. A brood consists of two or three. Swifts feed chiefly on flies, caught in flight *(top left on p. 449)*.

The Kingfisher family includes the native European variety, but the largest member is the Laughing Jackass or Kookaburra *(Dacelo novaeguineae)*, a powerful bird, almost 1 ft. 8 in. long, with a large head and heavy bill. It has a very strange voice that sounds like human laughter. Its food consists of small vertebrates, including snakes, and insects. This Kingfisher lives in Australia, Tasmania and New Guinea *(top right)*.

The Hoopoe *(Upupa epops)* measures about 11 in. and has pinkish brown plumage, the tail and wings have black-and-white bars. It has a rufous, black-tipped, erectile crest. An inhabitant of central and southern Europe, the warm parts of Asia, and North Africa, it nests in tree hollows, and sometimes under the roofs of houses, inside walls and in wood piles. Its diet consists of insects picked off the ground; in Europe it feeds its young chiefly with mole-crickets. It winters in the south *(bottom right)*.

The order Piciformes includes the Woodpecker family (Picidae). These have feet adapted for climbing trees, with two toes pointing forward and two backward, and a strong chisel-like bill for pecking holes in the wood.

Left, the Great Spotted Woodpecker (*Dendrocopus major*) which is 9 in. long. It is black-and-white, with crimson on the nape and beneath the tail. It is found over most of Europe and much of Asia. It favours rotting trees for making its nest hole, and feeds chiefly on insects it finds in the wood.

The Wryneck (*Jynx torquilla*) is about $6\frac{1}{2}$ in. long; its feathers are grey with brownish and rufous-yellow markings. It inhabits most of Europe, central and northern Asia, and north-west Africa, wintering in the south. It makes its nest in natural tree holes and feeds chiefly on ants, caught with its long, extensile tongue. The picture, bottom left, shows a Wryneck bringing ant cocoons to its young. If cornered and unable to fly off, Wrynecks spread their wings and tails, twist their heads from side to side, roll their eyes, and make a strange growling noise.

Hornbills (Bucerotidae) are related to the Hoopoes and Kingfishers. The Indian Hornbill (*Buceros bicornis*) is nearly 5 ft. long; its feathers are black-and-white and the tail long; the beak is huge and up to 10 in. in length. It inhabits the forests of India south-east to Sumatra, feeding on juicy berries and small vertebrates. At the nesting season the male walls the female up in a hollow tree, feeding her and the young through a narrow opening (*bottom right*).

Toucans (Ramphastidae) are classified with the Woodpeckers, to whom they are related. Of the five fairly similar genera and sixty species, the one shown here is the Green-billed Toucan *(Ramphastos discolorus)*. This is about 1 ft. 8 in. long, with an orange-yellow throat, turquoise-blue patch round the eye, and a green beak, orange on the sides and red at the tip. It inhabits the jungles of Central America, ranging from southern Mexico to Honduras. Though relatively enormous, Toucans' beaks are extremely light, being of honeycomb structure. Toucans live on fruit, insects and small vertebrates.

The order Passeriformes with over 5,000 species includes about three-fifths of all birds. The true songsters (Passeres) include the Reed Warbler (Acrocephalus scirpaceus), an inconspicuous brownish green bird, about 5 in. long, which inhabits almost the whole of central and southern Europe, the neighbouring parts of Asia, and north-west Africa. It nests among reeds, the nest being a cleverly constructed basket-like structure. The Sedge Warbler (left) feeds on insects, and migrates to central Africa for the winter.

The Wheatear (Oenanthe oenanthe) is nearly 6 in. long, grey above and buffish below. It has a black band through the eyes and a black tail-tip. Its range takes in the greater part of Europe, central and northern Asia, and North Africa. It nests in holes, either in rocks or in the ground, and feeds on insects. Wheatears fly south for the winter (below).

The most common central European representative of the Titmice is the Great Tit *(Parus major)*. It is $5^1/_2$ in. long, greenish above and yellow on the underside. The head is black and a black band stretches from the throat to the belly. Its cheeks are white. It is found throughout Europe and Asia except in the extreme north. It nests in hollow trees and eats chiefly insects *(above)*. There are many species of Titmice in other parts of the world; some of the American are called Chickadees.

The Penduline Tit *(Remiz pendulinus)* builds a very interesting nest *(right)*. Just over 4 in. long, it is light brown and buff with a black stripe across the eyes. It lives in eastern and some parts of southern Europe, and farther east across Asia to Japan, there being several varieties. Here it is shown just before the completion of its nest — all that remains to be done is to close the entrance, leaving a small round opening. This species leaves the colder countries in winter and moves south.

The long-tailed Tit *(Aegithalos caudatus)* is seen below bringing small spiders to its young. Including the tail, it is 5¹/₂ in. long, whitish-pink, white and black. It occurs throughout most of Europe, its range extending as far as eastern Asia.

The Waxwing *(Bombycilla garrulus)* is about 7 in. long, chestnut and grey, with black chin and reddish crest. The tips of the wing and tail-feathers are yellow, with bright red wing tips to the secondaries. It lives in northern Europe, Asia and America, and nests even within the Arctic Circle. It is seen in central and western Europe only in winter, when it seeks berries and seeds. In summer it also eats insects *(top left)*.

Top right, the Song Thrush *(Turdus ericetorum)*. It is 9 in. long, brown in colour with dark spots on the paler underside. It inhabits most of western, central and northern Europe, northern and central Asia, wandering south in winter. Living in woods and parks, it feeds on insects, worms, molluscs and berries. It ranks next to the Nightingale as a songster and is closely related to the North American Robin.

The Chaffinch *(Fringilla coelebs)*, 6 in. long, is distinguished by double white wing bars and white-edged tail. Living in Europe and western Asia it is partly migratory *(top left)*.

The Bullfinch *(Pyrrhula pyrrhula)* is nearly 6 in. in length. Cock birds have a beautiful red breast, the females are greyish-brown and black. European and Asiatic in range *(top right)*.

The White Wagtail *(Motacilla alba)* is 7 in. long.

It inhabits the whole of Europe and the adjacent parts of Africa, as well as North Africa. Partly migratory *(bottom left)*.

The Great Grey Shrike *(Lanius excubitor)* is $9\frac{1}{2}$ in. long and is found over most of the Northern Hemisphere. It is partly migratory. Its food consists of large insects and the smaller vertebrates *(below, with prey)*.

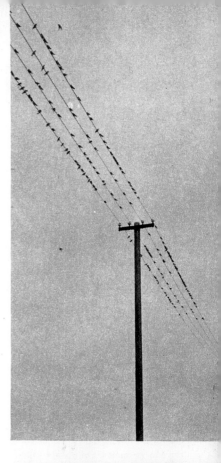

On the opposite page are the best-known of the larger European Passerines. At the top is the Raven (Corvus corax) which inhabits western North America and most of Europe except for some western parts. It is about 2 ft. 1 in. long. At left centre is the Jay (Garrulus glandarius) which measures 1 ft. $1^1/_2$ in.; next to it, the Magpie (Pica pica), 1 ft. 6 in.; bottom left, the European Starling (Sturnus vulgaris), $8^1/_2$ in., which is now a major pest species in North America. Beside it, the Rook (Corvus frugilegus), 1 ft. 6 in.

At the top of this page can be seen resting House Martins (Delichon urbica) and their nests. These birds nest nearly all over Europe, Asia and North Africa. They measure 5 in. At the foot of the page are Martins gathering material for nest-building. At top right, the smallest European Swallow, the Sand Martin or Bank Swallow (Riparia riparia), is seen perching on telegraph wires, and (bottom right) at the entrance to its nest. The picture below the text shows an earth bank with its nesting holes. The Sand Martin is under 5 in. long and is known as a summer migrant over nearly all the Northern Hemisphere.

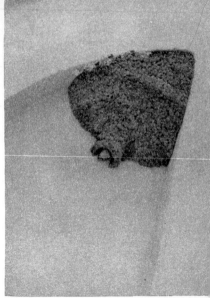

The largest European species is the Swallow itself (*Hirundo rustica*). It measures 7$\frac{1}{2}$ in. Above left, a Swallow's open, cup-shaped nest on top of a lamp-shade. The picture on the opposite page is of an adult Swallow. In summer this species is found all over Europe except the extreme north, in parts of Asia and North Africa and most of North America, where it is known as the Barn Swallow. All Swallows are useful because they catch large numbers of insects, especially flies.

Below can be seen Red-rumped Swallows (*Hirundo daurica*) – a slightly smaller species. In Europe it is a summer visitor to southern Spain and Greece, otherwise it lives in the warm parts of central and southern Asia, as far east as Japan. It has a glossy black cap and back, but may be recognised by the reddish-yellow rump. Its nests are built on ceilings or in caves and have a spout-shaped entrance *(above right)*.

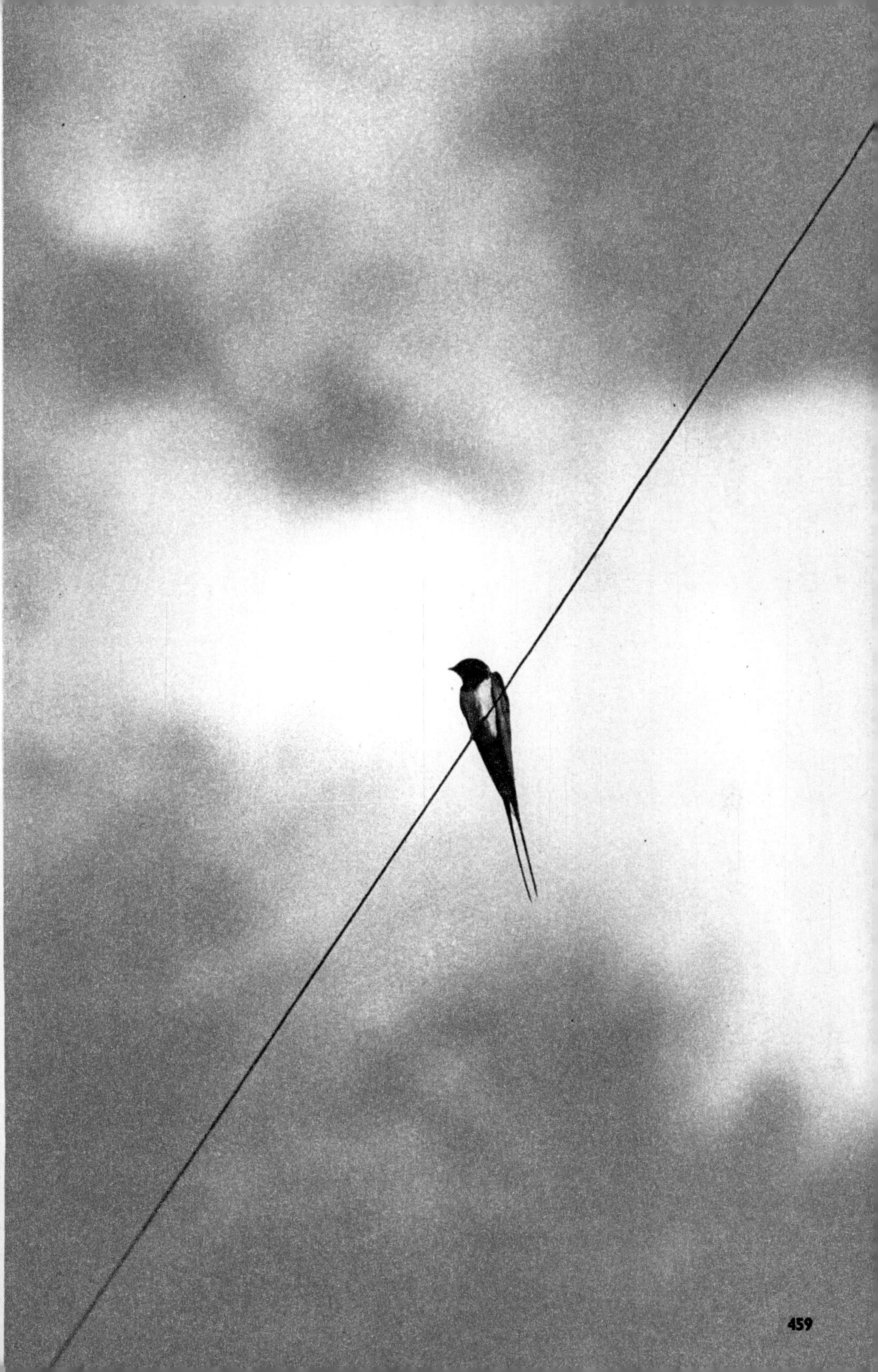

MAMMALS

The Mammals, class Mammalia, warm-blooded vertebrates that breathe air, have a four-chambered heart and a body covering of fur or hair; the young are born alive and are nourished by their mothers' milk. The ancestors of our modern mammals first came into existence perhaps sixty-one million years ago. during the Paleocene Period at the beginning of the Cenozoic Era — the Age of Mammals. They developed from reptilian-like forms. The Multituberculates, or Mesozoic mammals, lived some sixty million years earlier but they vanished, leaving a long period of time when there were no mammals on the earth. Mammals are the youngest and most highly developed vertebrates and include some 16.000 named forms of which 10.000 have become extinct.

Their size varies widely, the smallest mammal, a minute Shrew *(Suncus etruscus)* measuring a mere $1^1/_2$ in. (without tail) and weighing about $^1/_{18}$ oz., while the Blue Whale *(Balaenoptera musculus)* attains a length of 100 ft. and a weight of 150 tons.

The nearly six thousand species living today can be divided into two subclasses. The Prototheria include only a few primitive species which have retained some of the characteristics of reptiles. They lay eggs with soft, parchment-like shells, possess a cloaca, as well as a nictating membrane in the eyes, and they do not have a constant body temperature. One of these species is the nocturnal Australian Echidna *(Tachyglossus aculeatus).* It is about 1 ft. 6 in. long, inhabiting the sparse forests of Australia, Tasmania and New Guinea. It spends the day underground or hidden in a rocky cavity. It feeds on ants and termites *(top left).*

Below left, a nest with young of the Duck-billed Platypus *(Ornithorhynchus anatinus)* which when fully grown measures up to 1 ft. 8 in. long. It lives in Australia and Tasmania, being for the greater part an aquatic animal and feeding on worms, larvae, and molluscs which it finds in the mud. The females lay eggs out of which the young hatch, these being then fed on their mother's milk.

The second subclass, the higher mammals *(Theria),* is further sub-divided and the Metatheria includes the marsupials. In the order Marsupialia, while even the most primitive species bear live young, these are not fully developed at birth and the mother carries them in a marsupium or ventral pouch. The well-known, North American fur-bearing animal, Opossum *(Didelphis virginiana),* carries as many as sixteen young in this way. Without the tail, an adult Opossum is 1 ft. 8 in. long. It feeds on small vertebrates, chiefly rodents but is quite capable of killing off the entire population of a hen-house in a single night.

Left, a close-up of an Opossum, whose prominent eyes indicate that it is a nocturnal creature.

About 300 different species of marsupials live in the Australasian region and a few in South and Central America. The Koala (Phascolarctos cinereus), shown above, is a native of eastern Australia and attains a length of some 2 ft. An accomplished climber, it lives in eucalyptus trees. Kangaroos, best known of Australian marsupials, are vegetarians. Below is a female Red Kangaroo (Macropus rufa) with a large youngster in her pouch.

The Eutheria are the Placental mammals whose young develop in the womb of the mother and are fed through the placenta. The most primitive of these are the Insectivores – order Insectivora – with eight families, sixty-seven genera, and very many species, the number of which is still rather uncertain. It is widely distributed throughout the world except for Australia but is not well represented in South America. The best known members of this order are the Shrews and Moles.

The White-toothed Shrew (*Crocidura suaveolens*) measures nearly 3 in., its tail about an inch. It lives in gardens, meadows and on the fringes of forests in southern and south-eastern Europe and in parts of Asia. Its diet consists of insects and other arthropods, molluscs, and worms. As winter approaches, it seeks human habitations, where it eats hibernating insects and spiders. Red-toothed Shrews (*Sorex*) are common and widely distributed over the entire North American continent and average about 4 in. in total length.

The European Hedgehog (*Erinaceus europaeus*) is some 11 in. long. There are three forms living all over Europe, except for most of Scandinavia and Iceland. Hedgehogs are found in Asia and Africa. It frequents dry woods and undergrowth, feeding on various small creatures, in particular insects and their larvae, small vertebrates including snakes, and on fruit. Though not immune to snake venom, it will defeat an adder by its great nimbleness and the protection afforded it by its spines. In colder countries the Hedgehog hibernates in winter.

The Slender Loris.

The European Mole *(Talpa europaea)* is one of the best-known Insectivores. It is up to about 6 in. long, reddish-brown to black in colour with a coat of fine, short, velvety hair. It makes underground tunnels and feeds on earthworms and insects. It is found throughout Europe and eastwards as far as the Altai Mountains and Mongolia. The above picture shows molehills at the edge of a forest; below is the enlarged head of a Mole emerging from its burrow. The American Garden Mole *(Scalopus aquaticus)* has the highly specialised forelimbs, minute eyes and soft, velvety black fur of the European Mole, and has similar habits.

The Bats (Chiroptera) are an order containing some 750 species and some 2,000 named forms, the only mammals which can truly fly. Bats are divided into two suborders. The Microchiroptera are species which feed primarily on flying insects or fruit. Some of them, however, prey on smaller vertebrates, while others like the American Vampire *(Desmodus)* feed on the blood of larger vertebrates and even man. There are also species which catch fish on the surface of rivers or lakes and eat them in flight. The Fish-eating Bat *(Pizonyx)*, restricted to the Gulf of California, is a born fisherman. Many species are found in Europe, where the Long-eared Bat *(Plecotus auritus)* is one of the commonest. Its head and body measure about 2 in.; it has a greyish-brown fur above, paler on the underside. Its ears, the largest of all European species, are sometimes as long as $2^1/_2$ in. and touch at the base. When hanging asleep, the bat folds its ears backwards under the wing membranes, only the pointed tips protruding. The range of this species cover most of Asia as far as Japan, and it is very common in North Africa. It is pictured in flight *(top right)*.

Bottom left is the Long-eared Bat ($\times$ 2 approximately).

Top left, the head of the Lesser Horse-shoe Bat *(Rhinolophus hipposideros)* ($\times$ 2). This species lives in central and southern Europe, extending eastwards as far as the Himalayas. Members of this genus, like the American Leaf-nosed Bats, a fruit-eating species, have extraordinary and often highly complicated membranes around the nose which may help the bat in finding its way in the dark. It has been shown that Bats orient themselves in flight by listening to the sounds they emit, which are reflected by any obstacle. As well as twittering, squeaking, buzzing and whistling sounds audible to the human ear, they also produce ultra-shortwave sounds which are far beyond human range.

Horse-shoe Bats hibernate during the colder months of the year in caves, disused pits and underground galleries. They hang from the roof, often in large groups. The body temperature of sleeping Bats drops to approximately the temperature of their surroundings, while their pulse slows to about a twenty-fifth of normal. Bottom right, Lesser Horse-shoe Bats in a subterranean cave in Moravia.

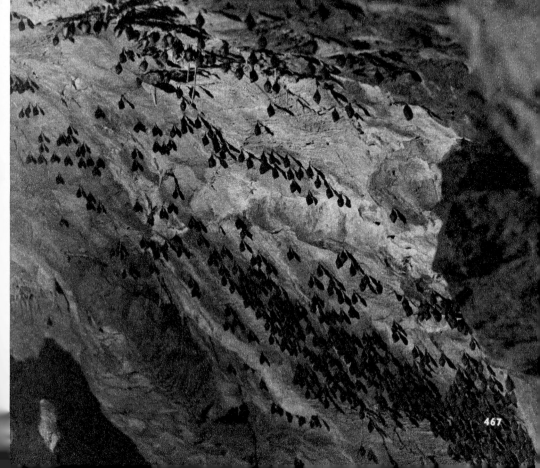

467

The Brown Bat *(Myotis myotis)* is about the largest species of Bat known to Europe, its body and head measuring about 3¹/₄ in. It inhabits western, central and southern Europe, and then east-wards the whole of central Asia all the way to India, and southwards to Ethiopia. Above, the head of *Myotis myotis*; right, a pair of these Bats hibernating in an abandoned gold mine. Other species of *Myotis* are quite small and one is the commonest Bat in the United States.

Bottom left is the head of Barbastelle *(Barbastella barbastella)* (× 3), a species of western, central and eastern Europe and as far east as the Caucasus. In summer, Bats spend the day sleeping in various hiding-places, such as attics, towers, behind window shutters, or in wood piles, etc. For the winter they seek out sheltered underground places with temperatures between 3° and 8° C.

The suborder Megachiroptera includes some nineteen genera, two hundred species, mostly larger Bats from the tropical regions of the Old World. They are mostly frugivorous, but those of the suborder Macroglossinae are nectar-feeding Bats, lapping the honeyed liquid from night-blooming flowers with their long tongues. The best known of the frugivorous Bats is the Malayan Fruit Bat or Flying Fox *(Pteropus vampyrus)*. It is about 1 ft. 3 in. long and has a wing span of almost 5 ft. Its colouring is reddish-brown and it lives in Malaya and Indonesia.

The order Primates includes Tree-shrews, Lemurs, Aye-ayes, Lorises, Monkeys and Apes. The sub-order Prosimii including the first four groups are classified between the Monkeys and the Apes and the Insectivores, and are considered to be the most primitive Primates. The great majority are species of Lemur, found on the island of Madagascar. The Slow Loris (Nycticebus coucang) is a Lemur about the size of a small cat. It is a nocturnal creature, inhabiting the jungles from Bengal southeast through to Borneo. It feeds on insects, lizards, birds, small mammals, and fruit.

The Slender Loris (Loris tardigradus) is only 10 in. long and brownish yellow. It spends the day curled up on a branch or in a hollow tree. At night it walks about in the branches, slowly and deliberately. It lives in southern India and Ceylon (left).

Above, the Potto (Perodicticus potto). It is usually brownish but its colour varies, as it does with the Lorises. It is a native of the dense forests of West Africa, the Congo, and some parts of East Africa. It is about a foot long.

Various species of Lemurs live in the mainland of Africa. The Senegal Bush Baby *(Galago senegalensis)* is about the size of a small squirrel and its usual colour is pale greyish-brown. It has bare, membranous ears, similar to those of the Bats, which it is able to fold during its daytime sleep. It is found in the grass woodlands in most of Africa south of the Sahara *(left)*.

Of the suborder Anthropoidea the broad-nosed Platyrrhines of the New World are considered the oldest and most primitive. The Three-banded Douroucouli or Night Ape *(Aotes trivirgatus)* is some 1 ft. 1 in. long, with a tail measuring up to nearly 1 ft. 8 in. It has striking yellowish-brown eyes in a black face. Its fur is greyish-brown on top and whitish to reddish underneath. It is the only nocturnal Monkey and it inhabits the forests of the northern parts of South America. It lives on insects, lizards, and fruit, as well as small birds which it catches while they sleep *(right)*.

The Woolly Monkey (*Lagothrix lagotricha*) is up to 2 ft. 3 in. long, its tail being as long again. This relatively slow-moving Monkey lives in small groups in the forests of South America, especially in the region of the Orinoco and Amazon rivers.

The natives call it Capparo or Barrigudo. Th[e] Monkey has a very strong and muscular prehensil[e] tail, bare on the inside of the tip. The Wooll[y] Monkey feeds on fruit, leaves, and shoots. I[n] captivity it becomes very tame and friendly.

The related Brown Capuchin Monkey (Cebus fatuel-
lus) is also found in the South American forests, but
in larger colonies.   It is not exclusively an arboreal
animal.   In size it is a little larger than a house
cat – 1 ft. 5 in. long and a tail of 1 ft. 4 in.   When
climbing trees, it uses its tail as a fifth limb, on
the ground it carries it curled in a flat spiral.   The
Capuchins seem to be the most intelligent South
American Monkeys (above).

The Catarrhines are the Old World Monkeys
– usually grouped in one superfamily, the Cercopithecoidea, which includes the Rhesus Monkey
(Macaca mulata).   Its body is some 2 ft. in length,
its tail nearly half as long.   It is greyish-yellow
and greyish-red in colour.   It is abundant in
India and neighbouring countries of south-
east Asia.   Below are three Rhesus females
with young.

The Stump-tailed Monkey (*Macaca speciosa*) is rather heavier than the Rhesus, its fur dark brown and sometimes long. Its face is red, and the tail even shorter than that of the Rhesus. It lives in mountain forests from Thailand through to western China.

Allen's Swamp Monkey (*Allenopithecus nigroviridis*) is a gentle, good-natured Monkey the size of a cat, having, however, a much longer tail. Its fur is greyish-brown with a greenish tinge. It lives in large packs in forests on the banks of the rivers Gabon and north-west Congo. These Monkeys utter a high-pitched whistle *(top right)*.

The sacred Monkeys of the Hindus – the Hanumans – are also classified among the Guenons (Cercopithecoidea). These are agile creatures living in packs in the tree tops, where they feed on leaves and shoots. According to an old Indian legend, the Hanuman once stole the rare mango fruit, which in those days grew only in the gardens of the giant of Ceylon. For this, the Monkey was cast into the fire, but it managed to escape with its life, only its face and limbs being scorched. That is why they are black to this day. The Madras Hanuman or Banded Leaf Monkey (*Presbitis priamus*) is up to 2 ft. 4 in. long, its tail being 3 ft. 4 in. This species chiefly inhabits the northern part of Ceylon.

The bottom picture shows a pair of Yellow Baboons *(Papio cynocephalus lestes)* from central Africa. They are up to 2 ft. 6 in. in length (the males are sometimes even bigger), with a slightly shorter tail. Their fur is olive-brown. Unlike most other Baboons, which because of their elongated head and strong teeth can do terrible damage when they become angry, this is a more amiable creature which may sometimes be allowed to roam freely among the visitors in zoological gardens.

479

The bottom picture shows an adult female Chacma Baboon (*Papio porcarius*). It is about 2 ft. 8 in. long, with a tail of no more than 1 ft. 2 in. Greyish-black in colour, it lives in the dry upland areas of South Africa. Baboons are predominantly vegetarian, but they also eat any small mammals and insects they find.

A young male Drill (*Mandrillus leucophaeus*) is illustrated in the top picture. It reaches a length of nearly 3 ft. and has a very short tail, measuring no more than 2 or 3 in. It lives in virgin forests of equatorial West Africa. The males are much larger and more powerful than the females. Old males are shy in the wild state and dangerously aggressive in captivity.

On p. 481 is a young adult Mandrill (*Mandrillus sphinx*). Somewhat heavier than the Drill, the Mandrill may be over 3 ft. long, the male having very vivid colouring. Its cheeks are a sky blue, the nose and mouth red with orange whiskers. The animal's buttocks are also very colourful. The Mandrill lives in very dense forests, mainly in the South Cameroons, Guinea, and the Congo. Like the Drill, it lives on the ground.

The Great, or Anthropoid Apes (Pongidae) include four genera of
Apes which bear the closest resemblance to Man. They are also
nearest to man from the point of view of development, having
features of their long-extinct common ancestors.

The Gibbons (Hylobates) are the smallest and most slender of the
Anthropoid Apes, being sometimes referred to as the Lesser Apes.
The Lar Gibbon, illustrated on the left *(Hylobates lar)* is about 2 ft.
8 in. in length. It has a dark face fringed with white, the body
colour dark grey or brownish-yellow. It is an arboreal creature
inhabiting the forests of Burma, Thailand and the Sunda Islands.

Gibbons are the most adroit
acrobats of the animal world,
and give the impression of flying
through the air as they swing
from branch to branch. Using
their exceptionally long arms
for this purpose, they can cover
distances of up to 45 ft. in a
single leap.

Orang-utans *(Pongo pygmaeus)*
live in Borneo and Sumatra. Their
exclusively arboreal mode of life
shows in their short legs and
exceptionally long and powerful
arms. Old males are giants
measuring up to 5 ft. 6 in. and
weighing as much as 200 lb. The
entire body and limbs are covered with long ginger-coloured
hair, their faces usually being
bare, greyish-blue in colour and
frequently adorned by a reddish
'beard'. Their diet consists of
fruit and other vegetable matter.
They build simple nests of
branches and leaves high up in
the trees. Orang-utans live up
to thirty years. In captivity
they will get used to a change
of diet and will take some meat.
In spite of the fact that Orang-
utans are protected by law, they
are in great danger of being
exterminated. The Orang-utan
in the picture on the right is a
seventeen-year-old male from
Borneo.

Head of an Orang-utan.

Head of an Orang-utan.

Gibbons are the most adroit acrobats of the animal world, and give the impression of flying through the air as they swing from branch to branch. Using their exceptionally long arms for this purpose, they can cover distances of up to 45 ft. in a single leap.

Orang-utans (Pongo pygmaeus) live in Borneo and Sumatra. Their exclusively arboreal mode of life shows in their short legs and exceptionally long and powerful arms. Old males are giants measuring up to 5 ft. 6 in. and weighing as much as 200 lb. The entire body and limbs are covered with long ginger-coloured hair, their faces usually being bare, greyish-blue in colour and frequently adorned by a reddish 'beard'. Their diet consists of fruit and other vegetable matter. They build simple nests of branches and leaves high up in the trees. Orang-utans live up to thirty years. In captivity they will get used to a change of diet and will take some meat. In spite of the fact that Orang-utans are protected by law, they are in great danger of being exterminated. The Orang-utan in the picture on the right is a seventeen-year-old male from Borneo.

The Great, or Anthropoid Apes (Pongidae) include four genera of Apes which bear the closest resemblance to Man. They are also nearest to man from the point of view of development, having features of their long-extinct common ancestors.

The Gibbons (Hylobates) are the smallest and most slender of the Anthropoid Apes, being sometimes referred to as the Lesser Apes. The Lar Gibbon, illustrated on the left (Hylobates lar) is about 2 ft. 8 in. in length. It has a dark face fringed with white, the body colour dark grey or brownish-yellow. It is an arboreal creature inhabiting the forests of Burma, Thailand and the Sunda Islands.

The Orang-utan is a slow-moving, circumspect animal which prefers solitude. It moves through the forest with the aid of its strong arms, the legs serving only to help it keep its hold. Its eyes are relatively small. Old males have huge cheek pads, more or less naked, and also a large throat pouch. Zoo keepers exercise great caution when handling old Orang-utan males because these powerful animals tend to be moody and unpredictable. Young ones become very tame and friendly in captivity. The Orang-utan is nevertheless less intelligent than the Chimpanzee or Gorilla (picture on p. 484).

Another Man-like Ape, the Chimpanzee (Pan troglodytes), has its home in equatorial Africa. The Latin nomenclature of the Apes was evidently invented before their life and habits were thoroughly investigated. Thus the Orang-utan was given the name pygmaeus (dwarfish), in spite of the fact that the male grows into a veritable giant, and the Chimpanzee was dubbed troglodytes (living in caves), though it lives in the dense undergrowth of the forest and not in caves at all. They move about in bands of up to fifteen led by a strong adult male, keeping mostly to the ground and feeding on fruit, plants and shoots. They vary very much in size but an adult male may weigh 180 lb. The Chimpanzee (above)

is considered to be the most intelligent of the Apes, easily tamed as a youngster and very playful and ingenious. Old individuals, however, can be dangerous in captivity owing to their unpredictable temper and enormous strength.

Largest among the man-like Apes is the Gorilla (Gorilla gorilla), the males growing to well over 6 ft. and weighing over 5 cwt. Like the Chimpanzee, the Gorilla inhabits the forests of equatorial Africa, but has a much smaller distribution and is found only in a few parts of the Cameroons, Congo, Gaboon and Uganda. Also like the Chimpanzee, they live in groups and feed on juicy shoots, fruit and other vegetable matter.

Young Gorillas will frequently raid birds' nests and eat the eggs or fledglings. They will also eat large insects. The Chimpanzee has a brain volume of 420 c.c., the Orang-utan 450 c.c., and the Gorilla 510 c.c., compared with about 1.500 c.c. in man. The above picture shows a two-year-old male Gorilla.

The Flesh-eaters, order Carnivora, are divided into two groups. The Land Carnivores, suborder Fissipedia, includes one hundred genera divided into seven families. Originally they were found practically all over the world except for Australia and New Zealand.

The Coyote or Prairie Wolf (*Canis latrans*) belongs to the Canidae. It is brown-grey, lives on the prairies of North America and resembles the Jackal. Like the Jackal, it is rather over 3 ft. 4 in. in total length. Coyotes hunt in packs, but are not dangerous either to man or to the larger animals. In captivity they are as affectionate as Dogs.

The largest of the few European canines is the Wolf *(Canis lupus)*. It is also found in Asia and North America. It is up to 4 ft. long, with a tail about 1 ft. 3 in. In winter it hunts in packs, attacking animals up to the size of deer and elk, though it is content with small vertebrates, carrion, and even beetles in times of scarcity. In many Asian countries Wolves present a considerable problem, being difficult to kill in the wilds owing to their extreme shyness and wariness *(top left)*.

The below picture shows Australian Dingoes *(Canis dingo)*. It is believed by some that a long time ago, before the first Europeans set foot in Australia, domesticated Dogs were brought there, most probably by natives from India. The Dogs reverted to the wild state and eventually became a distinct species – yellowish-brown in colour.

The domestic Dog *(Canis familiaris)* is descended in part from the Wolf. It has been known as man's faithful friend and helper for at least twelve thousand years. Some four hundred different breeds have come into being for various purposes, many of them simply as pets. The German Short-haired Pointer *(p. 489 top left)* is used by hunters to 'point' game and to retrieve shot birds. On the same page, top right is the Kuwasz Sheep Dog from the Tatra range of the Carpathians; bottom left is the St. Bernard, which has won much popularity by helping to rescue travellers lost in the Alps; bottom right is the English Pointer.

One of the most beautiful and intelligent breeds is the Alsatian or German Shepherd Dog, which is not unlike the Wolf in appearance. It is illustrated in the top picture.

Two black Dwarf Poodles, which are bred as pets, are illustrated below.

A young Golden Cocker Spaniel is illustrated in the top picture. It is one of the most popular of all breeds.

Bottom left is a Pekinese. These are small Dogs which came to Europe from China around 1860. They had been kept at the Emperor's court for the past two thousand years.

Bottom right is a large Royal Standard Black Poodle. An excellent watchdog, it is highly intelligent, agile and self-possessed. It stands 2 ft. high.

491

The Red Fox *(Vulpes vulpes)* is the only canine to have survived in any numbers in the wild state over most of Europe. It is also found in North America, Asia, India and North Africa north of the Sahara. It measures about 2 ft. 8 in., with a tail of up to 1 ft. 3 in. It is reddish in colour, greyish-white underneath, the tip of its tail usually white. It prefers wooded country, often in mountains up to a height of 7,500 ft. During the breeding season it lives in 'earths' which it burrows in the ground. It feeds on berries, insects, earthworms, snails, mice, frogs, rabbits, game birds and poultry. For its young, however, it will take mammals up to the size of fawns, and birds as large as geese *(top left).*

The greyish-black Silver Fox *(below)* is a well-known fur-bearing animal which is bred on special farms. A native of North America, it is one of the numerous subspecies of the North American Red Fox *(Vulpes fulva)* which is found over almost the whole of the Northern Hemisphere.

The Fennec (Fennecus zerda) is a small desert Fox about 1 ft. 6 in. long and with a tail of about 8 in. It is a sandy colour, and is best recognised by its large sensitive ears and enormous round eyes so typical of nocturnal animals. Its pads are hair-covered. The Fennec lives in North Africa inhabiting desert and semi-desert regions, where it feeds on large insects such as locusts. It also hunts mice, birds, and lizards, and is fond of dates and similar sweet fruit. It spends the day asleep.

The Cape Hunting Dog (*Lycaon pictus*), illustrated left, is up to 3 ft. 7 in. long, with a tail of up to 1 ft. 3 in. It is irregularly spotted black, white and yellow-brown, and has conspicuously large, round, erect ears. There are only four digits on its front paws. It inhabits open savannah country south of the Sahara as in East Africa. Hunting Dogs travel in packs, and are exclusively carnivorous.

The Raccoon-like Dog (*Nyctereutes procyonoides*), illustrated below, measures up to 2 ft. 4 in., of which 5 in. is tail. It is a sturdy, short-legged nocturnal animal, grey with some yellowish-brown hairs. It is a native of the Amur region of Asia, China, Korea and Japan. Its food consists of berries, garden fruit, insects, and small vertebrates. Bred for its fur, it is known also as 'Japanese Fox'.

The Ursidae (Bear family) have only one member still surviving in central Europe. This is the Brown Bear *(Ursus arctos)*, which is about 7 ft. long. Its fur is varying shades of brown, in some cases greyish. When young, it has a white collar band. In Europe it is now found only in the less inhabited places, in virgin forests and mountains, and through most of Asia as far as Japan; a closely related species is found in North America. Its diet ranges from berries and lichens to the flesh of live and dead animals. It is shown at top right.

Above left is the Himalayan Black Bear *(Selenarctos thibetanus)*, black, with a white V-shaped mark on its chest. It may exceed 6 ft. in length and is a good climber. Its habitat includes south and central Asia, from India to Japan, China and Thailand.

The Sloth Bear *(Melursus ursinus)*, below left, is roughly the same size but has a long muzzle and thick shaggy fur. It lives in the tropics of India and in Ceylon. An excellent climber, it feeds on fruit and other vegetable matter, sometimes also on insects.

The smallest of the Bears is the Malayan or Sun Bear *(Helarctos malayanus)*, only 4 ft. 6 in. long. It is black with yellow on the muzzle and on the chest *(below right)*.

The Baribal or American Black Bear *(Ursus americanus)*, illustrated in the top picture, is also black, with a yellow snout, and is about 6 ft. long. It inhabits North America, living in similar country to the European Brown Bear. It is a gentle creature with a fondness for fish.

The Polar Bear *(Thalarctos maritimus)* is the second largest living member of the Bear family, being up to 8 ft. long and weighing as much as 1.600 lb. Its colouring is yellowish-white. Its home is in the regions round the North Pole and on the shores of the northernmost continents. Its main food is seals, for which it lies in wait by their holes in the ice. Unfortunately, this beautiful animal, which is normally harmless to humans, has been ruthlessly slaughtered in recent years.

The bottom picture on the opposite page shows a couple of newly-born Polar Bears. For so large an animal they are surprisingly small, for each weighs only about 2 lb. The female suckles her young in a den in the snow in which gravid Polar Bears spend the worst part of the Arctic winter. Male Polar Bears do not hibernate.

The Raccoon family (Procyonidae), includes six American and two Asiatic genera. The Ringtailed Coati *(Nasua nasua)* is a semi-arboreal Raccoon-like animal about 2 ft. long, with a tail almost as long again. Its nose is extended into a sensitive, upturned proboscis. The colour of the fur is reddish-brown, paler beneath, and its tail has blackish rings. It inhabits the forests of most of South and Central America, feeding on fruit and insects, molluscs and small vertebrates.

A similar way of life, but more arboreal, is followed by the attractive Cacomistle *(Bassariscus astutus)* from the southern parts of North America, but it is a nocturnal creature which spends the daylight hours sleeping curled up in hollow trees and rock crevices. It is a far more agile climber than the Coati.

The Cacomistle, illustrated on the left, measures about 3 ft. in all, almost half being tail, which is thick, long and bushy. It serves as both rudder and parachute on the Cacomistle's acrobatic excursions in the branches of trees. Easily tamed, the Cacomistle is an amusing and friendly pet.

It was only in 1870 that an unusual animal living largely on bamboo shoots was discovered high up in the forested mountains of Tibet and China. This Giant Panda *(Ailuropoda melanoleuca)*, illustrated on the right, has a thick cream-and-black fur and is about 5 ft. 6 in. long. It is rarely seen in captivity, and then only at the world's largest zoos. It is rarely seen even in its native habitat owing to its extreme shyness. In the daytime it chiefly moves through tunnels it makes for itself in the dense tangle of mountain bamboo. It is found at altitudes of between 11,000 and 14,000 ft. above sea-level.

The Red Panda (*Ailurus fulgens*) is only about 2 ft. long, with a tail of 1 ft. 6 in. Its fur is a beautiful red colour, a shiny black on the underside and legs. There are yellowish-white markings on its head. It lives in the Himalayas, in Burma and China, in mountain forests up to about 12,000 ft. Though predominantly an arboreal creature, it frequently comes to the ground to look for bamboo shoots and hunt small vertebrates. Red Pandas live in pairs. They are more frequently to be found in the zoos than the Giant Panda.

The Raccoon *(Procyon lotor)* inhabits forests from Canada to Panama. It is some 2 ft. long, with a tail measuring about 10 in. Its fur is yellowish-grey, with individual dark brown hairs, and its head is whitish with a broad black stripe across the eyes. It lives near rivers and lakes and is an excellent climber and swimmer. It hunts at night and is well known for raiding chicken-houses and rabbit-hutches. Apart from these animals it also feeds on molluscs, cray-fish, fruit and berries, as well as other vegetable matter. It has a habit of washing its food and other objects in water with its front paws. In the north it hibernates in winter *(right)*.

The Weasel family *(Mustelidae)*, is represented in every part of the world with the exception of Australia, New Zealand and Madagascar. Its largest member is the Glutton or Wolverine *(Gulo gulo)* which attains a length of over 3 ft. including 6 in. of tail. It may weigh up to 30 lb. Its colour is dark brown, with broad yellowish bands on its face and flank. The Glutton is a native of the tundra and forests of northern Europe, Asia, and North America. It preys on a variety of animals, from lemmings to the large ungulates. Though it prefers fawns, it is said that it can kill fully-grown elks or reindeer by leaping on their backs and biting them in the jugular veins. It attacks these large animals in the water, where they are less able to defend themselves. The Glutton is expert at swimming, climbing and jumping, and is notorious for its ravenous appetite *(left)*.

503

The Ermine or Stoat (Mustela erminea) is illustrated above. The males are up to 11 in. long with a tail of about another 4 in. The females are a little smaller. Their colouring is brown with white underneath and the tip of the tail is black. In winter, however, the animal may change to white all over except for the black tail tip. Some forty-six different subspecies of this small beast of prey are said to live in various parts of Europe, right up to the far north, in North Africa, throughout central and northern Asia, and in North and South America. Its habitat is woods, farms and open country up to an altitude of nearly 10,000 ft.

It eats birds and mammals as large as hares, but its chief prey is mice. In the Middle Ages the fur of the Ermine was used for making clothes for royalty.

The Fitch or European Polecat (Mustela putorius) in the picture below is about 1 ft. 5½ in. in length, its tail measuring another 7 in. It is a shiny dark brown colour, paler on the sides, with white markings on the head. Some subspecies have been described in Europe and Asia. It hunts small mammals as well as larger birds, frogs and fish. It has highly developed glands under its tail which give off an unpleasant odour when the animal is annoyed.

The Red Panda.

South America and Mexico provide the home of the Grison (*Grison vittata*) which is illustrated in the top picture. It is a little over 1 ft. 4 in. long, its tail adding some 8 in. more. It is grey above and dark brown underneath. Unlike most of the Mustelidae, it is not a climber but keeps on the ground. It shows little fear of human beings. Its food includes various small animals and sweet fruits.

The Skunk (*Mephitis mephitis*), illustrated below, has exceptionally powerful anal glands. It is a member of the subfamily Mephitinae. Its body is about 1 ft. 4 in. long, the tail only slightly shorter. Coloured black and white, it lives on the ground in bush-covered country, especially in the vicinity of rivers and ponds, throughout North America, from Canada all the way south to Mexico. It feeds on small vertebrates and large insects. If pursued, the Skunk will usually not attempt to run away; instead, it turns its back on the

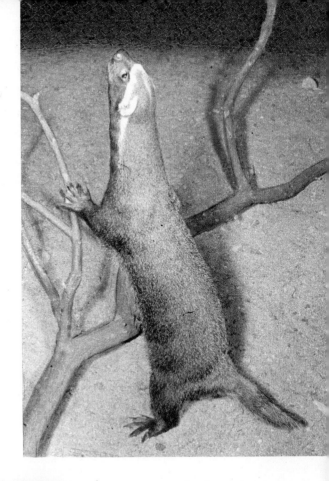

enemy, raises its tail and starts hopping up and down on the spot. When the pursuer approaches nearer, the Skunk emits the repugnant odour from its glands. It can 'hit' its target at a distance of several yards and thus more often than not save itself from its attacker. Its fur is valuable and it is bred on farms, where its glands are first removed by surgery.

The European Badger *(Meles meles)* is the largest European member of the Mustelidae family. It is some 2 ft. 6 in. long and has a tail measuring about 7 in. It may weigh up to 40 lb. Its long coarse coat is white, blackish-brown and light grey. It lives throughout Europe, with the exception of the extreme north, and in the temperate regions of Asia, ranging as far east as Japan. It inhabits forests and open woodlands, sleeping in the daytime and venturing out at night to seek its food. It eats whatever it can find, being both carnivorous and vegetarian. The sett in which it hibernates intermittently in winter is kept very clean. The American Badger *(Taxidea)* is well

known in the western United States and is similar in its habits to the European Badger.

The Pine Marten (Martes martes) is the best-known arboreal Mustelid in central Europe, with glossy brown fur, varying in shade from light to dark, and a large yellow spot on its throat. It is about 1 ft. 6 in. long with a tail of 10 in. During the day it sleeps in hollow trees, at night it hunts small vertebrates, being even more at home in the trees than the Squirrel, which is one of its favourite victims. It also eats insects and berries. It is becoming increasingly rare in its native forests in most of Europe, as well as some countries of Asia (above).

The picture below shows a young Ferret (Mustela furo). It is a domesticated breed, probably of the Russian or Steppe Polecat, which inhabits eastern Europe and the temperate regions of Asia. White all over with pink eyes, hunting Ferrets are used to drive wild rabbits out of their burrows.

The subfamily Lutrinae (Otters) includes some seven genera with many species adapted for a semi-aquatic life. They are found in suitable places all over the world except for Australia and New Zealand. Their bodies are long and streamlined, and covered with close fur. They have short limbs with webbed feet, and a muscular tail which serves as an excellent rudder.

The Otter (*Lutra*) is found in Europe, Asia, North America, and north-west Africa in a number of species and subspecies. It inhabits thickly over-grown banks of streams, in which it makes its den with an underwater entrance. The Otter's body is up to 2 ft. 6 in. and the tail is 1 ft. 4 in. – 1 ft. 7 in. long. The glossy brown coat including the chin and throat is much paler underneath. It feeds on fish, crayfish, frogs, small vertebrates and birds. Owing to the supposed damage it does to fisheries and because its fine fur is in great demand, it has been much reduced in numbers. It is now protected by law in many places.

The Family Viverridae, 'Weasel Cats', are for the most part small beasts of prey not unlike the Mustelidae, but they have certain feline characteristics. Some have partly retractile claws, a skeleton similar to that of the Cats, and slit-like pupils. They are the survivors of a primitive Carnivore family which used to live all over the world except Australia and the American continent. The Genet (*Genetta genetta*) is about 1 ft. 8 in. long, its tail being the same length. It is yellowish-grey with black markings. It is found in West, North and Central Africa and in Europe (in Spain and western France). A nocturnal animal, it climbs and jumps extremely well. It lives in open woodland or forests, hiding by day in hollow trees or among rocks.

On the left is a picture of a Genet. Its diet includes the larger birds and mammals, which it hunts like the Marten.

The Binturong (*Arctictis binturong*) is between 2 ft. 8 in. and 3 ft. long, with a tail which is almost as long. The fur is black and blackish-brown, greyish about the head. Sometimes it has a dark green tinge. Its whiskers are exceptionally long and the thick-set, compact body is reminiscent of the Bear family. It lives in the virgin forests of north-east India, ranging through to Indonesia. It spends the day sleeping in the tops of the trees. At night, guided by its sense of smell and touch, it goes in search of fruit and other vegetable food. It also hunts insects and tree frogs, robs birds' nests, and is fond of fish. Its prehensile tail helps it as it climbs about in the trees (*above*).

The Indian Mongoose (Herpestes edwardii), illustrated above, is about 3 ft. 4 in. long, almost half of this being its tail. Its coat is light grey, sometimes with a reddish tinge, and the limbs are black. It lives in India, Ceylon, Persia and Arabia, and has been introduced into many West Indian islands. Allied forms live in Europe and Africa. Extraordinarily agile, it feeds on birds, small mammals, and especially reptiles. It can fight and kill even the most venomous snakes.

The rocky and sandy regions of South-west Africa are the home of interesting animals about 1 ft. 3 in. long and with a tail of some 10 in. Their colour is greyish-brown with dark bands across the back. They live in colonies in burrows and are in the habit of sitting upon their hind quarters like Sousliks or Hares. They are called Meercats (Suricata suricata). Their diet includes small vertebrates and insects, and they are frequently kept as domestic animals (illustrated below).

The Hyenas (Hyaenidae), are scavengers and carrion feeders devouring dead animals before they begin to decompose. With their massive teeth and powerful jaws they can crack and crush even the heavy bones of game animals. The Aard Wolf *(Proteles cristata)* from South Africa, illustrated in the top picture, is an exception, having tiny teeth and weak jaws. It is smaller than the true Hyenas, being only about 2 ft. 8 in. long. It is a light yellow in colour with black stripes on the sides, and has a mane of long, bristly hair on its back. The ears are relatively large. The Aard Wolf digs extensive underground lairs which several of them share during the day. At night it hunts for insects, especially termites. Occasionally it will also eat carrion or the young of various mammals and birds.

The Striped Hyena *(Hyaena hyaena)* belongs to the subfamily of True Hyenas – Hyaeninae. It is about 3 ft. 4 in. long with a tail some 1 ft. 4 in. The coat is yellowish-grey, with black stripes running vertically on the back and horizontally on the legs. All Hyenas have shorter hind legs than the fore legs, so that they give the impression of squatting on their haunches. The Striped Hyena has a sparse mane and extremely powerful teeth. It lives in small packs mainly in the unforested parts of North and East Africa, extending as far as Abyssinia. It is also common in southern Arabia, Asia Minor, Afghanistan and parts of India. In the wild state it is a shy and non-aggressive animal which feeds on carrion. It travels in packs at night.

The Cat family (Felidae) are considered to be the most highly developed of the flesh-eaters. Their senses of hearing and sight are particularly acute; their peculiar lightness and elegance of movement, their agility, their ability to see in dim light, their retractile claws, and in most cases beautiful colouring – all these have earned them a leading place among mammals.

The Cheetah or Hunting Leopard *(Acinonyx jubatus)* has certain characteristics which distinguish it from the rest of the Cat family: it has only partly retractile claws, long legs, and altogether is built more like a greyhound. It is also the only big Cat which, when in a good mood, purrs like the smaller species. The Cheetah is about 4 ft. 6 in. in length, with a tail of some 2 ft. 4 in. Its colouring is greyish-brown, varying from grey to reddish, dotted with numerous small black spots, these variations in colour distinguishing the different subspecies. The underside of its body is white and it has black and brown round spots. A black stripe runs from each eye to the corners of the mouth. The Cheetah, the swiftest animal on foot, runs down its prey (it has been clocked at a speed of 75 miles per hour) and seizes it by a sudden, open attack. It inhabits Africa south of the Sahara, parts of western India, Afghanistan, Baluchistan, Arabia, and Turkmenia. Living in open steppe and savannah, it hunts mainly the smaller kinds of antelope. In captivity it will become very tame, but it does not breed and will not live to any great age.

The Wild Cat *(Felis silvestris)*, shown on the right, has many different subspecies throughout Europe and Asia, except for the tropical rain forests. In Europe, it has been exterminated in many countries, surviving only in some of the large tracks of forest. It is very much like the domestic Cat, though stronger and having a broader tail. Under the chin and on the underside of its body it is buff, and it has a round black spot on the soles of its feet. Its coat is yellowish-grey, with dark bands and spots. The Wild Cat is up to 2 ft. 1 in. long, with a relatively short tail of not more than 1 ft. 3 in. It feeds on small animals.

The Puma, or Mountain Lion *(Felis concolor)* is illustrated below left. It is up to 7 ft. 1 in. long, the tail measuring 2 ft. 6 in. It is found more or less throughout North and South America, where some thirty subspecies have been described, differing from one another mainly in their colouring, which varies from grey and brown to reddish. The Puma hunts all kinds of animals up to the size of sheep, but deer are its main source of food.

Bottom right is a picture of the Pallas's Cat or Manul *(Felis [Otocolobus] manul)*, a cat up to 1 ft. 9 in. long with a very broad tail measuring as much as 10 in. It has long, pale greyish-yellow fur and round pupils. It lives chiefly in the mountain steppes of China and Mongolia.

The Jaguar *(Felis [Jaguarius] onca)* from the lowland forests of the southern U.S.A. through to South America is seen on the left. It measures up to 5 ft. 10 in., its tail being some 2 ft. 1 in. It preys on animals up to the size of tapirs.

Above is the Snow Leopard or Ounce *(Felis [Uncia] uncia)*. Up to 3 ft. 9 in. long, with a tail of 3 ft., it is a pale greyish-yellow in colour, white underneath and spotted black all over. It inhabits the high mountains from the Altai to the Himalayas.

The European Lynx *(Felis [Lynx] lynx)* can be seen below. It still survives in some countries of northern Europe, in the Carpathians, the Balkans, and eastwards as far as China. A similar species is found in the New World. It is about 3 ft. 1 in. in length, with a short tail of only about 5 in. The tips of its ears are typically tufted. It preys on various animals up to the size of deer, but mostly on the smaller species including mice. The Canadian Lynx *(Felis [Lynx] canadensis)*, is widely distributed in the northern forests, while the Bay Lynx *(Felis [Lynx] rufus)* is common throughout the United States.

The Leopard or Panther *(Felis [Panthera] pardus)*, shown on the left, measures 4 to 5 ft. long and has a tail of up to 3 ft. Many subspecies have been described from Africa, Asia, India, the Sunda islands, China, Korea and Manchuria. It preys on birds, lizards and various mammals up to the size of a donkey. As a general rule its victims are antelopes and monkeys, but it is especially fond of domestic dogs. It usually avoids human beings.

The Ocelot *(Felis [Leopardus] pardalis)*, pictured above, is up to 3 ft. 4 in. in length, with a tail of about 1 ft. 4 in. Its colouring is very attractive, a tawny reddish-yellow with dark markings. Its eyes are bluish-grey. A number of subspecies are found in Central and South America and its range extends as far north as Texas in the U.S. It is chiefly a forest animal, hunting every kind of vertebrate up to the size of young pigs.

The Serval *(Felis [Leptailurus] serval)*, illustrated on the right, is buff with clear black spots. It is about 2 ft. 6 in. long and with a tail measuring some 1 ft. 3 in. It has large, erect ears and it lives in the open woodlands and mountains of Central and South Africa. It hunts small animals including mice, small birds and the larger insects. Like most Cats, it can become very tame in captivity.

The Lion *(Felis [Leo] leo)* is one of the largest among the Cats, some males reaching a length of 6 ft. 6 in., with a tail of 3 ft. In adults the coat is a sandy yellow or reddish-yellow. The mane of the males, when developed, is often much darker.

Many subspecies of Lion once roamed throughout Africa, Asia, and even in Europe. In Africa they have been exterminated north of the Sahara, and none survive in the extreme south. They survive only in the grassy plain and sparsely forested lowlands and hills of East, Central and West Africa, as far south as the Orange River. In India they remain only in the Kathiawar reserve northwest of Bombay, where a few dozen are carefully protected. Lions prey on ungulates up to the size of giraffes though they usually kill smaller animals. They will not attack adult elephants, rhinoceroses, African buffalo, and fully grown gorillas. In places where they are not persecuted they show little fear of man *(above*, a Lioness, *below*, a male Lion).

Head of a fully-grown Sumatra tiger.

The Jungle Cat (Felis chaus), above left, is up to 2 ft. 4 in. long, with a black-ringed tail measuring about 10 in. Its fur is greyish-brown, sometimes with faint stripes. It inhabits Egypt and Asia Minor as far as the Caucasus, ranging as far southeast as India and Ceylon. It hunts rodents and birds in marshes and cornfields.

Below is the African Golden Cat (Felis [Profelis] aurata) a slim Cat about 2 ft. 6 in. in length, with a small head and a tail of some 1 ft. 4 in. Its colouring varies greatly. It is most frequently a reddish-brown and pale underneath but it may be greyish, and the coat is often heavily spotted. It lives in the forests of equatorial Africa, feeding on birds and small rodents.

Top right is a well-known breed of the Domestic Cat (Felis domestica), the Siamese Cat. It has a light-coloured, close fur, a black-brown face and limbs. The tail is often kinked. Its eyes are blue.

The Tiger *(Felis tigris)* is the largest feline. Its size varies in the eleven or so existing subspecies, the smallest being the Sumatra Tiger *(Felis tigris sumatrae)*, illustrated above, which is about 5 ft. long with a tail of $2\frac{1}{2}$ ft. This Tiger weighs about 250 lb. The largest of the Tigers is the most northerly subspecies, the Siberian Tiger *(Felis tigris longipilis)*. It is said to reach a maximum length of 9 ft., with a tail of up to 3 ft. 8 in., and it weighs as much as 650 lb. In historical times Tigers were still living over a wide area from the eastern shores of the Black Sea through Asia as far as the Pacific. In the north they reached 50° N. latitude. Today the Tiger is found in the entire Indian region, in Mongolia, China, Korea, Manchuria, eastern Siberia, and south of the Caspian Sea; a few still survive in northern Iran, and occasionally a Tiger appears in Tadzhikistan, probably having come via Afghanistan from Pakistan.

The order Cetacea includes Whales, Dolphins and Porpoises, warm-blooded mammals that breathe air but never come ashore, even to breed. The Cetaceans are streamlined for speed and propelled by flukes. They have no external ear, no trace of external hind limbs, nostrils open in a blowhole on top of the head, and there is no connection between mouth and nose. Beyond the embryonic stage they do not have a covering of hair — thick blubber conserves body heat and body fluids. The order Cetacea consists of two suborders; one, the Odontoceti or toothed Whales, includes the mighty Sperm Whale *(Physeter)*, the source of ambergris. Also included are Dolphus Porpoises and the Narwhal *(Monodon)*, that has a single spirally twisted ivory 'tooth' on top of its nose. The Common Dolphin *(Delphinus delphis)* is illustrated on this page.

The suborder Mysticeti includes the whale-bone Whales, with two rows of horny blades hanging from the sides of the upper jaw. Cetaceans, which occur in all seas, oceans and larger rivers, are carnivorous and include not only the largest mammals but also the largest creatures that have ever lived – the average length of the great Blue Whale is 100 ft. and it weighs many tons. Large Whales consume about a ton of food daily, with a throat no bigger than a man's fist, except the Sperm Whale which can swallow a man. Feared by all warm-blooded marine life, the Killer Whale (Grampus) is found in all seas. Recognised by its very tall dorsal fin it reaches 30 ft., and the powerful jaws have 40 pointed teeth. It often hunts in a pack (above). Below, rising from an icehole.

Seals, sea-lions and Walruses, suborder Pinnipedia: the Aquatic Carnivora include some 30 species, divided into 16 genera and 3 families. Pinnipeds breed ashore.

Eared Seals, Sea-Lions and Fur Seals, family Otarii-dae, are more at home on land than the True Seal, and the hind limbs are capable of rotation forward.

The top picture shows the Cape Sea-Lion (Arcto-ephalus pusillus) from the coast of South Africa and adjacent islands. This species lives in the open sea and comes ashore in large numbers only in the breeding season. The Alaska Fur Seal (Callorhinus alascanus) visits the Pribilof Islands once a year to breed.

The True Seals (family Phocidae) are distinguished from the Sea-Lions by having no external ears. The Common Seal (Phoca vitulina), lower illus-tration, is up to $6\frac{1}{2}$ ft. in length and weighs about 2 cwt. It is greyish-yellow with brown and black spots. Its distribution takes in the North Atlantic coast, from Greenland to Portugal, and the entire coastal area of Asia and the Pacific along the length of North America and Mexico. It feeds on fish, molluscs and crabs.

Seals are very fast swimmers, so that when we watch them under water we do not see the movement of their limbs, and their torpedo-shaped bodies seem to dart through the water like arrows. Propulsion is centred in the turbine-like action of the hind flippers. On the left is a Common Seal swimming.

The picture above shows a young male Northern Elephant Seal or Sea Elephant *(Mirounga angustirostris)*. Adult males have snouts elongated into a down-turned proboscis about 1 ft. 4 in. long. The animal measures as much as 18 ft. and weighs over 3 tons. Sea Elephants spend about three months of the year on the shore, and the rest in the sea. Their chief food is octopuses and other cephalopods, and fish. These curious and interesting creatures, which are completely defenceless

and trusting when on dry land, survive only on Guadelupe Island off California, and on the western coast of Mexico, where they are protected by law. The ruthless slaughter of thousands of these and other Seals in past centuries for their skin and blubber or simply for fun, is one of man's most shameful acts.

The Walrus *(Odobenus)* can always be recognised by the pair of long white ivory tusks. It is at home on the Arctic floating ice. For all its crude, wrinkled, almost naked hide, the Walrus is a majestic creature, 10 or 12 ft. long and weighing between two and three thousand lb. The Walrus lives a community life; bulls, cows and calves live together and feed on shellfish dug from the ocean floor by means of their ivory tusks.

The Patagonian Sea-lion (Otaria) byronia) is a yellowish-brown giant covered with fairly long fur. The male attains a length of nearly 10 ft. and may weigh over a ton. Old males have a mane on their necks. This animal gives a resounding bellow, both in the wild state and in the zoo. Its home is around the south-western coast of South America, as far north as Peru, and south through Patagonia and Tierra del Fuego to the Antarctic. In the breeding season they come ashore in large herds, the females give birth to their young and are at once fertilised again. They

live in the sea and feed on cephalopods and other molluscs and fish. The top left picture shows an adult male.

The Hyraxes, order Hyracoidea, is the 'Coney' of the Scriptures. Three genera, nine species make up the family Procaviidae. Literally ungulates, these small creatures resemble tailless rodents, whose anatomical, physiological and ecological features seem to suggest relationship with the rhinoceros. Bottom left is the Syrian Hyrax (*Procavia syriaca*), which is up to 1 ft. 4 in. long, greyish-brown in colour, with hardly any tail. It inhabits the rocky regions of Syria and Palestine, living in colonies. It climbs even the steepest rock faces with absolute safety and can jump considerable distances. The soles of the feet are covered with bare, wrinkled pads which enable it to hold on to the smallest crevices in the rock The Hyrax – or Coney as it is popularly known – lives on berries, plants and lichens.

Elephants, order Proboscidea, are the largest and most powerful mammals in the world today. Anyone seeing an Elephant for the first time cannot help feeling that this is a creature from another age. That is, in fact, the truth, because their ancestors were already in existence early in the Tertiary period which began over fifty million years ago. From dozens of genera and many species in the family Elephantidae only two genera of Elephant survive today. A third, the Mammoth, became extinct when there was already human life on the Earth, man having perhaps played a considerable role in its extermination.

The Indian Elephant (*Elephas maximus*) is still found in the wild state in the damp forests of India, Ceylon, Burma, Thailand, Vietnam, and Sumatra. Elephants are not indigenous to Borneo. Adult males may be over 10 ft. long and up to $10^1/_2$ ft. tall. Their tails measure up to 5 ft. and their trunks $7^1/_2$ ft. The weight of these huge beasts is 4 to 5 tons. Elephants live on vegetable food, put into the mouth with their trunks. They live to about the same age as man. Wild Elephants are caught with the aid of tame decoys and are trained for various jobs requiring great strength.

The African Elephant *(Loxodonta africana)* has longer legs and is thus still larger than the Indian species. Old males of the original savannah form stand over 11 ft. at the shoulder, their tusks also reaching this length. The African species can readily be distinguished from the Indian by its much larger ears, which are a different shape, and the absence of the two rounded bosses on the forehead. The African Elephant once inhabited almost all the forests of Africa; today perhaps 200,000 of these animals remain in an area between 12° N. and 20° S. They live in savannahs and forests, one related species inhabiting the high forests. They are exclusively vegetarian, breaking off and stripping branches, tearing up bushes and clumps of grass, juicy shoots and wild fruits. They also eat bananas and other farm crops, frequently destroying more than they consume. The African Elephant, too, can be trained and used for work.

Most closely related to the Elephants, the Sirens, order Sirenia, have a restricted habitat — the shallow waters of bogs, harbours, estuaries and larger rivers. They can neither crawl up on dry land nor venture away from shore waters to the high seas where they would be devoured by sharks and killer whales. These strange, rather grotesque, almost formless creatures have a rounded body narrowed at both ends, no hind limbs, paddle-like fore limbs and a broad flat tail for propul-

sion in the water. The Manatee *(Trichechus)* is the best known and will reach a length of 7 ft. in Florida waters and weigh 300 or 400 lb. The Manatees occur in the warmer waters on both sides of the Atlantic Ocean. The Dugong or Halicore Dugong is found in the Australian waters, Indian Ocean and Red Sea. It may reach a length of 9 ft. The Sea Cow *(Hydrodamalis)* was a third member of the Sirenians but it was exterminated two hundred years ago. This remarkable creature reached a length of 30 ft. and weighed up to 4 tons. The Sirenians or Sirens are inoffensive creatures and feed on seaweed and sea grasses. Feeding, they stay down 15 minutes but can remain underwater for half an hour. They follow a process similar to the Elephants of tooth replacement. As the teeth wear down, the foremost and badly worn teeth are pushed out and a new tooth comes into place at the back of each row and starts on its journey forward until there is a full complement.

Odd-toed Ungulates, order Perissodactyla, are a fast disappearing group. Only the Horses, Tapirs, and Rhinoceroses are still in existence today. Only six genera survive of the 159 which existed in earlier times, mainly during the Tertiary. The present family of Horses (Equidae), with a single hoof on each foot, developed gradually from five-digit small animals such as the Dawn Horse which lived in the Eocene forests.

The Mountain Zebra *(Equus zebra)* is a rare species, and comparatively few specimens survive. The variety in the picture above (Hartmann's Zebra) is slightly more numerous, but even this is now considered to be in danger of extinction. The species is recognisable by the dewlap under its throat and especially by the characteristic arrangement of stripes on the withers in the form of a gridiron. It is only 4 ft. 2 in. high and lives in the mountainous western part of South Africa, in the Damara region. Like all Horses, the Zebras are vegetarian.

Largest of the Zebras is the Grevy Zebra (*Equus greyvi*) which stands up to 5 ft. at the shoulder. It has numerous narrow stripes and erect 'donkey's' ears, heavily haired. Of the Zebras it is the most amenable to taming and can be used as a draught animal or to carry burdens. It inhabits Abyssinia, southern Sudan, East Africa, and Somaliland, thus ranging the farthest north of all Zebras. It prefers hilly country, where it lives in small herds.

Above is the most numerous Zebra, the East African Zebra (Equus burchelii böhmi). It is beautifully striped black-and-white without the brown (shadow) stripes in between. Above its black mouth there is a brown spot. It lives in large herds together with antelopes and other ungulates in the East Africa Highlands.

The Kulan, Wild Ass, Onager and Kiang (Equus hemionus) stand about 4 ft. at the shoulder. The colour of the Wild Ass is a light yellowish-brown, white on the underside. The mane, tail and the stripe along its back are blackish-brown. The Mongolian Wild Ass lives in small herds in the vast steppes and mountains of Mongolian Kirgizia. Other varieties of the Wild Ass inhabit Iran, Afghanistan, Turkestan, Nepal, Sikkim, and Tibet where they are to be found up to a height of 16,000 ft. (below).

Several varieties of Eurasian Wild Horses lived over a wide area from eastern Asia to western Europe. Only one wild species has survived until modern times, since when one has entirely disappeared and the other two are artificially preserved in the last natural reserves and in zoological gardens. Top left is a herd of the Mongolian Wild Horse or Przewalsky Horse (Equus caballus przewalskii). This Horse stands between 4 ft. and 4 ft. 6 in. at the shoulder. In summer it is coloured a reddish-brown, in winter a lighter greyish-brown, the coat then also being longer. There is a dark 'donkey' stripe along its back, the legs are sometimes partly striped. The head above the nose is convex in shape. According to the most recent reports, there are now some forty specimens of this Horse living in the Dzhungara steppe on the borders of Mongolia and China, at an altitude of 3,000 to 4,500 ft.

The picture at the bottom of p. 534 is of a herd of Horses descended from the extinct Tarpan or European Wild Horse (Equus caballus gmelini). This was a European forest variety of the steppe Wild Horse. Its colouring was mousy grey, the legs were dark and striped, there was a dark stripe on its back, and it had an erect mane. This species of Horse survived longest in the steppes along the River Dnieper and in Poland. As a result of cross-breeding with the local domestic Horses it gave these many of its own characteristics. The last mare was killed by peasants in 1876. In recent years successful attempts have been made, through 'back-breeding', to produce a strain of Horse similar to the original.

Some five thousand years ago Wild Horses were domesticated in Europe and Asia. These were later introduced to America and Australia, where no Horses had lived in recent times. Over the centuries numerous domestic breeds have evolved in various countries, differing considerably in both appearance and quantities. Today they fall into six large groups, from one of which – the strong riding and draught Horse – stems the beautiful Lippizaner, a popular thoroughbred (top right).

Many different breeds of the Domestic Ass (Equus asinus) are found through most of the warmer parts of the globe. It is most probably descended from the Nubian Ass (Equus asinus africanus) and it would seem that it was domesticated even earlier than the Horse. Nowadays Donkeys are used in the Orient for riding and as draught animals, as well as to carry loads.

When a stallion is crossed with a she-Donkey the offspring is called a Minny. This is about the size of a Donkey, which it more closely resembles. Its ears, however, are shorter. When a Donkey is crossed with a mare the offspring is a Mule. Far larger than a Donkey, the Mule has long ears, slim legs, and is usually dark in colour like a Horse. The picture above shows a pair of Mules.

The Tapirs, family Tapiridae, are the second family of Odd-toed Ungulates. Though somewhat like pigs in appearance, they are in no way related to them. Their nose is extended into a short movable trunk. In the Tertiary era many species of Tapirs lived in various parts of the world, even in places where they are completely unknown now, such as North America, Europe and Asia. Today, only one species is found in Malaya and Indonesia, and three in Central and South America. The American Tapir *(Tapirus terrestris)* is nearly 3 ft. 4 in. high and some 6 ft. 8 in. long. It is a nocturnal animal, with a short, sparse coat which is brownish-grey in colour. It lives in damp forests in the north-eastern parts of South America, feeding on fruit and twigs. It is hunted by jaguars and pumas and by man. If caught young, it can easily be tamed and will be friendly and docile.

The Rhinocerotidae, the Rhinoceroses, are the last surviving members of a dying family. Of the species recorded, twenty-one have already become extinct, while the days of the remaining five are likewise numbered; only constant protection can save the Rhinoceros from complete extermination. Of these five species still living the most numerous is the so-called Black Rhinoceros *(Diceros bicornis)*, found today in certain parts of Central and East Africa. It is up to 11 ft. in length with a tail about 2 ft. long, and it may stand over 5 ft. at the shoulder. Its bare skin is a light brownish-grey, but it takes on various shades according to the mud or dust in which it has wallowed. It has two horns, one behind the other, the first of which may measure over 4 ft., though this is rare. The Black Rhinoceros lives in the open plain and in orchard bush. It eats leaves and twigs which it plucks with its prehensile upper lip, or on the roots and tubers which it digs out of the ground. It is predominantly nocturnal in habit, having poor eyesight but an excellent sense of smell. It rarely attacks man unless taken by surprise or wounded. Other Rhinoceroses are found in southern Asia, and the White Rhinoceros *(Ceratotherium)* is the largest, standing over 6 ft. at the shoulder and weighing up to four tons.

Even-toed Ungulates, order Artiodactyla, are the hoofed animals that have the toes even paired and include the Pig, Antelope, Deer, Camels, Sheep, Goats and Hippopotamus. The Pig family (Suidae) includes the Wart Hog (*Phacochoerus aethiopicus*), undoubtedly the most bizarre of the wild Pigs and larger and sturdier than the less grotesque Wild Boar. It is usually about 4 ft. 7 in. long and about 2 ft. 4 in. high. Its colour is greyish. It has large wart-like protuberances on its head and huge tusks. On its head and along the back there is a long, straggly mane. It inhabits much of Africa south of the Sahara, keeping mainly in the vicinity of water in open plains or woodland country. It digs deep holes in the ground which are a nuisance to travellers.

The Wild Boar *(Sus scrofa)* includes many subspecies living in Europe, northern Asia and North Africa. It has been introduced by man and reverted to the wild state in islands of the Malay Archipelago, in Australia, the West Indies and South America. The central European Wild Boar *(Sus scrofa scrofa)* inhabits the forests and unpopulated thicket country in central and southern Europe, where it is regarded as game *(left)*. An old boar is up to 5 ft. long and stands 3 ft. at the shoulder, in which case it will weigh anything up to 3 and even 4 cwt. The coarse bristles with which its body is covered vary in colour from blackish-brown to a light yellowish-grey. The Wild Boar is omnivorous, and wounded boars or sows guarding their young may be dangerous to man. The Wild Boar is the ancestor of the Domestic Pig *(Sus domestica)*.

The Peccaries, family Tayassuidae, are the American

counter species of Old World Pigs. Their range extends from the southern United States to Patagonia. There are two species, the Collared Peccary (*Tayassu tajacu*), and the White-lipped Peccary (*Tayassu peccari*).

The Hippopotamuses, family Hippopotamidae, today consist of only two species, both of which live in Africa. In prehistoric times Hippopotamuses also lived in Europe. The Hippopotamus (*Hippopotamus amphibius*) may be 13 ft. in length, with a height of 5 ft. and a weight of 2 to 3 tons. The colour of its thick, bare skin varies a great deal, from light reddish-pink to brown and greyish-blue. Hippopotamuses live in herds in the swamps, rivers and lakes of central Africa, chiefly in the inaccessible interior, and in reserves. They are vegetarians, coming out of the water at night to wander far in the search for food. The rest of the time they spend either in the water or on the low islands. If attacked or wounded a Hippopotamus will defend itself fearlessly and can inflict fatal wounds on human beings with its huge teeth, but where it is not persecuted it is mild and inoffensive. Pictured above and bottom left is a seven-year-old female Hippopotamus with a month-old baby in the Warsaw Zoo.

This is the Pigmy Hippopotamus (*Choeropsis liberiensis*) which is only 5 ft. long and 2 ft. 6 in. high, weighing at most 550 lb. *(left)*.

The suborder Tylopoda is a group of Camel-like animals in which the survivors are surprisingly few; two genera and not more than six species. Once widely distributed over the world, except the Australian region, the only truly wild forms are found in South America. Camels and Llamas are placed in a division of Tylopoda, family Camelidae. They have resilient, cushion-like soles for walking on sand or stones. The illustration underneath shows two Bactrian Camels

A small Hippopotamus living largely on dry land and feeding on shoots and other forest vegetation inhabits Sierra Leone, Liberia, Guinea and Nigeria.

(*Camelus bactrianus*) – animals up to 9 ft. long, and about $8\frac{1}{2}$ ft. at the shoulder. In the wild state they have short brown fur and small humps

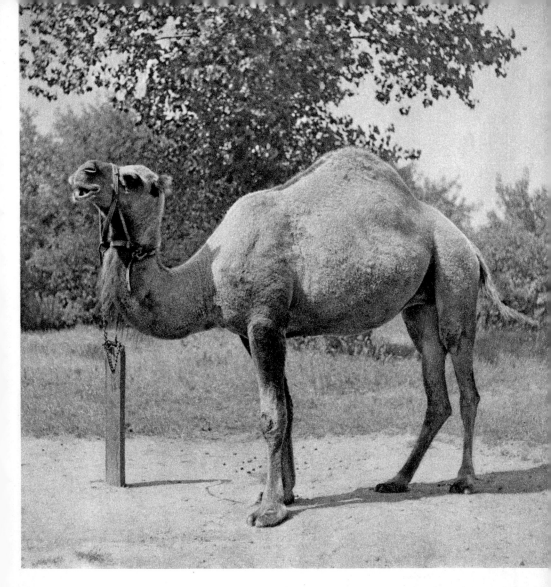

with clusters of hair on top. Domesticated forms have huge humps and, in winter, a long mane. Feral Camels are to be found living wild in the deserts of Mongolia and China, at altitudes between 4,500 and 6,500 ft. During the summer these animals graze on the vegetation of the Gobi Desert, moving to the shelter of the mountains for the winter. Bactrian Camels are used in the Orient as beasts of burden, carrying loads of up to 500 lb. on journeys as long as 20 miles a day.

The Arabian or One-humped Camel (*Camelus dromedarius*) stands perhaps a little shorter. Its coat is short and sandy brown in colour, though it is sometimes white or almost black. These Camels are known only as domestic animals. They are bred in North Africa, Arabia and eastwards as far as India, and have also been introduced into parts of southern Europe, America and Australia. A riding Camel can cover as much as 80 miles in a single day *(above)*.

The Llamas are the Camels of the New World. They are smaller and have no hump. In prehistoric times there were many members of the Camelidae family living all over the American continent, particularly in North America. Today they are restricted to the mountain plateaux in parts of the Andes in South America, mostly between 13,000 and 16,000 ft. above sea-level.

The Guanaco (*Lama guanacos*) inhabits the mountains of southern Peru and Chile, as well as the mountain plateaux of Patagonia. The Guanaco is about 7 ft. 6 in. in total length with a height of 3 ft. 9 in. Its colouring is reddish-brown, much paler beneath. All Llamas are extremely shy and possess exceptionally good eyesight and hearing.

Fawn of a Red Deer *(Cervus elaphus bactrianus)*. Photographed near the Amu Darja in Tadjikistan.

The Llama (*Lama glama*) is a tame, domesticated form of the Guanaco, sturdier and as much as 4 ft. 2 in. at the shoulder. Its fur is white, black, reddish-brown, and various combinations of these. The picture below shows the head of a domesticated Llama. On the mountain plateaux of Bolivia, Peru and other South American countries, Llamas are indispensable as beasts of burden.

The Alpaca (*Lama pacos*) is a domesticated form of another wild Llama, with a similar habitat to the Guanaco. The tame Alpaca stands about 3 ft. 8 in. at the shoulder. It has a fine, long coat which varies in colour, mostly white or black-and-white. Its meat is considered very good eating (*left*).

The Vicuna (*Lama vicugna*), a wild species, lives at excessively high altitudes in Peru, Bolivia and Chile. It is the smallest of the Llamas and was prized by the Incas for its soft fur.

545

The suborder Ruminantia comprises Ungulates which 'chew the cud', their stomachs being composed of three or four compartments. The partially chewed food is returned to the mouth to be more thoroughly masticatêd, and only then is it properly digested with the aid of bacteria.

The Deer family (Cervidae), consists of even-toed Ungulates with solid antlers that are shed every year in the winter and replaced by autumn. The Deer are concentrated in the Northern Hemisphere but range into South America and North Africa. Best known of the tribe is the Red Deer *(Cervus elaphus)*. There are many subspecies inhabiting forests in various parts of Europe, north-west Africa and Asia Minor, as well as the mountains and marshes of western and central Asia. The Wapiti, or American Elk *(Cervus canadensis)* is the New World representative. It was originally found through North America down to the northern frontiers of Mexico. The central European species, illustrated on the left, is up to about 6 ft. 8 in. long and nearly 5 ft. high at the shoulder. Its coat is reddish-brown in summer and greyish-brown in winter.

The Altai-Wapiti *(Cervus elaphus sibiricus)* known in Asia as the Maral, lives in the forests of the Altai mountain range, Tien-Shen and western Mongolia. It is yellowish in colour and has huge antlers which, however, do not usually form the so-called crown – i.e. are not branched at the ends of the tines, as is invariably the case with healthy European Deer. The Deer at top right is in velvet.

Bottom right is shown the head of a Milu or Père David's Deer *(Elabhurus davidianus)*. It is up to 4 ft. 4 in. high and 7 ft. 4 in. long, differing from all other Deer by having a long tail and unusual antlers forming long forks with no brow tine. Its original home was in northern China, Manchuria and Japan, but by 1865, when it was first described, it was no longer a wild animal but lived in the Emperor's walled hunting park. Today it is kept mainly in zoological gardens and on one estate in England (Woburn Park). It lived in swamps and fed chiefly on aquatic plants.

The Axis Deer *(Axis axis)* is a native of the temperate and southern regions of India and Ceylon. It has thin antlers bent back sharply, and is about 5 ft. long and less than 3 ft. 4 in. high at the shoulder. Its coat is always spotted, like that of the fawns of other species. Unlike the majority of other Deer, it is a diurnal creature *(left)*. Several different races of the Sika *(Cervus nippon)* live in southern China, Japan, Korea, Manchuria and the Amur region. It is up to 5 ft. long and 2 ft. 11 in. high. In summer its colouring is chestnut-brown with white spots arranged in lines, in winter it changes to a dark greyish-brown. On its rump it has a large white, black-bordered 'mirror'. In the U.S.S.R. it is kept in large numbers for its antlers, which are cut off before they are fully grown and are used to make a special preparation.

In various parts of the world there are numerous kinds of small Deer. One of these is the Barking Deer or Muntjac *(Muntiacus muntjac)*, a reddish-brown, smooth-coated animal about the size of a small Roe Deer, standing about 1 ft. 10 in. In the western United States the White-tailed Deer *(Odocoileus virginianus)* is the common species; it is easily recognised by its rather long, bushy tail, conspicuously white on the underside. The Mule Deer *(Odocoileus hemionus)*, of western North America, was so named because of its long, mule-like ears. The upper canine teeth of the males project and can serve as weapons. The Muntjac is a very active animal with a strong barking voice. In the wild state it lives on leaves, but in captivity it will eagerly devour large chunks of raw or cooked meat.

The picture at the bottom of p. 550 is of a group of Fallow Deer *(Dama dama)*. These lived originally in the Mediterranean region, including North Africa, Asia Minor and Persia. Later the species was introduced into other countries and it survived only as protected game. It is up to 5 ft. long and up to 3 ft. high at the shoulder. Its summer coat is reddish-brown with whitish spots, changing in winter to a dark greyish-brown, the spots being then almost indiscernible, but there are many colour varieties. The antlers are beautifully palmated.

Above is a group of Roe Deer *(Capreolus capreolus)*. It is up to 3 ft. 9 in. long, with no obvious tail, and $2\frac{1}{2}$ ft. high. There are never more than three tines on each antler. In summer the Roe Deer is reddish-brown, in winter greyish-brown; only the young fawns are spotted. It lives in forests throughout the greater part of Europe and adjacent parts of Asia, and is protected in many areas.

The largest living member of the Deer family is the European Elk, better known in America as the Moose (*Alces alces*). There are three distinct types, inhabiting north-eastern Europe, northern Asia and North America respectively. The Elk measures up to 9 ft. in length and 7½ ft. in height, such large specimens weighing about half a ton. Its antlers are either palmated, as much as 5 ft. 4 in. across, or smaller with a maximum of fifteen tines on each side and a weight of up to 60 lb. The Elk once lived over much of Europe but has been largely exterminated. Today it is again slowly extending its range from the region where it is protected and allowed to breed. It seeks out swamps and marshes, living chiefly on willows, the bark of trees, branches, reeds and aquatic plants.

The Caribou or domesticated Reindeer *(Rangifer)* is the most northern Deer, inhabiting the tundras and mountains of the Arctic region of Europe, Asia and America. In the Ice Age it was common throughout Europe. A number of different forms are recognised, differing among other things in size. It is usually up to 6 ft. 3 in. long, 3 ft. 7 in. at the shoulder, the tail a mere 6 in. The average weight is 300 lb. The Caribou is unique among the Deer family in that both sexes carry antlers. Though as a rule they are lighter, the antlers of adult females may become as strong as those of the males. Even today in Scandinavia, under inhospitable Arctic conditions, some people, especially Laplanders, depend on the Reindeer for their very existence.

The Giraffes and Okapis family, Giraffidae, whose ancestors once ranged over Europe and Asia, are now restricted to Africa. Giraffes are the tallest of all living mammals, achieving a height of up to 19 ft., 10 ft. at the shoulder. They have disproportionately long legs and neck, their body being under 7½ ft. long. The 30-in. tail has a tassel of hair at its tip. It weighs up to half a ton. There are variations in colour, the basic colour usually being a light yellowish-brown with large, dark brown spots more or less regularly distributed over the body. The short horns vary in number between two and four or even five, according to the type. In contrast to members of the Deer family, the Giraffe does not shed its horns. Today we include all but one of the types of Giraffe in a single species – *Giraffa camelopardalis*. The picture on the left is of a Masai Giraffe (*Giraffa camelopardalis tippelskirchi*). Above is the northern form, a native of Nubia and western Abyssinia – *Giraffa camelopardalis camelopardalis* – which has smaller, rectangular markings. Giraffes live in small herds in savannah and bush country, their diet consisting of the branches and leaves of acacia and other trees, plucked with their long, prehensile tongues. The female gives birth to a single young once every two years. The Giraffe can defend itself effectively with its front hoofs. The Reticulated Giraffe (*Giraffa reticulata*) is the most handsome variety.

The Bovidae, Hollow-horned Ungulates, the largest family among the Odd-toed Ungulates, include over fifty genera and about two hundred species varying widely in size, all of them exclusively vegetarian. They have permanent hollow horns which fit in bony cores. They can be roughly divided into Cattle, Antelopes, Sheep and Goats. Although some of the Antelopes are fairly large, they differ much more in their appearance than do the Cattle. The top picture on the opposite page

blackish-brown, the hind limbs black. The Nilgai lives in smallish herds in the tropical forests of India and eastern Bengal, generally near water.

Domestic Oxen were developed from the Wild Ox, Aurochs or Urus (Bos taurus primigenius) which was a native of Europe and did not become extinct until historical times. In the East various forms known as Zebu have evolved from the Indian Wild Cattle (Bos indicus). The Zebu is characterised

shows a Nilgai (Boselaphus tragocamelus). While some would consider it one of the Cattle, the slim legs, small head and thin horns of the males indicate that, in spite of its size ($7\frac{1}{2}$ ft. long, up to $4\frac{1}{2}$ ft. at the shoulder, and a tail of 1 ft. 8 in.), it should be and in fact is included among the Antelopes. The male's coat is dark grey with white marking on the legs, throat, head and the underside of the body. Its fore limbs are

by its long, erect horns, fatty hump and large dewlap. The colour varies, being most frequently greyish-yellow (illustrated above).

One African savannah form of the Zebu is the Anhole or Watussi Ox, bred by tribes in Uganda and Ruanda. It is usually brown in colour and has extraordinarily long spreading horns which are only slightly curved. Each horn may measure up to 5 ft. (lower picture on opposite page).

On the left is a one-day-old calf of the Zebu *(Bos indicus)*. Below, a picture of a Yak *(Bos grunniens)*, which reaches a length of some $10\frac{1}{2}$ ft., a shoulder height of 5 ft. 4 in. Its tail is like a Horse's and up to 2 ft. 11 in. long. The horns may measure almost 3 ft. The Yak weighs as much as $\frac{3}{4}$ of a ton. Today it lives in small herds in the eastern Tibetan mountains, 13,000 – 16,000 ft. above sea-level. Despite its considerable size it moves with great dexterity over the precipitous rocks among which it finds its food. Many domestic varieties have been developed in Tibet and north-eastern China, providing a livelihood for the inhabitants of these remote parts. Yaks are used for transport and as beasts of burden; they also provide milk, meat and skins. Even their droppings are used as fuel.

The Banting, or Tsine *(Bibos sondaicus)* is found from eastern India, through Burma to Indonesia. It is nearly 7½ ft. long and 5 ft. high, greyish-brown to reddish in colour with a white patch on the rump. The lower parts of its legs are white. Each horn, measuring about 1 ft. 8 in., curls upwards. The females are always lighter in colour than the bulls, as can be seen in the above picture. Most frequently the cow is pale reddish-brown. The Banting prefers jungle and lives in small herds near water, feeding on grass and leaves. It has been exterminated in many places. A domestic race is known as Bali Cattle.

The Indian Water Buffalo or Carabao (*Bubalus bubalis*) has a very wide range, covering the entire Indian Peninsula, and introduced into many of the warm regions of Asia, Asia Minor and parts of Africa and south-eastern Europe. It is some 9 ft. long, standing 6 ft. at the shoulder. Its skin is blackish-grey, its thin pelage being brownish. The Water Buffalo is a domestic animal in all these countries, being descended from the wild Indian Buffalo. The Pygmy Buffalo or Celebes Anoa (*Anoa depressicornis*) is the smallest of the wild Cattle, being only 3 ft. high at the shoulder. Small herds of this wild Buffalo can still be found in the jungle swamps of India, Burma, and some Indonesian islands. Both wild and domestic forms are very fond of water and mud – sometimes spending the whole day submerged up to the neck or muzzle. Above are specimens of the domestic form.

The North American Bison (*Bison bison*), shown on the right, is about 10 ft. in length, 5 ft. 8 in. high at the withers, with a tail about 2 ft. long. It may weigh up to a ton. It is blackish-brown and has a shaggy coat which falls off in large tufts in late spring. The Bison once roamed the vast prairies of North America in huge herds, from the Atlantic coast to the borders of Oregon and Nevada. They were gradually reduced as the country was colonised and modern weapons came into use, until the species was all but exterminated, surviving only in a few nature reserves. Now their numbers have again increased to about 30,000 head and are controlled at about that figure.

The largest wild Cattle of Europe is the European Bison or Wisent (*Bison bonasus*). Its body is 11 ft. long, it stands 6 ft. at the shoulder, and weighs about ³/₄ of a ton.

Not unlike the American Bison in appearance, it has a smaller hump and the rear part of its back does not slope as much as that of its American relative. Its colouring is chestnut brown, blackish-brown at the sides. Having once lived throughout Europe and the adjacent parts of Asia in dense forests, the Wisent survived until recent years only in East Poland, Lithuania, the Caucasus, and the western part of Byelo-Russia. It now lives, under careful protection, only in nature reserves, mainly in the Caucasus and in the Bialowiez forest in Poland, where the picture below was taken.

Reticulated Giraffes in their natural surroundings.

Antelopes are among the world's fastest and most graceful animals. They exhibit a great variety in size and form. The Royal Antelope is only 10 in. at the shoulder, while the Eland will weigh 1,200 lb. Some are solitary while others travel in herds of 1,000 or more. True Antelopes are concentrated in Africa, with a fair number in South-east Asia.

Largest of the Antelopes is the Giant or Derby's Eland *(Taurotragus derbianus)*, above. It is included in the subfamily Bovinae, and in the spiral-horned Antelope group. It attains a size of nearly 10 ft. and a height of 6 ft. It has spirally-twisted horns, very thick and up to 3 ft. in length. Its colour is yellowish-brown and yellowish-grey with a reddish tinge. On the underside it is yellowish-white, and it has several narrow, light-coloured lateral stripes on its back There are about two species divided into varieties of the Eland living south of the Sahara, in Kenya, the Cameroons, the Sudan, Senegambia, Rhodesia, and other parts of South-west Africa, up to a height of 12,000 ft. It feeds mainly on leaves and twigs.

The genus Oryx includes the straight-horned Antelopes in the subfamily Hippotraginae. Top left, p. 562, is a South African Gemsbok *(Oryx gazella)*. It is 6 ft. 8 in. long, 4 ft. at the shoulder, with a tail of about 1 ft. 4 in. The colouring is blackish-grey, white and black. It inhabits the semi-desert of South-west Africa. It sharp horns, which may attain a length of 4 ft., afford it very good protection, even against the lion.

The picture at the bottom of p. 562 shows the head of a female White or Scimitar Oryx *(Oryx algazel)*. The White Oryx measures about $6\frac{1}{2}$ ft. and is 3 ft. 6 in. high at the shoulder. Its horns may be anything up to 3 ft. 9 in. long. It is a native of the arid steppe country on the southern fringe of the Sahara, ranging from Ethiopia to Mauretania.

The Blackbuck (*Antilope cervicapra*) is about 4 ft. in length and 2½ ft. high. Its tail is a mere 6 in. The males have horns up to 2½ ft. long which have as many as three or occasionally more spiral twists. The male's coat is dark grey, sometimes almost black, with a white belly and markings on the head. The legs are usually brown. The female is as a rule light brown and hornless. These Antelopes live in herds on the plains of India. They can cover up to 20 ft. at one jump, reaching a height of nearly 7 ft. They are hunted with the aid of trained cheetahs or eagles. If given adequate space, they become very tame in captivity; on the other hand, when confined in narrow runs in small zoological gardens the males tend to be highly aggressive (upper picture).

The Brindled Gnu (*Gorgon taurinus*), illustrated below, is dark grey in colour with black stripes on the neck. Its tail and head markings are also black. Its body is over 8 ft. long, and it stands some 4 ft. 4 in. at the shoulder, with a 2 ft. tail. It lives in relatively large numbers in the open woodlands of Kenya south to the Orange River.

The tribe Strepsicerotini of the subfamily Bovinae includes several Antelopes with spirally twisted horns and broad hoofs, well suited to the swampy environment where they lead a secluded life.

One of these is the rare Sitatunga *(Strepsiceros spekei)* about 5 ft. long and 3 ft. 9 in. at the shoulder. Length of tail is about 6 in. The coat is brown with white markings, the horns are slightly twisted. There are several races living in swampy ground in the forest and among reeds and papyrus in Central and West Africa and as far south as the Zambesi. It frequently spends the day almost submerged in water, only coming out at dusk to graze. Its food consists of leaves, twigs and aquatic plants.

True Antelopes are not found on American soil. The Pronghorn *(Antilocapra americana),* often referred to as the American Antelope, is not an Antelope. It is unique in that it is the only hollow-horned Ungulate that sheds its horns annually; furthermore, it is the only animal with hollow horns that are branched. Living on the great open spaces of western North America, it is the swiftest runner in the New World and can maintain a speed of 60 m.p.h. for a considerable distance. The Pronghorns are in a family all their own, the Antilocapridae.

The subfamily Caprinae, a division of the Bovidae, includes the Sheep, Goats and Goat-antelopes.

The Saiga (Saiga tatarica) looks like an Antelope but is literally one of the Goat tribe. It is up to 4 ft. in length and 2 ft. 6 in. high. Its maximum weight is about 100 lb. The coat is short and yellowish-grey in summer, but paler in winter, when it also becomes longer and thicker. The males have lyrate, ringed horns up to a foot long which are light yellow in colour. The females are usually hornless. The Saiga's nose is large and swollen, having the appearance of a short proboscis lined with hair. This would seem to function as a dust and sand filter, very necessary in the steppes and desert which are its habitat. In earlier times the Saiga inhabited various parts of Asia and Europe; today it is confined to the Ukraine, Mongolia and Kazakhstan, where it survives only in protected herds (top left).

The Musk Ox (Ovibos moschatus) lives farthest north of the Ungulates on the barren wastes of Arctic America and Greenland. It is not an Ox but is closely related to the Chamois of Switzerland.

The Markhor (Capra falconeri) is nearly 5 ft. long and 3 ft. 4 in. at the shoulder. The horns of the male are also this length, and are twisted into a long straight screw-shape. The Markhor is found in a number of varieties in the mountain forests of Turkestan, Uzbekistan, Baluchistan, Kashmir, and Afghanistan. Its summer coat is light brown, the tail, beard and parts of its legs being dark brown. The colouring is paler in winter (bottom left).

The picture above shows the head of a kid be-longing to one of the many races of domestic Goats (Capra hircus). This is an African variety, the so-called Cameroon Goat, the smallest of all the dwarf forms, which when fully grown will not be more than 1 or $1^1/_2$ ft. high. The various types of dom-estic Goats may have come into existence in ancient times by crossing various mountain species, in particular the varieties of Wild Goat or Pasang (Capra hircus aegagrus) of the Mediterranean region and Asia Minor. The Bezoar stone, once famous as

an antidote for poison, was first taken from the stomach of Goats in Persia, now Iran.

The Rocky Mountain Goat (*Oxeamnos americanus*) is more closely related to the European Chamois than the true Goats. It is white except for the black horns and hoofs.

A young male Siberian Ibex (*Capra ibex sibirica*) is illustrated above left. This race may be some 5 ft. long, and up to 3 ft. 4 in. at the shoulder. Its horns are up to 4 ft. 8 in. long. It inhabits the high mountains of central Asia, being found at altitudes up to 15,000 ft. in the Pamir.

The Barbary or Aoudad Sheep (*Ammotragus lervia*), illustrated below left, seems to be an intermediate species between the Goats and the Sheep. It is about 5 ft. 4 in. long, up to 3 ft. 4 in. high, its tail being 6 in. and horns up to 2 ft. 9 in. in length. Its colouring is tawny. Old males, in particular, have fringes of long hair hanging from the throat and fore limbs almost to the ground. They have no 'beard', nor the characteristic odour of the Goats and Ibex. They live in the mountains of North Africa, ranging as far as Abyssinia.

The Bighorn Sheep (*Ovis canadensis*) will weigh up to 350 lb. and is native to the Rocky Mountains of western North America. It is a trophy much coveted by sportsmen the world over.

The Mouflon (*Ovis musimon*) is a wild Sheep about 3 ft. 7 in. long and 2 ft. 4 in. high. The large, curling horns may be up to 3 ft. 2 in. in length, the longest being those of 12-year-old rams. The females are almost or quite hornless. The Mouflon is brown in colour, white on the underside. Adult males have a white 'saddle' on their backs. This is one of the species from which the tame domestic Sheep may have evolved. It was once common in the mountains of much of southern Europe, but it is now confined to the rocky islands of Corsica and Sardinia. Since the end of the 18th century, however, it has been introduced into other countries, particularly in central Europe, where it has acclimatised itself in the forests and reaches a greater size and weight than in its original state (top right).

e Red Sheep *(Ovis orientalis)* is roughly the same e as the Mouflon, but is uniform in colour. Its rns are flatter and have a sharper front edge. lives at medium altitudes in the mountains of Cyprus, Asia Minor and Iran. There are several local varieties and other related species in Kashmir, Afghanistan, and Baluchistan. It may be the ancestor of the domestic Sheep to a greater extent than the European Mouflon, because tame Sheep have been and are bred far more extensively in Asia than in Europe *(below)*.

The order Edentata, the 'toothless' mammals, unites three families, all American, the Anteaters, Sloths and Armadillos. Originally the Pangolins of Africa and Asia and the African Aardvarks were included with the Edentates, but are now separated into two orders, Pholidota and Tubulidentata. Externally the three families are very dissimilar but related as a result of certain common anatomical features, such as the more complex and firmer linking of the dorsal and lumbar vertebrae. The Edentates are relics of prehistoric times, when some forms were of huge size like the Glyptodons (14 ft. long) and the Giant Sloth, Megatherium (20 ft. long). Only the Anteaters, family Myrmecophagidae, are actually toothless.

The Three-toed Anteater or Tamandua *(Tamandua tetradactyla)* belongs to the family Myrmecophagidae. The erect fur is a very light yellowish brown, glossy, with black on its neck and flanks. The animal is about 2 ft. long with a prehensile tail measuring another 1 ft. 4 in. It is arboreal and nocturnal, inhabiting the tropical forests of Mexico and South America, especially Brazil and Paraguay. Like all other Anteaters, the Tamandua has a long extendible tongue for capturing its prey – ants, and termites. The powerful claws on the forefeet tear open termite nests. The above picture shows a Tamandua with extended tongue, and on p. 571 the head only.

Bottom left is the Ant 'Bear' or Great Anteater *(Myrmecophaga tridactyla)*, a powerful animal up to 4 ft. 3 in. long with a tail measuring 3 ft. including the long hair. It has a large mane and a long snout. It weighs up to 100 lb. Its claws are used to break open the hard-boled termite nests in which its prey is to be found. The coarse, bristly coat is greyish-black in colour, with broad lighter stripes. The Great Anteater is a diurnal, terrestrial creature living in the open savannahs in South and tropical America, south to Paraguay and Argentina and north to Costa Rica. Anteaters have a tube-like head some 15 in. long with just a small opening the size of a lead pencil through which they push out 9 in. of their tongue.

A third member of the Anteater group is the Two-toed or Silky Anteater *(Cyclopes didactylus)*, not more than 15 in. long, strictly arboreal and ranging from Mexico to Bolivia.

The Sloths, family Brady-podidae, are not toothless, but their teeth are peg-like, deficient in enamel and without roots. They are arboreal, helpless on the ground, and move in slow motion. There are only two genera of these strange nocturnal beasts from the Central and South American tropics. They are perfectly suited to their arboreal mode of life.

The Unau or Two-toed Sloth *(Choleopus hoffmanni)* is up to 2 ft. 4 in. long and has no tail. Its fur is a light greyish-brown; when living in the wild this acquires a greenish tinge from various algae which grow on the hairs. Several other organisms including several species, also live in the fur. Because of the almost permanent 'upside-down' position – the Sloth hangs from the branches of trees by its long hooked claws – its long hair grows from the belly down over the sides. Its limbs are surprisingly strong and in defence it will sometimes also use its powerful teeth, of which it has twenty. The female bears one young which at first sits on its mother's abdomen and clings to her fur. The Sloth cannot walk in the normal way and will only crawl if it comes down to the ground. On the other hand it can swim and also turn its head through 270°. The second genus, the Three-toed Sloth or Ai *(Bradypus griseus)* is even more lethargic than the Two-toed Sloth.

In the Armadillos, family Dasypodidae, are included nine genera whose body is covered with a carapace of bony plates, the individual bands being connected by skin, so that the animal is able to curl itself up into a ball. Some species have as many as 104 tiny teeth: primitive peg-like structures devoid of enamel and without pronged roots. The Hairy Armadillo or Peludo *(Chaetophractus villosus)* illustrated is about 1 ft. 8 in. long. Its carapace is relatively flat and the Armadillo of this species cannot curl up like the others. It lives in the pampas of Argentina, Bolivia, Uruguay, and is of nocturnal habit. Armadillos dig very long tunnels even in hard, stony ground, mainly eating insects and small vertebrates, but they also take vegetable matter such as fleshy fruits and roots. Other members of the family range from the tiny Fairy Armadillo *(Chlamyphorus)*, 5 in. long, to the Giant Armadillo or Tatuasa *(Priodontes)* 5 ft. long. The Nine-banded Armadillo *(Dasypus)* ranges north to the southern United States.

573

574

The order Pholidota, Pangolins or Scaly Anteaters, has only one genus *(Manis)* which has seven species of strange animals inhabiting the warm parts of Asia and Africa. These largely nocturnal creatures feed on ants and termites, which they collect with their worm-like tongues, similar in both formation and use to that of the true Anteaters of America. The species shown opposite is the Common or Chinese Pangolin *(Manis pterodactyla)*, which is a native of India and Ceylon. It is a little over 3 ft. in length. The Pangolins are covered with a coat of chain mail made up of large, overlapping, sharp-edged, pointed scales that are used for attack as well as body protection. The largest Pangolin *(Manis gigantea)* reaches a length of 6 ft.

About half of all existing mammals in the world today are Rodents, order Rodentia. A typical feature is a pair of sharp, chisel-shaped incisors. Some of them are omnivorous, but in the main they live on vegetable food. The majority are small in size. The approximately five thousand various types of rodents are divided into three suborders: the Squirrel-like Rodents (Sciuromorpha), the Porcu-

pine-like Rodents (Hystricomorpha), and the Mouse-like Rodents (Myomorpha). The rodents are animals that gnaw. Characteristic of this order are the single pair of sharp, chisel-like incisor teeth at the front of the upper jaw in opposition to a similar pair in the lower jaw. These teeth are subject to excessive wear and continue to grow throughout life.

The Siberian Chipmunk or Borunduki *(Eutamias sibiricus)* is a north Asiatic ground Squirrel. It lives on the ground and in subterranean dens in not too dense coniferous forests, but it is also a proficient climber. Together with the tail it measures 10 in. Its fur is a tawny yellow colour with alternating black and light yellow stripes on the back. On the underside its body is white. The Borunduki eats berries, fungi, seeds and insects. Like most small mammals it is much preyed upon by the larger predators. There are similarly striped ground Squirrels in North America *(above)*. The American Chipmunks *Tamias* and *Eutamias*, brightly coloured, inquisitive, friendly little animals, are familiar figures throughout the United States and Canada.

The North American Flying Squirrel (*Glaucomys volans*) is about 5 in. in body length: it has furred membranes between front and hind legs on each side which it expands into a kind of parachute as it leaps through the air from one tree to another; its 4-in. bushy tail is used as a rudder. It feeds on berries, seeds and insects. This species has spread from North America, south to Guatemala *(above)*. Other species live in the forests of Northern Scandinavia and the Baltic countries, north Russia, Siberia and Japan, and others in South-east Asia, Indonesia, India, Ceylon, Kashmir and Tibet. Altogether we know eighteen species, the largest being the one from Ceylon and India, in which the body and tail each measure about 2 ft. These animals usually sleep throughout the day, setting out on their gliding journeys at dusk. They are greyish-brown, and inconspicuous. They eat berries, shoots and insects.

The Tree Squirrels (*Sciurus*) are the best known and most popular members of the gnawing animals. Only one species, the Pine Squirrel (*Sciurus vulgaris*) is found in Europe and Northern Asia; there are more in Africa and quite a few species in South America, but North America has an enormous population of Tree Squirrels: Red Squirrels, Chickarees, Grey Squirrels, Fox Squirrels, Tuft-eared Squirrels and others. All are diurnal and feed largely on seeds and nuts.

The Prairie-dog (*Cynomys ludovicianus*) is a North American species of Marmot, widespread in the prairies of western Texas and Kansas, in the upper reaches of the Missouri, and at the foot of the Rockies. Its name comes from its short barking call. Fully grown it measures about 1 ft. 2 in. with a 2-in. tail. The coat is tawny brown, with black and grey dapples on top and a dirty white on the underside. Prairie-dogs live in colonies called dog-towns; they make underground dens in which they hide from danger and hibernate in winter. They live on grass, which they dry and store in their dens for the winter period. In former times Prairie-dogs frequently became so numerous as to be a pest, but as man advanced into their native prairies, many colonies were wiped out.

The Hairy-nosed or Indian Porcupine *(Hystrix indica)* inhabits a large area from the southern Caucasus and northern Iraq through Iran and India all the way to Turkestan. It measures nearly 3 ft., being larger than the southern European and African species, which is only some 2 ft. 4 in. long. This Asiatic Porcupine has more brightly coloured spines and a very hairy nose and muzzle. Porcupines are solitary animals, hiding during the day in dens which they dig in the ground and going out at night in search of food, such as the fruits and roots of various plants. Several different species are found in the open forests in the warm parts of southern Europe, Africa and Asia.

The Canadian Porcupine (Erethizon dorsatum) is very similar to the Old World Porcupines, except that it is smaller and has more and smaller spines often almost hidden in its coat of coarse hair. It lives in the trees, feeding on leaves, shoots and the bark. Its rodent's teeth cause considerable damage in the forest, peeling off the bark to such an extent that the trees are killed. The Canadian Porcupine is about 2 ft. long with a tail of about 7 in. Its range extends over the forested regions of North America south to Mexico.

579

The Patagonian Cavy or Mara *(Dolichotis patagonica)* is a rodent from the steppes of Argentina and Patagonia, where it feeds on the tough grass. Its long legs and the colour of its fine, thick coat remind one of the Hare. Its body length is about 1 ft. 8 in. *(above left)*.

The Golden Agouti *(Dasyprocta aguti)* inhabits open and virgin forest from Mexico to the Amazon valley. It has a harsh, thick coat, tawny-yellow in colour. It measures about 1 ft. 4 in. It is very fond of berries and nuts, though it will sometimes also eat birds' eggs and fledglings *(bottom left)*.

The Capybara or Carpincho *(Hydrochoerus capy-* *bara)* is the largest living rodent, measuring about 3 ft. 4 in. and weighing up to a hundredweight. Its fur is greyish-brown in colour, thin and coarse. The Capybara lives in lakes and river valleys from Panama to Brazil, feeding on various fleshy plants. Its feet are webbed, enabling it to move with ease over marsh and swamp and to swim in the water. Small groups of Capybaras wander about in inaccessible swamps and reed-beds. Usually such a group consists of one male and two or three females, each of them with two or three young. In captivity they quickly become used to their new conditions and become very friendly towards their keepers *(above)*.

The European Harvest Mouse *(Micromys minutus)* is a miniature rodent. An adult measures a mere $2\frac{1}{2}$ or 3 in., a newborn Mouse not more than $\frac{1}{2}$ in., its weight being just $\frac{1}{28}$ oz. The adults have a close coat of fine hair, tawny brown in colour, while the young are more greyish. The species is widespread, ranging throughout Europe to Asia as far as Japan. Their usual home is in grassy swamps, where they make round nests in which they sleep and have their young. If they become very numerous they will migrate to the fields, but the damage done to the crops is offset by the quantities of harmful insects they eat. These charming little Mice are very adroit at climbing up the thin stalks of corn. They are rare in England. The American Harvest Mouse *(Reithrodontomys)* is represented by a number of species widely distributed in North America. It is larger than the European form and has a very long tail.

The pictures on the opposite page show two of the most harmful rodents in the world. At the top is the Black Rat *(Rattus rattus)*; at the bottom the Brown Rat *(Rattus norvegicus)*. The former is slightly smaller, measuring between $6\frac{1}{2}$ and 8 in., has large ears and a tail longer than its body. The Brown Rat is sturdier in build, up to 10 in. long, and has short ears and a tail shorter than the body. It is today more numerous than the Black Rat, and is responsible for many epidemics, especially in tropical and sub-tropical countries. The amazing fertility of these rodents necessitates a constant war against them if their numbers are to be kept in check.

Their well developed senses enable Brown Rats to travel concealed in the holds of ships and on trains. Thus, despite all efforts to exterminate them, they are now spread throughout the entire world.

The picture on the opposite page is of the Fat Dormouse *(Glis glis)* photographed at night. This is the largest of the Dormice, living in old parks, orchards and deciduous forests in central and southern Europe, around the Caucasus, in western Turkestan, and in Persia. It feeds on berries, shoots, and nuts. It spends the day sleeping in hollow trees, for its long winter sleep seeking warmer shelter underground or in old buildings.

585

The most attractive of the Dormice is the Common Dormouse (*Muscardinus avellanarius*). This nocturnal animal with large, bright eyes is under 3 in. long. Its fine, thick coat is brownish-yellow. It lives in central and southern Europe, in central Russia, and Asia Minor, also being found in Great Britain and the southern parts of Sweden. It frequents both lowlands and mountain woods, eating buds and berries, as well as its favourite food – hazel nuts. It builds neat little nests, either in the branches of a tree or on the ground, where it sleeps during the day. It hibernates in winter under leaves, roots, or piles of wood, building itself a round nest of grasses and leaves, curling up into a ball and sealing the entrance. This situation and the protection afforded by the sealed nest enable it to maintain adequate temperature and humidity during its winter sleep, which lasts several months.

The Asiatic Dormouse *(Dry-omys nitedula)* lives in the mountain forests of south-eastern Europe, being also known in the Alps, Carpathians, south-eastern Bavaria, southern Silesia, the Balkans, and south-west and central Asia. It has a typical black stripe running across its face from the nose to the ear. This Dormouse measures between 3 and 4 in., its bushy tail slightly less *(right)*.

The Coypu or Nutria *(Myocastor coypus)* resembles a large rat. Its body and tail each measure about 1 ft. 8 in., though specimens have been known to exceed 2 ft. 6 in. It has a fine, thick and long coat, chestnut-brown in colour. Orange-coloured incisors jut out of its mouth. The Coypu lives in the temperate zone of the southern part of South America, but it is today bred on farms as a fur-bearing animal in other parts of the world, including Europe. Escapees are now running wild in the United States. The fur is known as nutria *(below)*.

The famous builders of dams, the Beavers, are about 2 ft. 9 in. long and weigh up to about 80 lb. The above picture is of a Canadian Beaver (Castor canadensis). The European species (Castor fiber) has a somewhat paler fur and a more robust skull.

The Peruvian Cavy (Cavia porcellus) from South America is generally known in its domesticated form as the Guinea Pig, which has a wide range of colours and several different types of hair. These tame rodents, exclusively vegetarian in habit, are kept not only as children's pets but also as useful laboratory animals (below).

The Vizcacha (*Lagostomus maximus*) is about 1 ft. 8 in. in length. It has a fine thick coat, brownish-grey, with characteristic paler bands on its large, rather ugly-looking head. Entire huge 'villages' consisting of numbers of underground burrows at one time used to exist in the South American pampas from Patagonia to Buenos Aires, around which hundreds of thousands of these rodents could be seen grazing. Growing colonisation greatly reduced their numbers, and today they are fairly rare even in their original habitat (*above*).

The Chinchilla (*Chinchilla laniger*) is a silver-grey rodent, about a foot long, with the finest and densest coat of all mammals. Ever since the end of the 18th century the Chinchilla has been so assiduously hunted for its fur that the former hundreds of thousands, in strong colonies in the Cordilleras of South America, have been totally exterminated. The species survives only in small numbers in the coastal mountains of Chile and Bolivia, at altitudes of between 6,000 and 10,000 ft. (*below*).

Order Lagomorpha, Hares, Rabbits and Pikas. Characteristics of this order include large ears, short tail and large hind feet for hopping. While sharing with the rodents a few peculiarities such as chisel-like front teeth they followed their own line of development. Similarity between the two orders is coincidental and not a relationship. The best-known representative of this order is the European Hare *(Lepus europaeus)* of which some twenty-one subspecies are recognised not only throughout Europe but also in Asia Minor and East Africa. It has been introduced into Argentina, Australia, New Zealand and the United States. Thriving wherever it has sufficient food, the Hare continuously spreads farther afield *(left)*. Originally inhabitants of grassland, most Hares now live in fertile agricultural country.

In the northern parts of Europe and Asia lives the Blue or Variable Hare *(Lepus timidus)*. Its summer coat is tawny brown and it changes to snowy white in winter. The tips of its ears, however, remain black like those of the Common Hare. There are several geographic varieties *(below)*.

The European Wild Rabbit *(Oryctolagus cuniculus)* comes originally from Spain, having been introduced elsewhere as a small game animal. It does best in lowlands with sandy soil, in which it can easily make its burrows. Wild Rabbits live in large colonies, feeding on a wide range of plants and tree-shoots. Under favourable conditions the females breed as often as five times a year, giving birth each time to at least four, sometimes as many as twelve, young. In Australia the introduction of the Rabbit had catastrophic results owing to its rapid rate of breeding, but in Europe they seem to have sufficient enemies to keep their numbers in check. The Rabbit is smaller than the Hare, weighing only up to 4 lb. Its fur is greyish, and it has shorter ears without the black tips.

All the different varieties of Domestic Rabbits were developed from the European Rabbit (Orycto-lagus), bred for their flesh or fur. They are also used in research laboratories, helping mankind to fight disease. When Domestic Rabbits escape from captivity, they join their wild relatives and within a few generations lose all signs of domesti-cation. Nature adapts them by letting them revert to the protective colouring and size of the wild species, best suited to its mode of life. The European Rabbit lives in warrens or com-munity holes and is the only Lagomorph that is virtually a true Rabbit. All the other forms are Hares or Pikas. The Lagomorphs are spread over the temperate regions of the Northern Hemisphere and north into the Arctic and Green-land. Their range also covers most of Africa, but they are sparingly spread in South America. The Rabbits are well represented in North America with the Big-eared Jack Rabbits, Snowshoe Rabbits, Arctic Hares, Swamp Rabbits, Cottontails, Pigmy Rabbits and the Pikas (Ochotona).

INDEX